TEARS

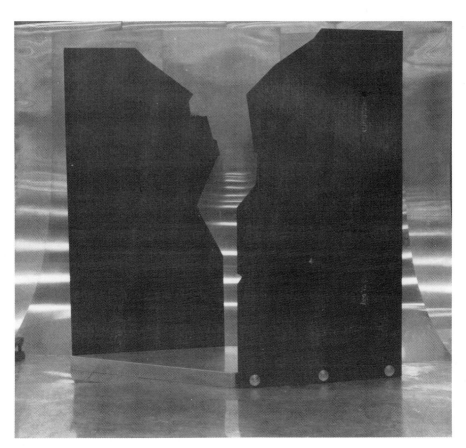

Figure 1. *The Silence of Jesus*, Enrique Espinosa.

TEARS

Mark C. Taylor

State University of New York Press

SUNY Series, Intersections: Philosophy and Critical Theory
Rodolphe Gasché and Mark C. Taylor, Editors

Several of these essays have appeared previously: "Archetexture of Pyramids," in Assemblage: A Critical Journal of Architecture and Design Culture, *vol. 5, pp. 17–27;* "Deadlines: Approaching Anarchetecture," in Threshold, *vol. 4 (Spring 1988), pp. 20–27;* "The Anachronism of A/theology," in Religion and Intellectual Life, *vol. 5, no. 2 (Winter 1988), pp. 22–36;* "Foiling Reflection," in Diacritics, *vol. 18, no. 1 (Spring 1988), pp. 54–65;* "The Nonabsent Absence of the Holy," in Phenomenology and the Numinous, *Duquesne University: The Simon Silverman Phenomenology Center, 1988, pp. 21–42; and* "The Eventuality of Texts," in Semeia.

Cover Photo: Michael Heizer, RIFT
 # 1 of Nine Nevada Depressions
1 1/2 - ton displacement in playa surface
52' × 1' 6" × 1'
Location: Jean Dry Lake, Nevada
Commissioned by Robert C. Scull
Photography by permission of the artist.

Published by
State University of New York Press, Albany
© *1990 State University of New York*
All rights reserved
Printed in the United States of America
No part of this book may be used or reproduced
in any manner whatsoever without written permission
except in the case of brief quotations embodied in
critical articles and reviews.
For information, address State University of New York
Press, State University Plaza, Albany, N.Y., 12246

Library of Congress Cataloging-in-Publication Data

Taylor, Mark C., 1945–
 Tears / Mark C. Taylor.
  p. cm.–(SUNY series, Intersections: philosophy and critical theory)

 ISBN 0–7914–0102–2.–ISBN 0–7914–0103–0 (pbk.)
 1. Literature–Philosophy. 2. Religion and literature.
 I. Title. II. Series: Intersections (Albany, N.Y.)
PN49. T35 1989
801–dc 19   89–4228
                                                CIP

10 9 8 7 6 5 4 3 2

For
Stephen Crites
and
John Maguire

Contents

Figures

Acknowledgments

It took me nearly twenty-five years to learn how to write a book. It is taking me even longer to learn how not to write a book. Many have contributed—wittingly and unwittingly—to this learning and unlearning. Family: Dinny, Aaron, and Kirsten; friends and colleagues: Thomas J.J. Altizer, Houston Baker, Kerry Batchelder, Jacques Derrida, William Eastman, Rodolphe Gasché, George Goethals, Ray Hart, Paul Holdengräber, H. Ganse Little, Francis Oakley, John Reichert, Carola Sautter, Stanley Tigerman, and Edith Wyschogrod. Thomas Carlson provided invaluable assistance in preparing the manuscript for publication. In the absence of an origin, beginnings proliferate—some can be named, others are unnameable. Though they will not always recognize themselves in these pages, this text began over twenty years ago in the classroom of two extraordinary teachers: Stephen Crites and John Maguire. Much could be said, nothing would suffice. Such debts can never be repaid.

M.C.T.

August 1988

*The names of minerals and the
minerals themselves do not differ
from each other, because at bottom
both the material and the print is
the beginning of an abysmal number of fissures. Words and rocks
contain a language that follows a
syntax of splits and ruptures. Look
at any* word *long enough and you
will see it open into a series of
faults, into a terrain of particles
each containing its own void.*

Robert Smithson

. . . my words are my tears.

Samuel Beckett

*The unsayable settles us in those
desert regions that are the home of
dead languages. Here, every grain
of sand stifled by the mute word
offers the dreary spectacle of a root
of eternity ground to dust before it
could sprout. In the old days, the
ocean would have cradled it. Does
the void torment the universe, and
the universe in turn vex the void?
Roots buried in sand keep longing
for their trees. The deepest weep
for their fruit. They are reborn of
their tears.*

Edmond Jabès

WILLIAMS COLLEGE WILLIAMSTOWN. MASSACHUSETTS 01267

DEPARTMENT OF RELIGION   *STETSON HALL*

May 5, 1988

Ms. Carola Sautter
State University of New York Press
State University Plaza
Albany, NY 12246

Dear Carola:

No! No, I will not write the introduction you request. You want
a book and I have struggled--perhaps vainly--not to write a book. You
say that it would be helpful to the reader to have an explanation of
the order of the essays and a brief description of the thematic unity
of the volume. But the "order" is random, arbitrary and there is no
unity, thematic or otherwise. Furthermore, I do not think I should
help the reader, even if I could do so. As Kierkegaard never tired of
telling us, the task of the author is not to make things easier for the
reader but to make everything more difficult.

And so, Carola, I must resist the temptation you pose. No, I am
sorry, I cannot, I will not. Though you do not agree, I hope you
understand.

Sincerely,

Mark

Mark C. Taylor

MCT/sb

1.

The Art of the Sacred

> He was locked in combat with something inac-
> cessible, foreign, something of which he could
> say: That does not exist . . . and which never-
> theless filled him with terror as he sensed it
> wandering [*errer*] about in the region of his
> solitude. Having stayed up all night and all day
> with this being, as he tried to rest, he was sud-
> denly made aware that an other had replaced
> the first, just as inaccessible and just as obscure,
> and yet different. It was a modulation of that
> which did not exist, a different mode of being
> absent, another void in which he was coming to
> life. Now it was certain, something was ap-
> proaching him, standing not nowhere and every-
> where, but a few feet away, invisible. . . . He
> felt ever closer to an ever more monstrous
> absence that took an infinite time to meet. He
> felt it closer to him every instant and kept ahead
> of it by an infinitely small but irreducible
> splinter of duration.
>
> Maurice Blanchot

Modernism . . . postmodernism . . . What *is* the difference? The difference seems to involve nothing other than the question of difference. The
question of difference, however, is inseparable from the question of presence
or, more precisely, the question of the possibility or the impossibility of
presence. To ask about presence is, of course, to ask about both space and
time. Might the difference between modernism and postmodernism have
something to do with different interpretations of space and time? And might
this difference approach or be approached in terms of art and the sacred?

1

In *The Sacred and the Profane*, Mircea Eliade attempts to define the nature of religion by examining different experiences of space and time. In contrast to "profane man" for whom space and time supposedly lack *qualitative* differentiations, religious man's experience of "space is not homogeneous; he experiences interruptions, breaks in it; some parts of space are qualitatively different from others. . . . This nonhomogeneity finds expression in the experience of an opposition between space that is sacred—the only *real* and *really* existing space—and all other space, the formless expanse surrounding it."[1] Sacred space is characterized by the *presence* of God or the gods. This presence establishes the *center*, which, for *homo religiosus*, constitutes the locus of the real. The temporal correlate of the spatial center is the origin—that is, the time of creation. Divine presence is most fully realized *ab origine*. The presence of this origin is not lost in the past but can return again and again. In contrast to the unpunctuated monotony of profane time, "*sacred time is reversible* in the sense that, properly speaking, it is *a primordial mythical time made present.*"[2] According to Eliade, the presence of the gods is *re-presented* in myths and rituals that recount and, more importantly, reactualize the primal reality that was totally present *in illo tempore*. Within the framework of myth and ritual, the past is a past *present* that eternally returns to renew and regenerate the here and now.

In the wake of nineteenth-century romanticism, it has become commonplace to suggest that one of the distinguishing characteristics of modernity is the displacement of religion by art. With the advent of what M. H. Abrams describes as "natural supernaturalism,"[3] artistic expression, rather than religious myth and ritual, becomes the means by which "the *real*" is embodied. The mythic and ritualistic functions of art create the possibility of representing a presence deemed sacred. The enjoyment of the work of art is supposed to satisfy the nostalgic longing for a presence once enjoyed but long since lost. As Thomas J. J. Altizer explains in a book that bears the revealing title *Total Presence*:

> The power of archaic or prehistoric art was discovered by the West at just the moment when the dominant Western images of God and man were undergoing a full process of either dissolution or transformation. That vast region of consciousness lying on yonder side of Abraham had long been unreal to us, and unreal because of the historical consequences of an original naming of God, a naming which gradually and progressively realized an individual and personal center of consciousness. Once that center burst asunder, as it did in the nineteenth century, then an original primordial identity came into view, and it was an identity lacking either a transcendent or an immanent center. Yet

modern painting is obviously not a simple repetition or resurrection of archaic art, just as modern literature is clearly not a simple reenactment or renewal of archaic myth. While there may well be decisive parallels between archaic art and myth and modern art and literature, there are also decisive differences, and one such fundamental difference is the virtual absence of a distinct form of the holy or the sacred from truly modern language and vision.[4]

Through a dialectical reversal, the *disappearance* of the distinct or separate form of the holy becomes the *appearance* of a radically new experience of the sacred. This new religious experience becomes possible only with the death of the transcendent God. The divine Other is negated in and through a complex incarnational process that comes to completion in modern art. "When modern painting seemingly has a wholly liberating or redemptive effect, as in Monet and Cézanne," Altizer contends, "it bears no signs of the holy, and in no way whatsoever exhibits even a shadow of God. This does not mean, of course, that God and the sacred are necessarily absent from these paintings. But it does mean that if they are present they are present wholly apart from their given and historical forms."[5] Indirectly extending Eliade's analysis of the sacred and the profane, Altizer concludes that the Parousia becomes fully actual in the "mythic" and "ritualistic" space and time of modern art.[6] The space of art is presence, its time the present. In the "Eternal Now" of the work of art, time and space, *sensu strictissimo,* are overcome. This presence/present is the complete self-embodiment of God in which the sacred is totally *present* as total *presence.*

But what if art does not draw one to the center or origin where presence is real and the real is present? What if art leads one to a time "before the beginning" that decenters every one and dislocates every One? Exploring "the space of literature," Maurice Blanchot writes:

> But where has art led us? To a time before the world, before the beginning. It has cast us out of our power to begin and to end; it has turned us toward the outside without intimacy, without place, without rest. It has led us into the infinite migration of error. For we seek art's essence, and it lies where the nontrue admits of nothing essential. We appeal to art's sovereignty: it ruins the kingdom. It ruins the origin by returning it to the errant immensity of an eternity gone astray.[7]

By "returning to a time before the world, before the beginning," art is, in a phrase of Hegel repeated by Blanchot, "a thing of the past." The interpretations of the past of art developed by Hegel and Blanchot differ significantly.

According to Hegel, art is past because it has been surpassed in philosophy. From this point of view, what is imperfectly represented in artistic images is perfectly presented in philosophical concepts. For Blanchot, by contrast, the work of art is "very ancient, terrifyingly ancient, lost in the night of time. It is the origin that always precedes us and is always given before us, for it is the approach of what allows us to depart—a thing of the past, in a different sense from what Hegel said."[8]

To imagine the past that art evokes without representing, it is necessary to think time in terms other than those characteristic of the Western philosophical and theological tradition. Blanchot suggests an alternative account of time when he writes: "Time, time: the step/not beyond [*le pas au-delà*], which is not accomplished in time, would lead outside of time, without this outside being timeless, but there where time would fall, fragile fall, according to this 'outside of time in time.' "[9] At first glance, this "outside of time in time" might appear to entail yet another dialectical reversal of time and space, which would lead to the enjoyment of presence undisturbed by absence. Blanchot insists, however, that the "outside of time in time" is not a timeless present in which presence is total but involves a radical temporality in which the present is never present, and presence is ever absent. "The time of time's absence is not dialectical. In this time what appears is the fact that nothing appears. . . . The reversal which, in the absence of time, constantly sends us back to the presence of absence, but to this presence as absence, to absence as affirmation of itself, as affirmation where nothing is affirmed, where nothing never ceases to affirm itself."[10]

The past of art, then, is not a past present that can be re-presented. To the contrary, art is bound to and by the "unrepresentable before" that is always already past. Paradoxically, by going back to this past, one encounters the future. In the irreconcilable contradiction of "an outside of time in time," the past for which we long eternally returns as the future that never arrives. If the encounter with the past has never really taken place, the past is always still to come and the present (as well as presence) forever deferred. Since the enjoyment of presence in the present (i.e., here and now) is impossible, *erring* is inevitable. As Blanchot explains:

> Error signifies wandering, the inability to abide and stay. For where the wanderer is, the conditions of a definitive here are lacking. In this absence of here and now what happens does not clearly come to pass as an event based upon which something solid could be achieved. Consequently, what happens does not happen, but does not pass either, into the past; it is never passed. It happens and recurs without cease; it is the horror and the confusion and the uncertainty of eternal repetition. . . . The wanderer's country is not truth, but exile.[11]

The space of erring *is not* presence and the time of erring *is not* the present. So understood, erring poses the question that haunts postmodern art: How can that which never is, has been, or will be present be re-presented?

Postmodernism is, in Stanley Tigerman's apt phrase, "historically allusive." Through the use of irony, parody, pastiche, and citation, postmodern artists attempt to draw attention to the historical dimensions of experience in a way that accentuates the contrasts and heightens the tensions between past and present. As Heinrich Klotz observes, such strategies "combine the memory of things long past with the drama of innovation."[12] This turn to the past is of more than historical interest. Historical images harbor vestiges of a yet more distant past—a past, which, I have noted, Blanchot describes as "terrifyingly ancient." This radical past that is never present but is always on the verge of arriving marks and remarks the approach of the sacred. The sacred that draws near in the never-present past and future differs from the sacred of modernity by infinitely deferring the perpetual presence of the Eternal Now. In an effort to glimpse the inscription of the sacred in postmodern art, I will consider a work by the French artists-sculptors Anne and Patrick Poirier: *Paysage foudroyé* [Thunderstruck landscape] (Fig. 2; 1982–83).

Having become convinced that the abstraction and formalism typical of so much modern art had run its course, the Poiriers sought alternative directions during the 1960s by turning to the anthropologist Claude Lévi-Strauss. With the help of Lévi-Strauss, they were able to arrange extended sojourns in foreign cultures during which they assisted various anthropologists by executing drawings and constructing scale models of tribal communities. In more recent years, this experience with anthropology has led to an interest in archeology that has manifested itself in a preoccupation with the ruins of the Greco-Roman world. The Poiriers repeatedly draw on the art and architecture of cultures distant in time and space. Their work is consistently excessive; the most impressive sculptures they have executed are either excessively large or excessively small. *Paysage foudroyé* combines the immense and the infinitesimal in a detailed depiction of the charred ruins of an imaginative Greek world from the ancient past. The extraordinary expanse (39 × 19 1/2 × 2 feet) and minute detail of this uncanny "landscape" combine to form a work that is deeply disturbing.

As if developing Blanchot's insight concerning the interplay of errancy and exile in the artistic imagination, the Poiriers preface one of the most extensive catalogues of their work by writing: *"From landscape to landscape, from ruins to gardens, our work is a series of errings: from lived landscapes to desired landscapes, from physical errings to mental errings, from exile to exile—real landscapes and oneiric landscapes mix and mingle."*[13] The Poiriers insist that their "fascina-

Figure 2. Anne and Patrick Poirier, *Paysage foudroyé*, [Thunderstruck Land-scape], courtesy of the artists and Galerie Daniel Templon, photographer, André Morain.

tion with ruined towns and buildings is not a morbid nostalgia for the past but a fascination for the architectural place itself. . . . In a ruin ownership is abolished, rules disappear, all at once the eye can see through the succession of spaces." The "succession of spaces"[14] exposed by the exploration of the arche-texture of ruins opens one to a past that is not only historical but is also psychological. As the architect of psychoanalysis so often stresses, the interpreter of dreams is always something of an archeologist. According to the Poiriers, "archeology, architecture, and mythology are metaphors privileged in order to try to set in space or put on stage the phenomena of the unconscious." The unconscious *partially* discloses itself in archetypes that haunt the human imagination and inform all its creations. "For our part," the Poiriers note, "this is what we seek in our errings across architectures, ruins, and gardens: to attempt to understand the relations of archeology and mythology with our mental universe. To try to penetrate, on the basis of physical and perceptible tridimensional images, 'poetic' spaces contained in a region of our being that is accessible only with great difficulty."[15]

Paysage foudroyé is an image of the aftereffect of the contest between Jupiter and the Giants. In the Poiriers' own words:

> The *Paysage foudroyé*–black, charred, in ruin–is the probable site of the battle of Jupiter and the Giants. A fictitious Mediterranean, an entirely mythical geography where different structures [are] assembled around a basin of black water. [These structures] do not refer to any locale in particular, but should evoke the viewer's memories of archeological landscapes.[16]

Thunderstruck Landscape is bordered by works figuring the death of two of the rebellious Giants. On the one side, the Poiriers place *Death of Mimas* (Fig. 3) and on the other, *Death of Enceladus* (Fig. 4).

The Giants were the sons of Gaia, goddess of the earth. With the encouragement of their mother, who had long been at odds with the sky gods, the Giants attacked the Olympian deities. After a prolonged war, the gods defeated the monstrous maternal envoys. Mimas was struck down by a thunderbolt released by Jupiter (or his Roman counterpart, Zeus); Enceladus was buried under Mount Aetna, whence he breathes flames through the volcano.

In *Death of Enceladus* two huge eyes, which are fragments of a much larger statue, emerge from a pile of white marble. In the midst of the rubble there is a miniature replica of a temple and at the top of the work there is a bronze arrow representing the deadly thunderbolt of Jupiter. *Death of Mimas* is formed by an enormous bronze eye with water constantly trickling out of it, and a large arrow on either side of it. Between *Death of Enceladus* and *Death of Mimas* lies the scorched earth of *Thunderstruck Landscape*. Representing no actual historical site, this deadly wasteland is the trace of a dark psychic space opened by a dreadful event (or nonevent) that "occurred" "before the world, before the beginning." As such, *Thunderstruck Landscape* is, in the strict Freudian sense of the term, *nachträglich*. Describing their "*gianto- machie*," the Poiriers write:

> The myth that guided the conception of this space is that of the battle of the gods and the Giants, a myth of violence and destruction. . . . It stages the combat between elemental and brutal forces attributed to the Giants, sons of Gaia, and the superior forces attributed to the gods of Olympus. In fact, perhaps [it stages] the incessant combat between the rational and the irrational, shadow and light, violent drives and sublimated drives.[17]

But even the struggle between such clearly defined opposites is not absolutely primal. These ruins are a sign—no more, no less—of an absent origin that recalls Blanchot's "origin that always precedes us and is always given before us." In their most revealing remark on *Paysage foudroyé*, the Poiriers suggest, but do not develop, the religious and psychological complexity of their work. "On the earth, scattered in the disorder, a sort of pulverization of sculptural, architectural, and human elements (or fragments), as if [they had been] struck by an enormous shaking of an invisible origin. In fact, it is a question of traces [*traces*] of a combat on an inhuman scale of which there remain only some signs, which, in this chaos, are difficult to decipher."[18] Like Derrida's "nonoriginal origin,"[19] the Poiriers' "invisible origin" is the condition of the possibility of binary opposites, like the rational and the irrational, light and shadow, presence and absence, and so forth. Contrary to expectation, the nonoriginal origin has always already "cast us out of our power to begin and to end; it has turned us toward the outside without intimacy and without rest." This "unrepresentable before" that is irretrievably past interrupts every present and disrupts all presence.

Perhaps the recognition of the impossibility of presence/present "written" in *Paysage foudroyé* helps to explain the tear trickling from the eye of Mimas. This tear might be the tear that issues from Bataille's thunderous "outburst of laughter,"[20] or the tear that is the tear (rip, *Riss*) that Heidegger identifies as "the origin of the work of art."[21] Bataille's tear is the trace of the sacred; Heidegger's tear the trace of the holy. This sacred—this holy—"is" nothing other than the "inhuman," "invisible origin" whose remains are traced in *Thunderstruck Landscape*.

Traced . . . . always already trac*ed* . . . . but only traced, for the *disaster* figured in burnt ruins is never present as such. It is "outside of time in time"—not as the total presence of an eternal Here and Now but as the eternal return of an absolute past that repeatedly approaches as the future that never arrives. Blanchot offers a powerful description of this uncanny disaster.

> The disaster ruins everything, all the while leaving everything intact. It does not touch anyone in particular; "I" am not threatened by it, but spared, left aside. It is in this way that I am threatened; it is in this way that the disaster threatens in me that which is exterior to me—an other

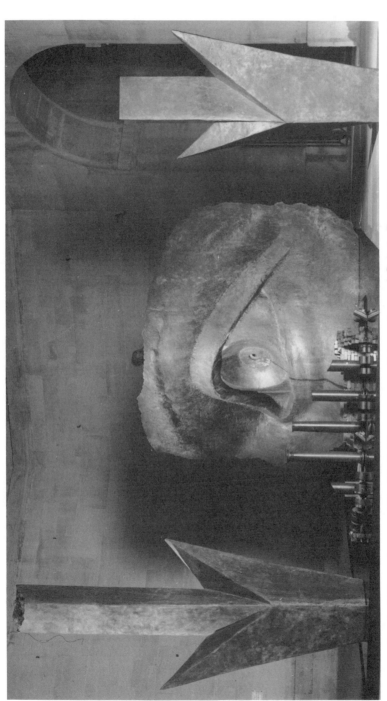

Figure 3. *Death of Mimas*, Anne and Patrick Poirier, courtesy of the artists and Galerie Daniel Templon, photographer, André Morain.

than I who passively become other. There is no reaching the disaster. Out of reach is he whom it threatens, whether from afar or close up, it is impossible to say: the infiniteness of the threat has in some way broken every limit. We are on the edge of the disaster [*au bord du désastre*] without being able to situate it in the future: it is rather always already past, and yet we are on the edge or under the threat, all formulations which would imply the future—which is yet to come—if the disaster were not that which does not come, that which has put a stop to every arrival.[22]

Suspended between *Death of Mimas* and *Death of Enceladus, Paysage foudroyé* marks the "site" of a holocaust that is an absolute Disaster. In the postmodern world, the Disaster takes place (without taking place) *in* art *as* art. The time of the disaster is a time without present; its space, a space without presence. Forever exiled, the artist goes back, back to a past more ancient than every past, where one encounters a future more distant than every future. To approach the *paysage foudroyé* that marks and remarks the space of postmodernism, one must follow Thomas the Obscure by going back to the future that always approaches but never arrives:

Thomas sat down and looked at the sea. He remained motionless for a time, as if he had come there to follow the movements of the other swimmers and, although the fog prevented him from seeing very far, he stayed there, obstinately, his eyes fixed on the bodies floating with difficulty. Then, when a more powerful wave reached him, he went down onto the sloping sand and slipped into the midst of the currents, which quickly submerged him. The sea was calm, and Thomas was in the habit of swimming for long periods without tiring. But today he had chosen a new route. The fog hid the shore. A cloud had come down upon the sea and the surface was lost in a glimmer that seemed the only truly real thing. Currents shook him, though without giving him the feeling of being in the midst of the waves and of rolling in familiar elements. The conviction that there was, in fact, no water at all turned his effort to swim into a frivolous exercise from which he drew nothing but discouragement. Perhaps it would suffice for him to master himself to drive away such thoughts, but his eye found nothing to cling to, and it seemed to him that he was staring into the void with the intention of finding help there. It was then that the sea, driven by the wind, broke loose. The storm tossed it, scattered it into inaccessible regions; the squalls turned the sky upside down and, at the same time, there was a silence and a calm that gave the impression that everything was already

Figure 4. Anne and Patrick Poirier, *Death of Enceladus*, courtesy of the artists and Galerie Daniel Templon, photographer, André Morain.

destroyed. Thomas sought to free himself from the insipid flood that was invading him. A piercing cold paralyzed his arms. The water swirled in whirlpools. Was it actually water?[23]

Or something Other? To err in the spacetime of this uncanny Other is to draw near the sacred by patiently awaiting what never arrives.

2.

Archetexture of Pyramids

If the subject is archetexture – the *arche* of texture as well as the texture of the *arche* – if the subject is, in one way or an other, the *arche* or the beginning, then where is one to begin? How is one to begin? I will try to begin by exploring something near and dear to all of us . . . a pocket. What is a pocket? The question seems banal. But is it? Are we sure we know what a pocket is or is not? Are we confident we can comprehend the implications of its precious contents – a pocketbook? Can there be such a thing as a pocket book? Or does the pocket make the book impossible? Is the pocket inside or outside? Is it, perhaps, neither inside nor outside but rather "invaginated" – inside out and outside in?

In an essay entitled "Living On/ *Border Lines,*" Derrida briefly touches the question of the pocket in the context of his consideration of Maurice Blanchot's haunting *récit, L'arrêt de mort:*

> That they, these two other women, others of the other, should not merely resemble each other but should be the same: this is what he desires, what he would die of, what he desires like the death that he would "give" himself. This is absolute terror: the boundless abyss of that which is single, unique – the other death, laughable, the most simply insignificant death, the most fatal. And immediately *la Chose* is its double. It remains [*reste*] its double. . . .
>
> At about ten o'clock Nathalie said to me:
> "I telephoned X., I asked him to make a cast of my head and my hands."
> Right away I was seized by a feeling of terror. "What gave you the idea of doing that?" "The card." She showed me the sculptor's card which was usually with the key in my wallet.
> Should we say that he gave her the idea of or desire for the death mask, as he had wished to embalm the other woman, in order to preserve both of them, to keep them alive-*and*-dead, living on? Yes *and* no. Yes, because it is indeed thanks to him, next to him, *on* him, that she *finds*

13

this "idea." No, because she *finds* them only by *stealing* them from him, from a place where he was hiding them, in a crypt, a crypt next to his body, clinging to his skin, the wallet, an object that is detachable from him, neither clothing nor itself a body, a safe containing other detachable objects, a card, keys, they operate, orient, open, close; they make something readable or keep it secret.[1]

By digging into our pockets, Blanchot and Derrida suggest, we find a crypt. Is this really so? Let's see. Dig into your pockets or into your supplementary pockets–your pocketbooks–and pull out a dollar, a single dollar bill. Hold it for a moment.

Derrida begins, or more precisely delays beginning, *Of Grammatology* with a textual supplement that he labels "Exergue." "Exergue," which derives from the Greek *ex*, "out of," plus *ergon*, "work," probably was intended to be a rendering of the French *hors d'oeuvre*. The "exergue" is a small place, usually on the reverse of a coin or metal, for any minor inscription. Our basic token of exchange no longer is metal but now is paper. We trade in papers that are signs whose value is arbitrary. There is no stable referent, no "transcendental signified" that secures the signs we swap. Our currency floats freely. The sign of the groundless sign that "grounds" our economy is a barred S–$. This $ is and is not the same sign that Lacan uses to mark the split or cracked subject. The | of the $ subverts everyone by re-marking the archaic tear–the preoriginal wound–of "castration" reflected by inscription within the symbolic order. If grammatology begins with an exergue, it might be possible to open a consideration of the text-ure of the *arche* by examining the exergue of the treasure tucked away in our pockets. But what treasure?

. . .

Hors d'oeuvre

The root of "pocket" is *beu*; *bhel*, *bhleu*: swelling, flowing, flowering. Greek, *phallos*; *phallus*. Ithyphallic (*ithy*: erect; carried at festivals of Bacchus. Latin, *follis*: bellows. *Follicle*. *Folly*; *fool*: windbag. *Foolhardy*. *Foolproof*. *Foolscap*, from the early watermark design on the paper. Germanic, *poach*, *pouch*; *poke*, its dimunitive *pocket*.

The question of the pocket is, at least in part, a question of jewels–hidden jewels that might or might not be (un)covered. (Remember Dupin.)

. . .

Capitalism (and, for reasons that will soon become apparent, it is important to remember the association of the capital and the head, established by
way of the Latin *caput,* meaning "head"–though we also recognize other
meanings of kaput) can be understood as an "ontotheological" economy. "Ontotheology" is Heidegger's term for the dominant philosophical tradition in
the West. This economy is political, social, psychological, religious, and artistic. The guiding principle of this tradition is fundamentalist belief–that is,
belief in the fundaments named Identity, Unity, Being, and Presence. The
God in whom ontotheology trusts is the omnipresent ONE. This ONE is the
principle that founds every united state. The ideal of the capitalist economy is
printed on the scroll held in the beak of an eagle: *E Pluribus Unum;* From
Many, One. All of this is, of course, on the exergue of the dollar.

But there is something else on the underside of the dollar. To the left of
the ONE there is inscribed the backside of the Great Seal. The face of the
Seal, which is to the right of the ONE, bears an image of the eagle–the very
eagle that is supposed to bring oneness from manyness. This exergue within
an exergue is strange: it includes a pyramid that is, in words Hegel uses in the
Phenomenology to describe the role of the unconscious in the struggle between
Antigone and Creon, "a pyramid with its very tip knocked off."[2] Above the
decapitated pyramid on the backside of the foundation of capitalism is an eye
in the middle of a triangle. Whose eye is this and what does the triangle imply? The *Journals of the Continental Congress* tell us that the eye is God's and suggest that the triangle represents the trinity. The image of the eye within a
triangle surrounded by rays of the sun is a common symbol for the all-seeing,
panoptical, penal, eagle-eye of God. God's eye is always the *right* eye. But is
the eye in the exergue the *right* eye? We cannot be certain. It is possible,
perhaps likely, that William Barton, designer of the seal, borrowed the
triangulated eye from the apron of the Freemasons. The "father" of the country, whose image adorns the face of the dollar and whose monument is a
monumental obelisk, was a Mason. Washington is often pictured standing
erect with a Masonic apron veiling his jewels.

In a well-known etching (see Fig. 5), the nation's first president is wearing an apron (embroidered by Madame Lafayette) that resembles a pocket
turned inside out or a pouch hanging below his waist. Masonic aprons usually
depict "small temple buildings reminiscent of the Panthéon in Paris; and columns topped with [fruit, as well as] landscape scenes with Egyptian elements
such as sphinxes and obelisks."[3] Almost every apron design includes an
eye–a single eye–in the middle of a triangle, inserted between two erect columns. Examining these eyes carefully, one makes a surprising discovery: the

Figure 5. George Edward Perine, *Washington as a Mason*.

Masonic eye is often the *left* eye. The right eye is a traditional symbol of the sun, day, and the future, but the left eye is a common image of the moon, night, and the past. Might this gazing eye approach from a past that has something to do with the strange *arche* for which we are searching? In view of the image of the pyramid under the eye, it is perhaps noteworthy that the Egyptian god of the moon is Thoth, the nocturnal representative of Ra (the god for whom obelisks usually are constructed). The figure of Thoth, Derrida explains:

> is opposed to its other (father, sun, life, speech, origin or orient, etc.), but as that which at once supplements and supplants it. Thoth extends or opposes by repeating or replacing. By the same token, the figure of Thoth takes shape and takes its shape from the very thing it resists and for which it substitutes. But it thereby opposes *itself*, passes into its other, and this messenger-god is truly a god of the absolute passage between opposites. If he had any identity—but he is precisely the god of nonidentity—he would be that *coincidentia oppositorum* to which we will soon have recourse again. . . .The god of writing is thus at once his father, his son, and himself. He cannot be assigned a fixed spot in the play of differences. Sly, slippery, and masked, an intriguer and a card, like Hermes, he is neither king nor jack, but rather a sort of joker, a floating signifier, a wild card, who puts play into play.[4]

From pocket, to crypt, to jewels, to dollar, to exergue, to eagle, to pyramid, to triangle, to eye, to Thoth—the Egyptian god who invented writing. This course seems errant and the question of archetexture remains obscure. Things might become a bit clearer if we move from capitalism to a distant capital, a capital from which we really have never been very far. With this move, I am trying to think the *space* of postmodernism by rethinking the problem of *time*. To think time radically is to think something like the archetexture of pyramids. It is possible to think this cryptic archetexture by exploring the architecture of the capital—the capital named Paris. This is, of course, an enormous undertaking. I will limit my remarks to a certain axis near the center of the city: Etoile–Place de la Concorde–Louvre. In exploring this axis, my guides will be Merleau-Ponty, Bataille, and Derrida. By considering the archetexture of the capital, I hope to be able to rethink the System of the philosopher in whom ontotheology comes to closure: Hegel, whose name, Derrida tells us on the first page of *Glas*, sounds like the imperial Eagle. My question is whether the archetexture of the pyramid subverts the System of the philosopher who brings *modern* philosophy to completion and thereby marks the opening of the space of postmodernism.

The Etoile is located at the center of a circle from which rays extend and to which they return to insure the orderly circulation of traffic. In the midst of this circle stands the Arc de Triomphe. *Etoile* means star. But it also can designate a star that is a crack in glass. Hence *étoiler* means to star and to crack, and *étoilement* can mean either starring or cracking. At the other end of Les Champs Elysées (which means, of course, the Elysian Fields) is Place de la Concord. In the middle of it there is an Egyptian obelisk covered with hieroglyphics and capped by a pyramid. This obelisk stands on the site once occupied by the guillotine–the place of decapitation where reason finally lost its head. Beyond Place de la Concord, at the end of the axis opposite Etoile, is the Louvre. In the middle of the Louvre there is arising, at this very moment, a pyramid–a *glass* pyramid. Etoile . . . obelisk . . . pyramid–a glass pyramid. This axis might be understood as the figure of a critique of Hegel that culminates in a cryptic text named *Glas*.

Modern philosophy, which reaches closure in the absolute self-consciousness seemingly achieved in Hegel's System, is a *philosophy of the subject*. The modern subject is both *constructive* and *reflexive*. This subject posits itself in its thinking and doing, and returns to itself through an act of recollection that reduces all differences to its own complex identity. The subject of speculative philosophy is a *specular* subject that sees *itself* reflected everywhere–in nature as well as history, in objects as well as other subjects.

Hegel gives his most concise definition of this subject when he describes spirit as "pure self-recognition in absolute otherness."[5] It is important to realize that the Hegelian subject or spirit (for our purposes, these two categories can be used interchangeably) must not be understood simply in individual terms. The subject is *absolute*–it is both universal and particular. In the Hegelian dialectic, part and whole are isomorphic. For both the universal and the particular subject, the recognition of self in other is the sublation (*Aufhebung*) of otherness through which self-identity is achieved. The subject's movement from and return to itself can be understood in terms of space and time. The goal of philosophy is the enjoyment of presence.

Presence, of course, has both a spatial and a temporal dimension. The absolute subject becomes itself in the processes of nature and history. Spirit realizes itself first by externalizing itself in space, as nature, and in time, as history, and then returning to itself in and through human self-consciousness. This circular process reaches completion in the absolute knowledge of Hegel's System. The philosopher's knowledge of the absolute is at the same time the absolute's knowledge of itself. In theological language, human self-knowledge is God's self-knowledge and vice versa. The subject–both human and divine, for in the final analysis these two are one–becomes totally *present* to itself in and through acts of representation in which the subject re-presents itself to itself.

The total presence of the subject is the Parousia–the appearance of essence, which is the realization of the salvation promised in the Christian religion. With the arrival of the eschaton, space and time are, in effect, overcome. Absolute knowledge is the perfect copulation of subject and object, self and other, which issues in certain conception. The certainty of this conception overcomes the uncertainty of Cartesian doubt.[6]

Hegel's *final solution* has always met with suspicion on the part of many of his most sensitive and insightful interpreters. The sensualism of Feuerbach, materialism of Marx, and individualism of Kierkegaard all ask what the System leaves out. Nowhere have these questions about Hegel's System been developed with greater rigor than in French literature and philosophy. The works of many of France's most important twentieth-century writers can be understood as extended responses to Hegel's philosophy. For these thinkers, Hegelianism does not end with his System but extends into this century in the guise of Husserlian phenomenology and structuralism. If Hegel is understood as a protostructuralist and structuralism as latter-day Hegelianism, poststructuralism can be read as an extended critique of Hegel's systematic philosophy. Because Hegelianism is the culmination of modern philosophy, poststructuralism is, by extension, postmodern. By concentrating on the work of Merleau-Ponty, Bataille, and Derrida, it is possible to see the way in which the critique of Hegel continues to shape the current critical landscape. Though not immediately apparent, all of this *does* have something to do with the archetexture of pyramids.

Merleau-Ponty is rarely considered in the context of poststructuralism. This is understandable, for clearly he cannot be classified as a poststructuralist. Nevertheless, his late writings anticipate many of the most important insights of recent critics of structuralism. In his early work, *Phenomenology of Perception*, Merleau-Ponty outlines the genesis of the subject of modern philosophy: "The Cartesian doctrine of the *cogito* was . . . bound to lead logically to the assertion of the timelessness of spirit, and to the admission of a consciousness of the eternal. . . . Eternity, understood as the power to embrace and anticipate temporal developments in a single intention, becomes the very definition of subjectivity."[7] By constituting or constructing its world, the subject appears to be freed from the uncertainties and vicissitudes of temporal existence.

In his important posthumous work, *The Visible and the Invisible*, Merleau-Ponty describes the eternal vision of the reflective subject as "high-altitude thought [*la pensée en survol*]," which results from the sovereign gaze of "the eagle." The perfect knowledge revealed to the "eagle-eye" of the reflective philosopher realizes the dream of the Western philosophical tradition. There is, however, a high price to be paid for this vision—a price that is nothing less than time itself. The *birth* of eternally constructive subjectivity is the *death* of the passionate temporal subject. "It is the dream of philosophers," Merleau-Ponty explains, "to conceive an 'eternity of life,' lying beyond permanence and change, in which time's productivity is pre-eminently contained, and yet a thetic consciousness *of* time that dominates and embraces it merely destroys the phenomenon of time."[8] Merleau-Ponty is convinced that this dream cannot be realized, for he discerns an unavoidable "blind spot" in the philosopher's eagle-eye.

Claims to the contrary notwithstanding, absolute knowledge remains forever inaccessible to the temporal subject. Echoing Heidegger's insistence that ontotheology constitutes itself by forgetting its origin, Merleau-Ponty contends that the philosopher who claims to know universal truth forgets the inescapable nonknowledge from which his reflection repeatedly departs. The experience that nourishes reflection cannot itself be known. In an effort to return to what the speculative philosopher represses, Merleau-Ponty charts a course that leads from the Etoile, along Les Champs Elysées to Notre-Dame and back again. Those who follow this route discover that the return of the repressed is the re-turn of time, which exposes the irreducible absence *of* space. As we will see, the "of" in the phrase "absence of space" must be read in at least two ways.

The achievement of the total self-consciousness requisite for absolute knowledge presupposes that the reflective subject returns to itself from its self-objectification in objects of knowledge. As I have stressed, if knowledge is not to be incomplete, the self must discover *itself* in everything that appears to be other than itself. In one of his richest and most influential criticisms of the reflexivity of self-consciousness, Merleau-Ponty writes:

> The philosophy of reflection . . . thinks it can comprehend our natal bond with the world only by *undoing* it in order to remake it, only by constituting it, by fabricating it. . . . It is, therefore, essential to the philosophy of reflection that it bring us back, this side of our *de facto* situation, to a center of things from which we proceed, but from which we were decentered, that it retravel, this time starting from us, a route already traced out from that center to us. . . . For the movement of recovery, of recuperation, of return to self, the progression toward internal adequation, the very effort to coincide with a nature, which is already ourselves and which is supposed to unfold the things and the world before itself . . . these operations of re-constitution or reestablishment, which come second, *cannot* in principle be the mirror image of its internal constitution and its establishment, as the route from the Etoile to Notre-Dame is the inverse of the route from Notre-Dame to the Etoile; the reflection recuperates everything except *itself* as an effort of recuperation, it clarifies everything except its own role. The eye of spirit or the mind's eye also has its blind spot but, because it is of spirit or of the mind, it cannot be unaware of [this blind spot], nor treat it as a simple state of non-vision. . . . If it is not unaware of itself . . . reflection cannot feign to unravel the same thread that the mind would first have woven.[9]

In this important passage, Merleau-Ponty argues that the irreducible temporality of subjectivity "decenters" self-consciousness in two ways. In the first place, reflection is secondary to an experience that eludes conceptual comprehension. This inaccessible origin of the world of experience effectively deconstitutes or deconstructs the subject's constitutive or constructive acts. In the second place, the achievement of self-consciousness takes time. Merleau-Ponty uses the imaginary journey from the Etoile to Notre-Dame and back to suggest the inevitable *delay* between the constituting act and the return of the constructive subject to itself through the process of re-collection. The interval between the centrifugal and centripetal moments of self-consciousness disrupts the coincidence of origin and conclusion in the life of the subject. As a result of this delay, the consummation of the union of subjectivity and objectivity remains a dream whose realization is perpetually "deferred," or to use Merleau-Ponty's term, *différée*. Temporal deferral opens a space in the subject that self-consciousness can never close. This invisible space blinds the speculative philosopher. The blindness uncovered by Merleau-Ponty preoccupies Bataille.

The goal of speculative philosophy is *concord*. Through rational mediation, the philosopher attempts to reconcile hostile opponents that are engaged in a struggle or battle for mastery. The French word for battle is *bataille;* the French name of the place of concord is Place de la Concord. As I have already noted, in the middle of Place de la Concord (on the site once occupied by the guillotine) there is an obelisk that previously stood in front of a temple in the Egyptian village of Luxor, located next to Thebes, which was the home of Oedipus. In a brief essay bearing the seminal title "Rotten Sun," Bataille suggests a startling series of associations that begin to illuminate this obelisk:

> In mythology, the scrutinized sun is identified with a man who slays a bull (Mithra), with a vulture that eats the liver (Prometheus); in other words, with the man who looks along with the slain bull or the eaten liver. The Mithraic cult of the sun led to a very widespread religious practice: people stripped in a kind of a pit [a pit that anticipates the pit in Derrida's important essay on Hegel's semiology, entitled "The Pit and the Pyramid"] that was covered with a wooden scaffold, on which a priest slashed the throat of a bull; thus they were suddenly doused with hot blood, to the accompaniment of the bull's boisterous struggle and bellowing. . . . Of course the bull himself is also the image of the sun, but only with his throat slit. . . . One might add that the sun has also been mythologically expressed by a man slashing his own throat, as well as by an anthropomorphic being *deprived of a head*. All of this leads one

to say that the summit of elevation is in practice confused with a sudden fall of unheard-of violence. The myth of Icarus is particularly expressive from this point of view.[10]

I can only begin to point out the complexity of the network of images that Bataille is suggesting: a petrified column erected in honor of the sun god, Ra; speculative philosophy as the purest light of reason, which perfectly expresses the truth anticipated in the incarnation of the Son of God, the light of the world; the obelisk marking the site of the terrifying end of the rebellion against the grandson of the Sun King; the obelisk as Hegel's own example of the sign of a sign, which, like his other illustration of the sign, the pyramid, is an empty tomb or a dead letter yet to be elevated or res-erected to reason according to which perfect harmony is a function of complete copulation–the copulation of subject and object that gives birth to thought through effective conception; the incised obelisk covered with hieroglyphics, which is a strange reminder of Egypt, land of Oedipus; a stone column-petrification as the image of castration–castration, which is also figured as decapitation; decapitation as the undoing of the capital, the capitol, and capitalism–especially the capitalization of the I; castration as the cruel cut that makes copulation and conception impossible; the scaffold as the sacrificial altar, which is the place of excessive transgression. One could go on, but this is enough to suggest some of what is at work in Bataille's text.

Let us return to Icarus. Having flown too close to the sun, his wings melt and he falls (it is important to note that the French word for fall, *tombe*, is also the word for tomb, *tombe*), into the sea. (Inasmuch as we are already engaged in the oedipal triangle, I should stress that the French word for sea, *la mer*, is homophonic with the word for mother, *la mère*. The reader who knows Lacan's work will be able to extend this series of associations. It is clear that Bataille and Lacan shared more than a woman named Sylvia.) Bataille relates Icarus and his "high-altitude" flight [*survol*, the same word we have already discovered in Merleau-Ponty] to the soaring of the eagle. This eagle is, for Bataille, as for Merleau-Ponty and Derrida, the image of the philosopher–Hegel.

In an essay entitled simply "The Obelisk," Bataille approaches Hegel's speculative philosophy by way of a consideration of the obelisk with a pyramid at its top, located in the middle of Place de la Concord. According to Bataille, the obelisk "is without a doubt the purest image of the head and the heavens." Recalling a "petrified sunbeam," the firmly fixed obelisk is the "Egyptian image of the IMPERISHABLE." As such, it "is the surest and most durable obstacle to the drifting away of things."[11] When the obelisk is understood in this way, it is possible to interpret Hegel's speculative philosophy as something like an obelisk. As I have already suggested, Hegelian recollection purports to take perishable temporal and spatial existence up into the eternal life of the concept. As Merleau-Ponty points out, the completion of philosophy presupposes the repression of time. But *can* time be forever repressed?

Over against the obelisk of speculative philosophy, Bataille sets "The Pyramid of Suleri." This pyramid is the pyramidal rock in the lake of Silvaplana that occasioned Nietzsche's ecstatic experience of the eternal return. For Bataille, the pyramid of Suleri is the figure of the eternal return of time, which frustrates the monumental desire of the philosopher. Describing Nietzsche's shattering experience, Bataille writes:

> In order to represent the decisive break that took place . . . it is necessary to tie the sundering vision of the "return" to what Nietzsche experienced when he reflected upon the explosive vision of Heraclitus, and to what he experienced later in his own vision of the "death of God." . . . TIME is the object of the vision of Heraclitus. TIME is unleashed in the "death" of the One whose eternity gave Being an immutable foundation. And the audacious act that represents the "return" at the summit of this laceration only wrests from the death of God his *total* strength, in order to give it to the deleterious absurdity of time.[12]

"The deleterious absurdity of time," embodied in Nietzsche's eternal return, involves a fall that, Bataille insists, is *final*. This is the fall from which the philosopher is always attempting to recover—*la tombe* he is always attempting to re-cover. But his efforts are futile, for the repressed—that is to say, time—eternally returns. The eternal return of the fall of time is marked by a *tombe* /tomb—a tomb in the form of a pyramid. This pyramid is the crypt of the ONE that founds and grounds Western philosophy, religion, psychology, society, and culture. The sound (and it is important to remember that in French the word sound is *son*, the English word "son") of this empty tomb, if such empty space sounds, is *glas*, and *glas* is the death knell of the West.

Pursuing a style of questioning initiated by Heidegger, Derrida repeatedly attempts to think what the Western philosophical tradition has left unthought. Heidegger argues that though ontotheology is preoccupied with the question of Being, or more precisely with the presence of Being in all beings, philosophers working in this tradition never raise the question of the origin of the presence of Being as such. From Heidegger's point of view, what needs to be thought is the difference in and through which both Being and beings are determined. He labels this difference the "ontological difference." Though persuaded that Heidegger remains bound to and by the tradition he attempts to dismantle, Derrida recognizes the importance of Heidegger's interrogation of Western philosophy and culture. Indeed there is no single thinker who is more important for Derrida than Heidegger. Derrida's writings can be read as various efforts to think the *difference* that Heidegger describes as the unthought of Western philosophy. This difference is, in Maurice Blanchot's term's, "the non-absent absence" that is the space of time and the time of space.[13]

To think difference "as such" or to think difference *as difference* is to think a difference that is neither an identity nor its binary opposite, a difference. To suggest this irreducibly liminal difference, Derrida coins the neologism *différance*, which, he insists, is "neither a word nor a concept." This curious nonconcept is intended to underscore two contrasting dimensions of *différer:* "temporalization" and "spacing." As the irreducible margin along which time and space interweave, *différance* is the matrix of all presence and absence. In his essay entitled "Différance," Derrida explains:

> In constituting itself, in dividing itself dynamically, this interval is what might be called *spacing* [espacement], the becoming-space of time or the becoming-time of space (*temporalization*). And it is this constitution of the present, as an "originary" and irreducibly nonsimple (and therefore, in the strict sense of the term, nonoriginary) synthesis of marks, or traces of retentions and protentions . . . that I propose to call archi-writing [*archi-écriture*] or archi-trace [*archi-trace*]. Which (is) (simultaneously) spacing (and) temporalization.[14]

With the question of *différance*, we return to the problem of the *arche*. *Différance* is, in some sense, the *arche* of both the differences and the identities that make up the world of experience. This *arche*, however, is a strange source, for it is neither simply an origin nor a ground. To the contrary, it is a "nonoriginal origin" that escapes the polarity of ground and grounded. As the condition of the possibility of presence and absence, *différance* itself is neither present nor absent. Because it is never present, it cannot be re-presented or represented. *Différance* is, to borrow a phrase from Emmanuel Levinas, the "unrepresentable before." This unrepresentable before is an *absolute* past—a past that never was, is, or will be present. The nonpresence (which is not exactly an absence) of this *arche* disturbs all presence and disrupts every present:

> "Older" than Being itself, Derrida explains, such a *différance* has no name in our language. But we "already know" that if it is unnamable, it is not provisionally so, not because our language has not yet found or received this *name*, or because we would have to seek it in another language, outside the finite system of our own. It is rather because there is no *name* for it at all, not even the name of essence or of Being, not even that of *différance*, which is not a name, which is not a pure nominal unity, and unceasingly dislocates itself in a chain of differing and deferring substitutions.[15]

Différance is, then, the impossible "name" of the nameless. The difference between *différance* and *différence* is a single letter—the letter with which writing begins, A. With this A, Derrida attempts to write that which spells the end of every philosophical system based upon the principle of the ONE, which is otherwise known as Identity, Unity, Being, and Presence. This *différance*, however, is not simply *outside* or *opposite* the structure it calls into question. If it were merely outside or opposite, *différance* would still remain *within* the structure of binary opposition. *Différance* is, paradoxically, inside as an outside that forever subverts the opposites it nonetheless makes possible. So understood, *différance* is something like a pocket—a nonphallocentric pocket that is "invaginated" . . . outside turned inside, inside turned outside.

To discover *différance* in the midst of the economy of ontotheology, we need only go back to our own pockets and look again at the exergue of the ONE dollar bill. A reexamination of the pyramid with the tip knocked off imprinted in the exergue of the exergue to the left of the God in whom we trust (i.e., the ontotheological God of Oneness) unexpectedly discloses the letter A. Might this A be the A of *différance?* Perhaps. Consider Derrida's comment in the opening pages of "Différance":

> Therefore, preliminarily, let me recall that this discreet graphic intervention [i.e., the substitution of the *a* for the *e* in *différance*] came to be formulated in the course of a written investigation on a question about writing. Now it happens . . . that this graphic difference . . . , this marked difference between two apparently vocal notations, between two vowels, remains purely graphic: it is read, or it is written, but it cannot be heard. It cannot be apprehended in speech, and we will see why it also bypasses the order of apprehension in general. It is offered by a mute mark, by a tacit monument, I would even say by a *pyramid*, thinking not only of the form of the letter when it is printed as a capital, but also of the text in Hegel's *Encyclopedia* in which the body of the sign is compared to the Egyptian Pyramid. The *a* of *différance*, thus, is not heard; it remains silent, secret and discreet, as a tomb. . . . And thereby let us anticipate the delineation of a site, the familial residence and the tomb of the proper in which is produced, by *différance*, the *economy of death.* This stone—provided one knows how to decipher its inscription—is not far from announcing the death of the king.[16]

Glas, which means, among many other things, death knell, is the inscription of *différance*, the writing of an economy of death that is *l'arrêt de mort*—a death sentence. This sentence of death is written in the form of a pyramid—an empty tomb that is the mark of the inescapability of the time of death rather than the sign of the effective death of time. Toward the end of *Glas*, Derrida returns to the eternal return of time by suggesting an unex-

pected relationship between absolute knowledge and Saturn. To appreciate
the force of this passage, it is necessary to note that Derrida abbreviates absolute knowledge, *savoir absolu* as *Sa*, which is homophonic with *ça*, the
French word for id. It is also useful to recall that in one of his more effusive
moments, Hegel describes the *Phenomenology of Spirit* as "the bacchanalian
revel in which no member is sober":

> One could speak as well–the two words are closely related–of *Sa*'s
> saturnalia. Festival in honor of Saturn: the Italic god who had been
> identified with Kronos (an empty play on words and this was the time
> that one here would come to celebrate as *Sa*). He would have taken
> refuge in Italy after his son had dethroned him and thrown him down
> from the heights of Olympus. With the aid of his mother, Gaia, he
> himself had cut off the testicles of his father. It is again Gaia who already
> put the sickle between the hands of her son. It is, perhaps, she again
> who joins forces with Zeus, her grandson, against Kronos, her son, and
> made him drink a *pharmakon* that forced him to vomit all the children he
> had eaten. Saturn [i.e., *Sa* or *savoir absolu*], absolute knowledge would,
> then, be a deposed father [perhaps a dead king], whose Latin reign,
> nevertheless, had permitted the memory of a mythic golden age. He
> had become the god of agriculture, and more precisely, armed with a
> sickle and billhook, he used to preside over the cutting of the vine. Like
> Dionysus-Bacchus, he was closely associated with wine.[17]

Sa, it appears, is the play of Saturn, Kronos, and Dionysus-Bacchus.

If read in a certain way, this suggestion can be reconciled with Hegel's
System. Hegel is persuaded that the proper dialectical interpretation of
religion culminates in the absolute religion, Christianity, which is the
Vorstellung or representation of absolute knowledge. Derrida reformulates
Hegel's claim: "The absolute religion is not yet what it is already: *Sa*. The absolute religion (the essence of Christianity, the religion of essence) is already
what it is not yet: *Sa*, which itself is already no longer what it still is, the absolute religion."[18] The liminal nonplace of *Vorstellung* is *time*. In Hegel's own
terms, time is the *Dasein* of the concept, or as Derrida phrases it, "time is the
concept itself, which *is there* (*der* da ist)."[19] "The *Da* of the concept (time),"
Derrida explains, "marks the incompleteness, its interior default, the semantic void that holds it in motion. Time is always of this vacancy with which *Sa*
affects itself. Because it affects itself with this, *Sa* empties itself, with a view to
determining itself, *it procrastinates, it gives itself time*. The *Da* of *Sa* is nothing
other than the movement of signification."[20] For Hegel, the "vacuous" movement of signification ends in the semantic plenitude of knowledge. In the

Figure 6. Beverly Pepper, *Ternary Altar*, courtesy of André Emmerich Gallery, 1985.

fullness of time, the unsettling emptiness of temporal representation becomes the reassuring fullness of eternal presentation. This atemporal present/presence marks the advent of the Parousia.[21]

From Derrida's perspective, the realized eschatology of the System is an impossibility. In an effort to expose this impossibility, Derrida abbreviates "the absolute of the already-there of the not-yet or of the yet of the already-no-more [*le déjà-là du pas-encore ou l'encore du déjà-plus*]" with "*pas-là* (the being-there [*da*] of the not [*pas*], which, being there, is not, is not there)."[22] *Pas-là*, not there: this abbreviation provides a concise summary of Derrida's critique of Hegelianism and all it represents:

> Knowledge, truth (of the) phantasm (of) (absolute) philosophy–(absolute) religion, this proposition delineates no limit, is the infinite proposition . . . of speculative dialectics. The infinite circle of auto-insemination that entails the *paideia* of every seminar in its phantasm. What can there be outside of an absolute phantasm? What is one still able to add? Why and how to desire to get out of it?
>
> It is necessary to delay–to give oneself time. The remain(s) of time.[23]

The *pas-là* (the not there) is the remain(s), which "is" both "always already" and forever "remain(s)." This restless remainder (the French word is *reste*, which can be either a noun or a verb) repeats the excessive alternation of *fort/da* in which the *da* (the there) of the *fort* (the gone) is the *fort* (the gone) of the *da* (the there). The ceaseless play of this *fort/da* is the eternal return of time. Forever beyond the pleasure principle, the repetition of *fort/da* binds us to death. Death, however, is never present, though it is not absent. As the nonabsent absence that forever haunts presence–my presence and my present–death approaches yet never arrives. This approach is the apocalypse of apocalypse, the end of the end that exposes an unending opening, which is an incurable wound. This petrifying wound, this mortal tear, is figured in an A that sometimes is sketched as a pyramid with its tip knocked off.

Our wandering–our erring–has taken us from the Etoile, to Place de la Concord, to the Louvre. Etoile, shattered glass. Place de la Concord, pillar of stone with a pyramid at the tip. Louvre, a glass pyramid. If the tomb in the form of a glass pyramid has anything to do with what Derrida describes as the "pyramidal silence" of the A of *différance*, then the glass pyramid opening in the middle of the grandest monument to art might be read in terms of the pyramidal text named *Glas* (and, of course, vice versa). This text opens the *arche* of every text–an *arche* that is the nonoriginal origin eternally returning as the end that never arrives. The dilemma the postmodern architect faces is how to inscribe the space of this time–the nonpresent space of a time that never was, is, or will be present. This is also the dilemma of the writer. In some sense, every text implies the arche-text-ure of pyramids and every arche-tect is a writer.

3.

Deadlines:
Approaching Anarchetecture

.
.
.

Prison House

.
.
.

Dead Lines

"Sometimes she is far away, very far away," she said, making an impressive gesture with her hand.

"In the past?" I asked timidly "Oh, much farther away!"

I pondered, trying to discover what could really be farther away than the past. Meanwhile, she seemed all of a sudden afraid that she had thrown me slightly beyond the limits.

Maurice Blanchot

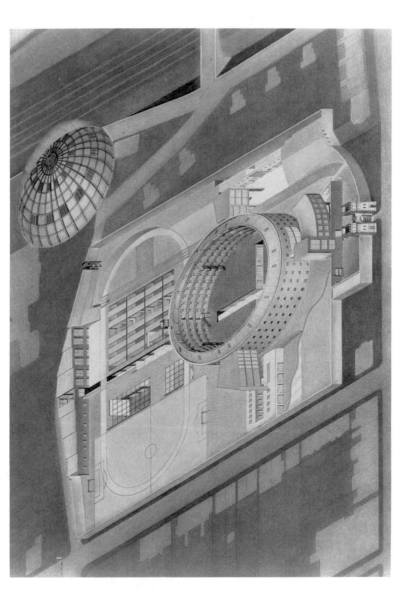

Figure 7. Rem Koolhaas with Stefano diMartino, "Project for Alterations to Arnheim Prison," Netherlands, 1979.

.
.
.

Time . . . what time? Comes . . . from where? The past? What past? Or beyond? Beyond the limit? Of what?

What is a deadline? Is it temporal? Or spatial?
>Temporal: A time limit, as for payment of a debt or completion of an assignment.
>
>Spatial: A boundary line in a prison that prisoners can cross only at the risk of being shot.

Neither simply temporal nor spatial, the deadline is the intersection of time and space that interrupts the present and dislocates presence. As the crossing of time and space, in which time is spaced and space timed, the deadline is a THRESHOLD—an irreducible threshold that is never present as such. To cross the threshold of the deadline is to run the risk of being shot—shot dead

But what is the prison that the deadline surrounds? Who or what is the jailer? Perhaps, but only perhaps, for in this case insiders *cannot* know, the prison house is language and the jailer the penal eye/I of reason. The eye of reason that guards the prison house of language must be panoptical:

>Bentham's *Panopticon* is the architectural figure of this composition. We know the principle on which it was based: at the periphery, an annular building; at the center, a tower; this tower is pierced with wide windows that open onto the inner side of the ring; the peripheric building is divided into cells, each of which extends the whole width of the building . . . All that is needed, then, is to place a supervisor in a central tower and to shut up in each cell a madman, a patient, a condemned man, a worker, or a schoolboy.[1]

If the prison house is constructed by securing the deadline, then can the gaze of reason really be panoptical? Or is such vision but a dream—a dream of the master who is never really master even in "his own" house? What if the circle of the prison house is redrawn as an ellipse—an ellipse without a penal tower in its midst? Is the figure of the ellipse the (re)inscription of an unavoidable ellipsis or vice versa?[2] Is the ellipse/ellipsis what the deadline surrounding the prison house of language is constructed to erase?[3] Is the ellipse/ellipsis the blind spot that drives reason mad by exposing its impotence? Might this im-

potence be traced by decapitating the prison rather than the prisoners . . . as
when Bentham is refigured by Koolhaas and diMartino? In such a prison
house the gaze would always be the gaze of Medusa

.

.

.

Deadlines. . . . Dead Lines: How to draw? How to speak? How to
write? Are such lines (simply) graphic? Or are they inevitably elliptic–even
cryptic?

.

.

.

The Present/Presence of the Modern

.

.

.

Modernity is preoccupied with the presence of the present and the present of presence–the *hic et nunc, ici et maintenant.* The word "modern" derives
from the Latin *modernus,* which means "just now." The modern is of the present and not of the past. The present/presence of the modern is affirmed by
the negation of the past. Rupture is announced in the dictum: "Make it new!"
Or so it seems. It is, of course, possible for the repressed to return unexpectedly. What if the presence of the modern, which seems to arrive in the
break with tradition, turns out to be the culmination of the tradition itself?

The search for the new is the search for originality. The original is not
derivative; it is primary not secondary, independent not dependent . . . on an
O/other. In different terms, to be original is to be present at an origin or an *arche*
that is nothing O/other, or more precisely, is nothing other than oneself.
So understood, the achievement of originality has always been the dream of
Western theology, philosophy, and art. As Heidegger points out: "What
characterizes [Western] metaphysical thinking, which grounds the ground for
beings, is the fact that metaphysical thinking departs from what is present in
its presence, and thus represents it in terms of its ground as something
grounded."[4] During the modern era, the quest for grounding presence takes
the form of the search for a subject that is truly original. Descartes's inward
turn to the subject reaches a certain closure in Hegel's dialectical philosophy

where the subject comes to completion in and through "pure self-recognition in absolute otherness." In this panoptical gaze, subject and object achieve perfect transparency. The logos of the object and the logos of the subject join to form a consciousness that is, in fact, self-consciousness. The subject becomes *present* to itself *here and now* in everything that seems to be other than itself. When all difference returns to identity, the subject is grounded in nothing other than itself. The self-grounded subject is origin-al. Such originality has been the end of the Western tradition from the beginning. Sometimes, however, the end is not the end.

The modern philosophy of the subject extends into the twentieth century in forms of reflection as seemingly different as phenomenology and structuralism. Following Hegel, Husserl regards philosophy as a "universal science" that seeks perfect clarity and certainty by uncovering the "absolute foundations" of knowledge. A phenomenon, for Husserl, is an entity *as it appears to consciousness*. The task of the phenomenologist is to *describe* all being as being-for-consciousness. Through this description, it becomes apparent that every object of experience is the product of a constituting subject. This subject is "the transcendental ego" that projects the world of experience through its "intentional" activity. In examining the object of consciousness, the phenomenologist does not look for empirical data but seeks the ideal logos that, having been constructed by the transcendental subject, constitutes the objectivity of the object. Husserl labels the essential structure of the object its 'eidos.' The eidos is the unchanging form that secures the spatial and temporal presence of the object. The phenomenological eidos is reinscribed in the patterns and codes uncovered in structural analysis. For the structuralist, the object of investigation—be that object a text, a work of art, or psychological and historical processes—is essentially formal. Interpretation moves toward something like eidetic vision in which the knowing subject sees the formal structure that is *present* in the known object. This unifying vision presupposes the isomorphism of subjectivity and objectivity. In a manner reminiscent of Hegel, a structuralist like Lévi-Strauss insists that knowledge must become encylopedic.

It would be a mistake to think that the modern philosophy of the subject that seems to reach closure in Hegel's System resurfaces in this century only in philosophy and the social sciences. It is possible to understand the formalism of abstract art and high modern architecture as the refiguration of philosophical phenomenology and linguistic structuralism. As the phenomenologist attempts to bracket the natural attitude of consciousness and the structuralist struggles to suspend historical supplements in order to discover the essential form of the object, so the modern architect seeks to manifest the transparency of structure by erasing historical reference. In the absence of quotation, the structure of the architectural object is supposed to be self-

Figure 8. Walter Gropius, *Bauhaus*, Dessau, 1927.

referential. The self-referentiality of the created object is the perfect reflection of
the reflexivity of the creative subject. The *arche* of the modern architect is nothing
other than the creative subject of modern philosophy. The erasure of history
in the construction of pure form represents an effort to secure a present/
presence that is undisturbed by the past. The search for this "now" is what
defines modernism. What most modernists do not understand is that the
present/presence of this "now" remains thoroughly traditional. The repressed
returns to establish continuity where there had appeared to be discontinuity.
Just as an end sometimes is not an end, so a beginning sometimes is not a
beginning.

Presence of the Past

·

·

·

The question of the modern is, at least in part, a question of language. As a question of language, it is inseparable from the problem of translation. Language *always* requires translation. Even when no other language is involved, an Other that is not precisely language's Other is repeatedly implied. Thus there is always something missing in translation, always something that remains untranslatable.

When modernity, which is bound to and by the structure of self-referentiality, becomes reflective by turning the question of translation back on itself, language fails. If language fails, how is "modern" to be translated—translated into the language of the philospher in whom modernity comes to closure—the philosopher who insisted that the only truly philosophical language is German? "Modern" does not really need to be translated, for the German word is the "same" as the English: *modern*. The German *modern*, when used as an adjective, means modern, up-to-date, progressive; fashionable, stylish; elegant. But *modern* is duplicitous; it is also a verb that means decay, rot, molder, putrefy. How is one to read the difference between "modern" and *modern*? Are modern constructions—architectural and otherwise—built to repress or wipe away *der Moder*? From what crack does the repressed *Moder* return—always return? Is this crack the fault of modernity that marks the opening of the postmodern?

·

·

·

In 1980 Paolo Portoghesi, Charles Jencks, and others organized the Biennale of Architecture in the old Arsenale in Venice around the theme "The Presence of the Past." More recently Heinrich Klotz mounted an extensive exhibition, first shown in Frankfurt, entitled "Die Revision der Moderne: Postmoderne Architektur 1960–1985." These two shows amply illustrate the remarkable changes architecture has undergone over the past two decades. Gone are the simplicity and formalism of the International Style. Instead of structure purified of decoration and ornamentation, we discover forms, sometimes irregular or even fragmented, cluttered with details that are historically allusive. The shift from the modern to the postmodern involves a return to or of history. Rather than trying to affirm the present by breaking with the past, the postmodern gestures of citation and quotation repeatedly invoke the presence of the past. Tradition returns but with a difference. In their writings, Jencks and Klotz have done much to illuminate the complex relationship between modernism and postmodernism.

As early as 1978, Jencks defined postmodernism as "double coding: the combination of Modern techniques with something else (usually traditional building) in order for architecture to communicate with the public and a concerned minority, usually of other architects."[5] The strategy of communicating on different levels at the same time represents an effort to overcome purported inadequacies of modernism. "Modern architecture," Jencks maintains, "had failed to remain credible partly because it didn't communicate effectively with its ultimate users . . . and partly because it didn't make effective links with the city and history."[6] By joining past to present and present to past, the postmodern architect constructs a double code, which, according to Jencks, is intended to communicate in different ways to different people. The polymorphous perversity of architectural forms generates a polysemy that is creative rather than destructive. Such plurivocality seems to undercut the possibility of univocality. It is, however, important to understand the precise nature of the polysemy Jencks identifies. Each message in the double code is, in principle, understandable. The duplicity of meaning results when different messages are conjoined. Jencks's double code, therefore, simultaneously multiplies meaning and *controls* its proliferation.

When plurivocality is radicalized, single-mindedness becomes impossible. Equivocality displaces univocality, and truths that once seemed certain begin to appear undeniably fictive. Anticipating much of Jencks's argument, Klotz contends that postmodernism represents "an architecture of narrative, symbolism and fantasy."[7] Klotz recognizes that the rehistoricization of architectural form through supplementary details and ornaments involves neither a reactionary response to modernism nor a nostalgia for the simplicity and security of earlier times. The past that returns in historical citation is transformed through its reinscription. When quoted by the postmodern architect, the past is, in effect, rewritten as fiction. The past that is present as fiction is never simply re-presented. Rather, representation itself is refigured in and through repetition. The implications of the refiguration of representation, which prepares the way for the presence of the past in postmodern architecture, can be seen by noting central insights that emerge in contemporary semiology. Signs, we have learned, do not re-present objects or events that once were present. To the contrary, the sign is always the sign of a sign. Forever entangled in the play of signification, we never have access to things themselves and thus cannot penetrate naked reality. What we often naively take to be objectivity is actually nothing other than a sign or set of signs whose signature has been forgotten. Inasmuch as we deal only with signs and never with "reality" as such, our knowledge is inescapably fictive. Unlike (almost all) their predecessors, postmodernists not only recognize but gaily embrace the fictions among which they are destined to err. It is, of course, Nietzsche who is the most prescient precursor of this postmodern understanding of understanding.

> Against positivism, which halts at phenomena–"There are only *facts*"–I would say: No, facts is precisely what there is not, only interpretations. We cannot establish any fact "in itself": perhaps it is folly to want to do such a thing. . . . Insofar as the word "knowledge" has any meaning, the world is knowable; but it is *interpretable* otherwise, it has no meaning behind it, but countless meanings.–Perspectivism.[8]

Nowhere have the implications of Nietzsche's fragmentary account of interpretation been more artfully expressed than in the poetry of Wallace Stevens. In a poem entitled "Asides on the Oboe," Stevens rereads Nietzsche's perspectivism in terms of poetic fiction:

> The prologues are over. It is a question, now,
> Of final belief. So, say that final belief
> Must be in a fiction. It is time to choose. . . .
> The impossible possible philosophers' man,
> The man who has had the time to think enough,
> The central man, the human globe, responsive
> As a mirror with a voice, the man of glass,
> Who in a million diamonds sums us up. . . .
> It was not as if the jasmine ever returned
> But we and the diamond globe at last were one.
> We had always been partly one. It was as we came
> To see him, that we were wholly one, as we heard
> Him chanting for those buried in their blood,
> In the jasmine haunted forests, that we knew
> The glass man, without external reference.[9]

Postmodern fictions are as fragile as the glas(s) man who makes them. This fragility is the result of the recognition of fiction as fiction. In the postmodern world, belief is both impossible and unavoidable. The fictions we fabricate do not refer in any straightforward way to things or events "out there" in the "real" world. That world, like Kant's thing-in-itself, is completely inaccessible and hence functionally nonexistent. In different terms, the concept of reality or the notion of the true world is nothing but another fiction that we invent (usually unknowingly) to check and balance the signs from which there is no exit. Stevens summarizes the complex interplay between fiction and belief in an in.portant posthumous text: "The final belief is to believe in a fiction, which you know to be a fiction, there being nothing else. The exquisite truth is to know that it is a fiction and that you believe in it willingly."[10]

If one follows the leads of Nietzsche and Stevens, it becomes apparent that it is not only the past that is fictive. If signs are always signs of signs, then in the final analysis (but, of course, there is no final analysis, for analysis is inevitably interminable) everything is fictive. The recognition of the inescapability of fiction issues in what can best be described as *ironic self-consciousness*. Rather than nostalgic or reactionary, the presence of the past in postmodern architecture is ironic. Irony, as Kierkegaard citing Hegel insists, is "infinite and absolute negativity."[11] As such, irony entails a paradoxical strategy for relating to the world of experience in which one simultaneously sustains a certain attachment while remaining somewhat detached. In the ironic gesture, one distances oneself from that to which one nonetheless relates. The duplicity of this negativity renders it infinite or absolute. Never merely negative, irony harbors a positivity that results from doubling negation. While realizing the fictiveness of the signs with which one deals, the ironist acknowledges their necessity. Signs that are negated as real or true are reappropriated as fictive, which is not to say false.

The positivity involved in absolute negation, however, is more profound than the return of the sign as sign. Irony, I have suggested, is a form of *self-consciousness*. From the ironist's point of view, ironic self-consciousness is *more complete* and thus *higher* than nonironic awareness. It is precisely the sophistication of ironic consciousness that transfigures the past in its quotation. Ironists "know" something that those they cite do not know or did not know: ironists "know" that they believe and that they can believe in nothing other than fictions. The negation and reappropriation of the past is, therefore, the assertion of the subject's own ironic self-consciousness. The performance played out on the postmodern stage unexpectedly displays a subject that affirms itself in and through a negation that is absolute or infinite.

If, however, the negativity of irony is the covert positivity of subjectivity, then are the fabrications of "the glass man" really different from glass constructions in the International Style? As modernism unwittingly perpetuates the tradition from which it struggles to escape, so postmodern architecture (as traditionally understood) is actually an extension of the most basic philosophical presuppositions of modernism. The end of both modern and ironic self-consciousness seems to be Stevens's glass man, without external reference. Contrary to expectation, when everything becomes transparent, (the) all becomes obscure. To be without external reference is to be locked up in a prison house. For the ironic postmodernist, as for the visionary modernist, this prison house is *language*. With this insight, apparent opposites collapse into a surprising identity. Fictive perspectivism becomes indistinguishable from absolute idealism. The idealist's claim, that objectivity is truly subjectivity and vice versa, returns in the ironist's confession that signs are signs of signs. Though seemingly partial, the gaze of the ironist is, in its own way, panoptical. Affirming itself in every negation, the ironist extends rather than subverts the modern philosophy of the subject. In seeing through everything, the glass man sees *himself*–sees himself more truly than anyone before him:

> He is in the transparence of the place in which
> He is and in his poems we find peace.
> He sets this peddler's pie and cries in summer,
> The glass man, cold and numbered, dewily cries,
> "Thou art not August unless I make thee so."
> Clandestine steps upon imagined stairs
> Climb through the night, because his cookoos call.[12]

"August": the cry of a subject still too august.

.

.

.

Future of the Past

.

.

.

> The threshold . . . sustains the middle in which the two, the outside and the inside, penetrate each other. The threshold bears the between. . . . The threshold, as the settlement of the between, is hard because pain has petrified it. But the pain that became appropriated to stone did not harden into the threshold in order to congeal there. The pain presences unflagging in the threshold, as pain.[13]

The pain of the threshold issues from the *Riss* that both opens and faults the work of art. The sign that de-sign-nates this *Riss* is the tear that is a tear. The pain from which this tear flows is unknown to the ironic subject. The tears of the pain of difference rend the subject of modern philosophy (and architecture). The *Aufriss* of the *Riss* not only "draws and joins" but also draws and quarters. The tear of difference is neither more nor less than an evasive line that marks the nonsite of death. This aberrant line, which, of course, neither exists nor does not exist, "is" a deadline. The deadline that can never

Figure 9. Ueli Berger, *Riss,* Bern, 1970.

be met marks the threshold of the prison house of language. Neither the classical modern nor traditional postmodern architect dares transgress this limit. To entertain such transgression, one would have to imagine the cryptic drawing of deadlines.

Figure 10. Arata Isozaki, *Future City*, Tsukuba Center Building, 1985.

The failure of modernism is undeniable in Ibaraki. As Heidegger insists, the atomic age is the inevitable end of the Western theological and philosophical tradition. The bomb is the actual embodiment of the struggle for mastery that comes to a devastating conclusion in the modern subject's will to power. If irony is interpreted as an extension of the will to power in which the self affirms itself through infinite and absolute negation, then Hiroshima and Nagasaki might be understood as the end of modernity and the anticipation of the end of postmodernity. In the flash of the bomb, calculative-technological reason turns on its creator with tragic consequences. What can possibly rise from such ruins?

Ibaraki represents an attempt to answer this urgent question. But the "answer" is a failure; in the effort to erase the past, the errors of modernity are repeated. In contrast to many towns, villages, and cities of the past, Ibaraki has neither a definite center nor obvious boundaries. Near what might once have been the center, the planners of the new city placed the Temple of Reason: the uni-versity. This university, however, quickly became a place of death. The young, in distressingly large numbers, began committing suicide on the university grounds. Having become concrete, the lines of the modern city became all-too-literally deadlines. How, asked city dwellers, can such terrifying deadlines be erased without leaving a trace?

Though atomic fission seems to make fusion unachievable and centeredness impossible, for many people some kind of center appears necessary to human survival. Yet any simple return to a past center of orientation is unthinkable. The center that once seemed secure must be redrawn in such a way that it can simultaneously be affirmed and denied. In his Tsukuba Center Building (1979–1983), Arata Isozaki attempts to accomplish this double gesture by a nonnostalgic return to the past. He refigures the decentered city around a *fictive* center established by historical citation. In the midst of Ibaraki, Isozaki recreates the center of the world. More precisely, he reconstructs the center of the center of the Eternal City–Rome–by replacing the Place of Death with a representation of the Campidoglio. In this return, the past is supposed to be refigured so as to transfigure the present.

But Isozaki seems uncertain about the success of his "solution" to the problem of the destruction of modernity. He offers a *supplement* to his "Center Building." This supplement is a painting that reinscribes (which *is not* to say represents) the reconstruction of the reconstructed city. The title of the supplement is *The Future City*. The city of the future is a city in ruins. Isozaki gives no explanation . . . just an image. In his painting, the city is precariously perched on the brink of a cliff. The buildings–even obviously postmodern buildings–are all decapitated. Through the middle of the reconstructed center runs a deep *Riss* or fissure. This fault, which extends through the buildings, past the limit of the city, to the edge of the cliff, and beyond, is *black*. What is this tear? What future does it portend?

The ruined city of the future, Isozaki implies, has been struck by a strange disaster. Unlike the catastrophe wrought by the bomb, Isozaki's uncanny disaster does not destroy everything but, in a certain sense, leaves things unchanged. What kind of a disaster is both destructive and nondestructive? Maurice Blanchot probes but never actually answers this question.

> The disaster is the gift; it gives disaster: as if it took no account of being or non-being. It is not advent (the proper of what arrives or takes place)—it does not arrive or happen. And thus I cannot ever happen upon this thought, except without knowing, without appropriating any knowledge. Or again, is it the advent of what does not arrive or happen, of what would come without arriving or happening, outside being, and as though by drifting away? The posthumous disaster? . . .
> The disaster is not somber, it would liberate us from everything if it could just have a relation with someone; we would know it in light of language and at the twilight of language with a *gai savoir*. But the disaster is unknown; it is the unknown name for that in thought that dissuades us from thinking of it, distancing us by its proximity. Alone in order to be exposed to the thought of the disaster that disrupts solitude and overflows every variety of thought, as the intense, silent and disastrous affirmation of the outside.[14]

Disaster . . . the unknown name for that in thought that dissuades us from thinking of it . . . does not arrive or happen . . . is the advent of what does not arrive or happen, of what would come without arriving . . .

What does not arrive or happen is yet to come. The exteriority of the disaster is a future that can *never* become present. As I have stressed, this future is, for Blanchot, inseparably bound to an extraordinary past that has never been and can never be present. Forever eluding any form of presentation, this past repeatedly approaches as a future that never arrives. This never-present past, which is always on the edge of the present as the never-present future, is the "terrifyingly ancient." The disastrous implications of this *futur antérieur* can be partially clarified by examining the relationship of Blanchot's "terrifyingly ancient" to Emmanuel Levinas's "unrepresentable before."

Much of *The Writing of the Disaster* is written in response to Levinas. In his most philosophically astute work, *Otherwise than Being or Beyond Essence*, Levinas develops an indirect critique of the tendency of structuralists to concentrate on synchronic form rather than historical and temporal development by formulating a complex analysis of diachrony. Instead of envisioning past and future as modalities of the present, Levinas points toward an irreducible past that was never present. He labels this past *anarchie*. This anarchy is an *an-arche* that signals a "deep formerly" (*profond jadis*), which is not a " 'modification' of the present":[15]

Incommensurable with the present, unassemblable in it, it is always "already in the past" behind which the present delays, over and beyond the "now" that this exteriority disturbs or obsesses.[16]

Like the Lacanian unconscious, which is something other than the Freudian preconscious, the trace of Levinas's anarche is a past "more ancient than every representable origin, a pre-original and anarchical *passed*."[17] Instead of an absolute origin (*arche*), the *an-arche*, which is *toujours-déjà*, renders impossible every origin and all originality. In the wake of the trace of this past, everything and everybody is ever after–that is, never primary, always secondary. That the subject is irreducibly secondary implies, for Levinas, a passionate submission to what cannot be understood within the framework of experience or reception–with all the intentionality, self-awareness, and self-containment that such experience would imply:

Passivity, "more passive than all passivity," consisted in suffering–or more exactly in having suffered already in an unrepresentable past–which never was present–an unassumable traumatism, struck in the "in" of the infinite, devastating presence and waking subjectivity to the proximity of an other.[18]

To suffer this unnamable alterity is to undergo an "experience" that does not *take place* (*qui n'a pas lieu*). The anarche to which the suffering subject is subjected is unending and thus infinite. It "is" nothing other than the *in-fini* itself. Having been submitted to an "experience" that does not take place, "I," as subject, am always already subjected to the *In-fini* that is (impossibly) placed "within" me:

The *in* of the infinite designates the depth of affection with which subjectivity is affected by this placing of the Infinite in it, without prehension, or comprehension. Depth of an undergoing [*subir*] that no capacity embodies, that is no longer upheld by any foundation, where all processes of investment fail and where all the locks that close the interior of interiority [*arrières de l'interiorité*] break open. Setting without gathering [*mise sans recueillement*], devastating its place as a devouring fire, catastrophizing the place, in the etymological sense of the word.[19]

The *in-fini* "within" is the disastrous "outside" that tears open property lines and prison walls that would de-fine, bound, and authenticate the place of interiority presupposed by experience proper. Unhinging the prison gates, that which is placed "within" the subject, without any possibility of receiving it, opens (the) one by an opening of opening itself–a tear that devastates, consumes, "catastrophizes" the very ground or place by which interiority and exteriority are rendered discrete.

Anarche . . . Anarchie . . . Devastating (non)place . . . catastrophizing, traumatizing the place . . . every place. The "writing of the disaster" is inscribed in deadlines that form and deform *Death Sentence[s]*.[20] Perhaps these deadlines are drawn in the dark fault of Isozaki's *The Future City*. But why did Isozaki draw or paint this future of the past as a supplement to a city he had rebuilt? Why didn't he construct the *Riss* that is the deadline marking the limit of the modern and its return in the postmodern?

The tear that inscribes the deadline cannot be *constructed* but can only be *deconstructed*. Never present and yet not absent, the *anarche* that faults every modern and postmodern construction can never be figured as such. *If* the past that approaches in the disastrous future is to be solicited, it must be *between* lines that remain irreducibly cryptic. Fault is always dark–as dark as the night beyond night whose darkness cannot be dispelled by day.

Postmodernism, at least in architecture, is, in a certain sense, over before it begins. Instead of reversing the assumptions of modernism, the postmodern return to the past actually extends the modern philosophy of the subject. Nothing O/other can happen until contemporary architects begin to reconceive space by rethinking time. In *anarche*, time is spaced and space is timed. This anarchic threshold harbors a space without presence and a time without the present. Architects–classical, modern, and postmodern–can never represent this unrepresentable before. *Anarche* can be figured, if at all, only in anarchetecture. Rather than resecuring foundations and reestablishing centers, the anarchetect makes everything tremble . . . even if ever so slightly. The fear of this trembling subverts the self-certainty of modern man.

.

.

.

deadlines

.

.

.

What is this life, where the only certainty is the only thing one cannot with any certainty learn about: death; for when I am, death is not, and when death is, I am not.[21]

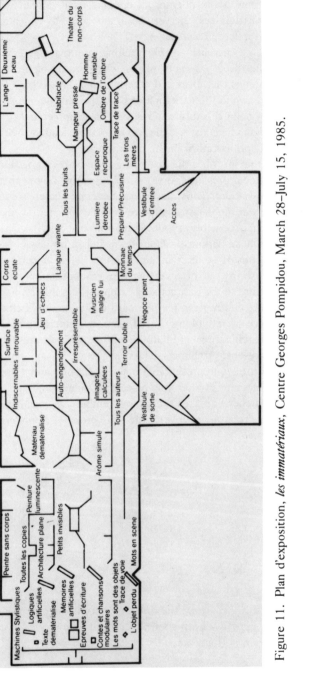

Figure 11. Plan d'exposition, *les immatériaux*, Centre Georges Pompidou, March 28–July 15, 1985.

Figure 12. Peter Eisenman, Romeo and Juliet Palace in Verona, *Moving Arrows, Eros, and Other Errors* (The text superimposed on Eisenman's drawing is from Blanchot's *Le pas au-delà*, p. 49.)

.

.

.

Why hasn't it been built?
Can it be constructed?
Only deconstructed?
Time will tell.
If, that is,
time can
tell

.

.

.

D
E
L
A
Y
D
E
F
E
R
R
A
L
A
L
W
A
Y
S
L
A
T
E
D
E
A
D

L
I
N
E
S
C
A
N
N
E
V
E
R
B
E
M
E
T

.
.
.

4.

Messages from/to the Post Age: A Letter to Peter Eisenman[1]

January 8, 1988

Dear Peter,

Playing on/off a House of Cards

This "book" is a disaster! But is it disastrous enough? The question concerns the architecture of the text (a text that sometimes harbors a nostalgia for the book – but I defer for a moment) and the text of archetexture.

The columns are unstable. They are never in the expected place. When the page is turned, the column is not there or is not where it "should" be. Columns that are not columns support nothing – if, that is, nothing can be supported. It is always possible, of course, that nothing is insupportable.

Colors: red, white, and blue (and black)
red and white; black and blue

If "meaning" were differential the spacing of terms would make a difference.

If the text is read as red, white, and blue, it is magisterial. If it is read as black and blue, it wounds.

51

Do the colors of the columns subvert their instability? What if colors had also alternated? Then the text would have been yet more difficult to read.

Is the text textual enough? "Although attitudes and methods have changed somewhat over time, the project of this book has nevertheless remained single-minded." You give away too much. Why the need to see the unity of the *book*. Might you misread your misreading here?

Reply/Repli

Fin again/Begin again . . . at the fin. With a repli of/to the p.s. Blue (why?) gas . . . becoming uncorked. Loses definition. The absence of (read at least doubly) definition erases foundations. Why is the floor of House VI blue? Perhaps this is where the uncorked gas ends up. If so, the floor is not a floor.

G(l)as(s) House

What a gas! To build a glass house that is not a glass house as a commentary (before it had been read) on a glas book that is not a glass book. *Glasarchitektur* is not transparent and is not opaque in the way the modernist thought it was. A deconstructive architecture must be a Glas-architektur. This is, of course, the most difficult construction. If "glass is above all the enemy of secrets," then the task is to de-sign a glass house, which in and through its ostensible transparency, inscribes a secret. Where to look for the "archetype"? Not only *Glas* but, more importantly, "Fors." I enclose "Secretions."

Anxiety needs to be thought more rigorously. Most of the reflection on anxiety has come out of the existentialist tradition. This is not the reading you are after. Anxiety must be thought with and through the erasure of the individual. The difference between existentialist anxiety and this other anxiety is the difference between early and late Heidegger. Read: "What is Metaphysics?" This is one crack in Heidegger's project—a crack that inscribes the anxiety that eventually becomes "The Origin of the Work of Art."

The disappointment of the Krauss and Tafuri essays is that they are already old. Thus some of the misreadings are not productive. Krauss is simply wrong when she identifies structuralism and postmodernism. And yet her reading of the critique of idealism is on target. Moreover, her recognition of the relationship between pleasure and decipherment on the one hand and blockage and what we now can call *jouissance* on the other is suggestive. I could write more, for hers is a fine essay.

You are more interested in dirt—or at least now realize that you have always been more interested in dirt—than Tafuri allows. Indeed, to move toward the grotesque you now seek is to move toward dirt. Perhaps that dirt is the absent presence in all the white of those early houses. When you fully acknowledge this (but what might this mean?), the gas in the blue vial becomes the vile gas of a fart. Until you allow space for that stench, you cannot be as grotesque as you claim to want to be.

With sincere appreciation for the disastrous gift of this disastrous text . . .

Mark

5.

p. s.
fin again

The question would be this: why does laughter
here traverse the whole of the experience which
refers us to *Finnegans Wake,* and thus not letting
itself be reduced to any of the other modalities,
apprehensions, affections, whatever their richness, their heterogeneity, their overdetermination? And what does this writing teach us of the
essence of laughter if it recalls that laughter to
the limits of the calculable and the incalculable,
when the whole of the calculable is outplayed
by a writing about which it is no longer possible
to decide if it still calculates, calculates better
and more, or if it transcends the very order of
calculable economy, or even of an incalculable
or an undecidable which would still be homogeneous with the world of calculation? A certain
quality of laughter would supply something like
the affect . . . to this beyond of calculation, and
of all calculable literature.

Jacques Derrida

Voice

In the wake of Finnegan, I hesitate to beginegan. I hesitate . . . (in
order) to begin. After "Joyce and the End of History," I hesitate to begin.
After all, after "all in all," I hesitate to begin.[1] I hesitate to begin by voicing a
question . . . voicing a question that is nothing other than the question of
voice. I am especially hesitant to begin with voice and its "I" when the book
proper begins with vision and its eye (i.e., "The Birth of Vision"). I

hesitate . . . to question . . . for my question involves a certain hesitation. I hesitate to add such an insignificant p.s. to such a significant book. Nevertheless, I begin again[2] with a question: Who is speaking in *History as Apocalypse?*

Though I begin with the question of speaking, my hesitation involves the question of writing. Is it possible to write after someone (but who?) has said it all by saying the All? Or is it possible to write only after someone (but who?) has said it all by saying the All? If I am to begin again, my writing will have to be after All . . . after the End. My writing will have to be something like a postscript, which, after all, might already have been written by an other. Preoccupied with an after that might be before, my hesitation concerning the book is a "hereistance," which at the *fin* again returns as the "*nat* now" of every here. Such hesitation gives one pause. Perhaps this delay allows the time and space for the outbreak of *le rire déchirant*—the laugh that displaces every possible "restricted economy" with an impossible "general" "echonomy." Arguing that *Finnegans Wake* is "the 'writable' text par excellence," Jean-Michel Rabaté maintains that this "text hesitates between the *writable/unreadable*, which the reader must rediscover at the cost of an excessive investment or an 'ideal insomnia,' and the *readable/risible*—that 'readable' which attacks us brutally in the laughter that takes us unaware when we are faced with a sentence or a word. As Freud well said, the more one looks for the meaning of the joke, the less one laughs, for laughter comes from an economy—in *Finnegans Wake*, an impossible economy. The paradoxical economy of *Finnegans Wake* carries along a perpetual mobilization and a cumulative discharge that is liberated in fits and starts in the laughter that surges up now and then, is triggered off by the sense of a suddenly significant nonsense, without a place consecrated by the wit and prepared in advance for the reader, without the author having foreseen the points of intersection of the crazily interwined series."[3] If the text that is supposed to mark "The End of History" is read as writerly, can there ever be apocalypse here, now? In the "risible universe" of the *Wake*, perhaps "*The* End" is impossible, or is possible only as the eternal return of the fin again.

I begin again by repeating or returning (for the repetition of [the] return remains in question as questioning) to the question of voice: Who *is* speaking in *History as Apocalypse?* For anyone who has read the remarkable series of books beginning and ending (for the moment!) with the question (if it is a question) of apocalypse—a series extending from *The New Apocalypse*[4] to *History as Apocalypse*—there can be little doubt about the name of the speaker. The identity of Altizer's voice is obvious. The words that constitute his lexicon are unmistakable: source, ground, first, primal, origin, original, immediacy, here, now, real, actual, integral, whole, full, complete, totality, absolute, pure, center, organic, ultimate, final, end, identity, voice, speech, presence, above all presence—total presence. The presence of Altizer's voice establishes his undeniable identity. Or so it has seemed until this book. Now we learn that the presence of identity itself is becoming a thing of the past. *History as Apocalypse* begins (more precisely, almost begins, for the decisive words form the opening of a "Prologue" that falls between a "Preface" and the first chapter) by observing that we are losing our identity—"our primal identity." "No greater danger lies before us today," Altizer writes, "than that of the loss of our deeper or primal identity, an identity that has always been the center of mythical and ritual traditions throughout the world, just as it has been the center of our imaginative and intellectual creations" (p. 7).

History as Apocalypse marks the culmination of Altizer's effort to recover this primal identity. But questions remain. After finishing the concluding chapter, which ends with " 'Lff' is all in all," "we can ask ourselves if eschatology is a tone, or even the voice itself. Isn't the voice always that of the last man?"[5] And who is the last man? Perhaps he is the one who, after having proclaimed the good news of the death of God, repeats the words of Nietzsche:

> I am the last man. No one speaks to me except myself alone, and my voice reaches me like that of a dying person. With you, beloved voice, with you, last breath of the memory of all human happiness, allow me still this commerce of a single hour. Thanks to you I delude my solitude, and I penetrate into the lie of a multiplicity and a love, for my heart loathes believing that love is dead; it does not support the shudder of the most solitary of solitudes, and obliges me to speak as if I were two.[6]

" . . . as if I were two." Why "as if"? Is this "as if" related to the quotation marks that sometimes surround the word *other* in Altizer's writings? If the marks between which the *other* is suspended are erased, it becomes possible to reread "the last man" as *Le Dernier Homme*—a text written by one who, in the most solitary of solitudes, writes but *never* speaks.[7]

The question of "the narrational voice"[8] emerges outside the book proper in the gaps that simultaneously separate and join Preface, Prologue, and chapter 1. Moving from one to the other, the voice of the author slips from "I" to "we" to "anonymity." The Preface is filled with proper names (my "own" among them). There is, however, one noteworthy name missing from this list: Thomas Jonathan Jackson Altizer. Altizer's name does not appear in the Preface or anywhere else *in* the book. Unlike most authors, he does not sign the Preface and does not specify the place (here) or time (now) of writing. In the prefatory remarks, the author appears only through his substitute—the pronoun "I." It is with the "I," the repetition of the "I," that the Preface ends. "And I owe a particular debt to . . . to say nothing of the deep gratitude I owe . . . " (p. 5). This remark suggests that the authorship of the "I" involves a restricted economy in which expenditure repays debt. Having declared books balanced and accounts closed, the "I" disappears.

Between the last sentence of the Preface and the first sentence of the Prologue (a gap marked by the white space of two empty pages), a significant shift occurs. The Prologue begins with the following words: "No greater danger lies before us today . . . "(p. 7). In the brief space of two blank pages, "we" replaces "I." After the Preface, the "I" never again appears in the book. The narrational voice of *History as Apocalypse* is the first person plural: *we*. The disappearance of the "I" is the condition of the possibility of the appearance of the "we." But who are we; what is the "we"? At first glance, it seems that we are author and reader. But the matter is not so simple. As *we* move from Prologue to chapter 1 (it is important to recall that everything prior to this point falls outside the book strictly so called), the identity of the "we" becomes obscure. "The Birth of Vision" begins anonymously: "Beginning is anonymous" (p. 17). The anonymity of the beginning is the end toward which the book relentlessly moves.

These shifts in narrational voice provide a prolepsis of the argument of the book as a whole. Altizer charts what he describes as the "eternal voyage of universal humanity" (p. 16) as it moves from the emergence of the "I" to the disappearance of the individual subject in the anonymity of an all-encompassing "we." This journey to and from selfhood unfolds in the Western epic tradition:

> It is the Western literary tradition, and more particularly the Western epic tradition, that most fully embodies and makes manifest the historical evolution and realization of self-consciousness. Here, one discovers a historical origin or beginning of the individuality and interiority of consciousness, an interiority and individuality of consciousness that passes into self-consciousness with the advent of Christianity and then into an integral, necessary, and final movement and destiny of self-consciousness with the birth, evolution, and resolution or consummation of the Christian epic tradition. Our individual and interior consciousness begins with Homer; at least, there is no available evidence of its prior appearance. So likewise an interior and individual consciousness ends with Joyce, or so it would seem in our perspective, and certainly nothing in our world offers any possibility of going "beyond" *Finnegans Wake*. Consequently, *The Iliad* and *Finnegans Wake* mark the historical boundaries of our consciousness and self consciousness, thereby giving our consciousness an integral and individual identity that otherwise would be absent. [pp. 9–10]

History as Apocalypse is inscribed within the tradition it describes. More precisely, this monumental book is an epic of epics. By rereading "the Christian epic tradition" as "an organic and historical whole," Altizer creates an epic work, which, he insists, is something other than merely his own. The narration of this metaepic is intended to fill the gaps between "I," "we," and the "anonymity" of "universal humanity." Insofar as the subject of this epic is one (and/or the One), Altizer's story is also our own. The "I" of the author and the "I" of the reader join in the narrational "we" of the book. At the end of the book, voice becomes One. As the reenactment of the entire epic tradition, *our* reading of the epic of epics brings to closure not only this tradition but individual selfhood.

It is clear that Altizer models his pedagogy on the writings of Hegel. *History as Apocalypse* represents something like a combination of the *Phenomenology of Spirit*, the *Lectures on Aesthetics*, the *Lectures on the Philosophy of Religion*, and the *Philosophy of History*. The questions raised by the narrational voice of *History as Apocalypse* repeat and extend difficulties surrounding the phenomenological "we" in the *Phenomenology of Spirit*.[9] For the book to be written, the author must, yet cannot, identify with the reader. On the one hand, if instructing author and instructed reader are at the same stage of consciousness, the author cannot write the epic of epics. On the other hand, if author and reader are not one, the "we" who is supposed to narrate the book is unreal—more fictive than actual. The possibility of the fictive status of the narrational voice raises the prospect that the book itself might be fiction. Altizer repeatedly asserts that the story being told is *history* rather than fiction. But even after the end of the book, questions linger. These questions return repeatedly.

The Hegelianism of Altizer's strategy is not surprising to those who are familiar with his earlier work. Altizer is, without a doubt, our most Hegelian theologian. From the outset, the form and content of his position have been shaped by a creative appropriation of Hegel's insights. There are, of course, significant differences between Hegel and Altizer. Most importantly, while Hegel maintains that philosophy brings to completion the truth represented first in art and then in religion, Altizer translates Hegel's philosophical wisdom into religious images that achieve fulfillment in modern art. Altizer insists that his reversal of Hegel's argument perfects rather than overturns the Hegelian dialectic.

Although *History as Apocalypse* draws together a line of analysis that has been unfolding throughout Altizer's works, it stands in a special relationship to his two most recent books, *The Self-Embodiment of God* and *Total Presence*. Presented as a drama in five acts (Genesis, Exodus, Judgment, Incarnation, and Apocalypse), *The Self-Embodiment of God* articulates the bare dialectical structure of Altizer's position. In *Total Presence* Altizer attempts to render concrete his relentlessly abstract language by suggesting the way in which the

Christian Logos is concretely realized in and through the historical process. Falling between his earlier speculative work and his latest "historical" analysis, *Total Presence* can best be understood as a transitional work outlining the argument more fully developed in *History as Apocalypse*. The movement from abstract speculation to concrete analysis is made possible by an examination of language. The subtitle of *Total Presence* is, significantly, *The Language of Jesus and the Language of Today*. A consideration of Altizer's account of language in this book helps to clarify the argument of *History as Apocalypse*. The language of Jesus, we discover, *is* the language of today, and the language of today is the language of the here and now. Today, here and now, presence is total presence.

According to Altizer, "there is virtually unanimous scholarly agreement that the parabolic language of the Gospels is closest to the original language of Jesus."[10] Furthermore, the language of parable is the language of *presence*. "Pure parable embodies an auditory as opposed to a visual presence, an immediate sounding which commands and effects a total attention. One hears a parable, and does so even in reading, for parable sounds or speaks an immediate presence."[11] The eschatological presence embodied in parabolic speech is the product of the perfect union of God, self, and world. In the word of the parable, "world speaks in voice itself, and as voice as well. True parabolic speech is the speech of world itself, a speech wherein and whereby world is totally actual and immediately at hand. Then speech is world and world is speech at once." The immediacy of the here and now present in speech erases "every trace of a beyond which is only beyond."[12] The absence of every beyond realizes the total presence of the Kingdom of God. For Altizer, the Kingdom of God is nothing other than the enjoyment of a presence that is total. This pure presence becomes actual *in* speech *as* speech.

But is Jesus's parabolic *speech* really present? Altizer is forced to admit that Jesus's speech is present only as absent. The original speech of pure parable has always already disappeared in the written text of scripture. Altizer acknowledges that "the very act of writing deeply transforms a purely parabolic language." Within Altizer's dialectical scheme, the transformation of speech into writing is in effect the fall that sets history in motion:

> For the pure parable so centers the attention of its hearer upon its enactment as to end all awareness of a meaning or an identity beyond its immediate arena of speech. In this sense parable, or pure parable, is present only in its enactment, only in its telling or saying. Therefore, it can pass into writing only with a loss of its original immediacy, a loss which occasions a reversal of itself, a reversal effecting its fall into the

language of simile and metaphor, a fall culminating in its full reversal in allegory.[13]

This remark suggests that the threefold dialectical structure of Altizer's epic of epics can be read in different ways: immediacy, division, reunion; prehistory, history, posthistory; life, death, life; birth, death, rebirth; assertion, negation, negation of negation. . . . These and other formulations of Altizer's trinitarian construction can be summarized in terms of speech and writing: speech, writing, speech. Though pure speech is always already lost in impure writing, the origin is present in the end even as the end is present in the origin. The perfect coincidence of Alpha and Omega makes it possible to recover pure speech and thus enjoy the total presence of the Kingdom of God.

> To confine the identity of Jesus to words or text is to lose that identity, a loss which has occurred again and again in Christian history, but most obviously so in the modern world. Hence, in attempting to recover the parabolic language of Jesus we must not confuse that langauge with the words of the synoptic texts. Nor may we allow the form or forms of the synoptic parables to determine or mold our sense of the original identity of the parable, for it is now clear that these forms or structures are movements away from the original parables. But if we can see that the parable itself is a reversal of all given or manifest meaning and identity, and that the synoptic parables move in the direction of reversing the original parables, then in this movement of reversing reversal we can apprehend a decisive way of returning to an original parabolic language.[14]

The language of Jesus can be present *only* as the language of today. To recover original parabolic language, it is necessary to reverse the reversal of speech in writing in and through a writing that is truly speech. Altizer is convinced that such a reversal has been realized in the major works of modern literature. "Literary language," he argues, "has returned or become open once again to its original oral source, and voice itself has been reenacted in the text, even if such a reenactment gives the text the form of antitext."[15] *Finnegans Wake* is the nonwriterly "antitext" in which the fallen written word is resurrected as the voice of pure speech.

The voice of *Finnegans Wake* is not the voice of Joyce or his "I," but is the voice of anonymity itself. The uniqueness of "the Joycean epiphany . . . lies not in the interior individuality of the artist, but rather in the fullness of a language that unites an exterior totality with a cosmos of interior and immediate centers."[16] The unity of interiority and exteriority in modern poetic language brings to completion the identity of God, self, and world declared but not totally realized in the parabolic speech of Jesus. When voice is totally present, it transcends its individual ground in a universal presence that is completely anonymous. Altizer summarizes the conclusion of *Total Presence* by responding to his own rhetorical question:

> Is it possible to conjoin an understanding of the actual advent of a universal hand and face and voice with a realization of the actual disappearance of an interior center of self-consciousness? By this means we could realize that the negation and transcendence of an individual and interior self-consciousness goes hand in hand with the realization of a universal humanity, a humanity that can neither be named nor apprehended by an interior and individual voice. We might also thereby see that it is precisely the individual conscience and the individual consciousness that are the deepest obstacles to the realization of a universal humanity, a humanity that can be born only by a negation and transcendence of every previous historical configuration and voice of consciousness.[17]

The birth of universal humanity is impossible apart from the death of the individual self.

Self Sacrifice

The self whose death marks the advent of the Kingdom of God is the self that is born in Pauline Christianity. Greek and Jewish culture prepare the way for the individual subject but, Altizer contends, self-consciousness *sensu strictissimo* first emerges in the letters of Paul. As Paul makes clear, the self is born guilty. In the Hegelian language that Altizer borrows to explicate Paul, self-consciousness is unavoidably "unhappy." "Thus self-consciousness as such initially appears as a dichotomous consciousness, a doubled and divided consciousness which is itself only insofar as it is not itself, which is for itself or manifest to itself only insofar as it is against itself, only insofar as it is a pure and total negativity" (p. 66).

Altizer's characterization of self-consciousness is obviously Hegelian. The subject becomes itself through a process of *inner* division in which otherness is initially posited as difference and finally returned to the sameness of self-identity. It is *as if* the self-conscious subject were two. The appearance of duplicity, however, is misleading, for the subject is really one. The identity of the subject is secured by the purity and totality of negation. Pure negativity is *doubly* negative. While self-consciousness achieves initial articulation in the negation of immediacy, the divided self is itself negated through a dialectical process in which opposites are reconciled. Altizer describes the "pure negativity" of self-consciousness in a telling passage that deserves to be quoted at length:

> When pure negativity passes into the very center of consciousness, it realizes itself as the consciousness of itself, as a doubled and divided consciousness, a self-alienated consciousness whose alienation lies at the very center of itself. Then self-alienation becomes manifest and real as the source and ground of consciousness itself, and the otherness of death and guilt become real as the otherness of consciousness itself, an otherness which knows itself as its own "I." Now absolute otherness is "I" myself, it is wholly internalized and interiorized as the integral otherness of itself. Finally otherness is itself only insofar as it is within itself, only insofar as it is finally irrevocably within. Thereby a within is fully actualized which is its own otherness, an otherness which is itself, which is "I." The actualization of this dichotomy is the actualization of a pure internal and interior dichotomy, a self-dichotomy which is self-consciousness. For consciousness can be conscious of itself only by being other than itself, only by realizing itself as its own otherness, an otherness which is the object of consciousness, but simultaneously the subject as well. [p. 76]

Within the structure of self-consciousness, otherness is always the subject's "own other." Difference, therefore, is an inward difference, which, in the final analysis, is identical with the subject itself. Unreconciled otherness constitutes what Hegel describes as "the bad infinite" that must be negated if the true infinity of subjectivity is to become actual.[18] The other to which the self becomes reconciled is not only an other subject but is the entire cosmos, which now becomes totally manifest as the self-embodiment of God. The subject's self-realization is, paradoxically, at the same time its self-negation. In negating its own other, the self negates itself. The death of the "I" is the birth of universal humanity, which is present only in complete anonymity. "The anonymity of humanity" is the real presence of "the anonymity of God."[19] In the presence of this anonymity, "difference as difference" comes to an end. As we have been led to suspect, difference disappears in speech. Describing apocalypse in *The Self-Embodiment of God,* Altizer writes:

> Hence difference as difference becomes unsaid when it is fully spoken. But it is unsaid only in being actually unsaid. The silence of the unsaid is now actually spoken, and when it is fully spoken it passes into total speech. Total speech can only be the disembodiment, the actual negation, of difference. When speech is fully embodied in pure voice, it is disembodied from difference, or disembodied from all difference which

is only difference. But that disembodiment from difference is also the full actualization of difference. Now difference is fully actual by having come to an end as difference, by having come to an end as a difference which is other and apart.[20]

The self-sacrifice of the subject repeats and extends the Christian drama of incarnation, crucifixion, and resurrection. The death of the individual self who is only himself completes the death of the transcendent God who alone is God. God is emptied into man and man is emptied into God. This kenotic process can be described both abstractly as the negation of negation, which issues in absolute reconciliation, and concretely as the death of death, which brings life eternal. When negation is negated and death gives way to life, loss is turned to gain. In Altizer's restricted economy, there is a return on every investment and a profit from every expenditure.

The "total and actual presence" of the resurrection presupposes the reversal of the fall of speech into writing. The reversal cannot occur apart from the emergence of a form of writing that is essentially speech. Altizer is convinced that precisely such a speech event takes place in the "liturgical language" of *Finnegans Wake:*

> [The] wholly worldly or fleshly language of the *Wake*, is also a language which at least by intention never strays from an actually spoken speech. Writing or scripture finally ends in *Finnegans Wake*, for this is a text in which a written or writable language has wholly disappeared as such, and disappeared to make way for or to awake that primal and immediate speech which is on the other side of writing or text, and on the infinitely other side of that writing which is Scripture or sacred text. [p. 237]

In the wake of self-sacrifice and the self-sacrifice of the *Wake*, the voice of *History as Apocalypse* becomes the voice of all, or more precisely, the voice of the All, which is embodied in everyone: "Here Comes Everybody" . . . "H.C.E." . . . *Hoc est corpus meum*. . . . Take read, this is my body, broken for you.

To read is to hear, and to hear truly (or to hear the Truth) is to hear the pure voice, which, once having been present in the parabolic language of Jesus, now returns in the poetic language of Joyce. The language of *Finnegans Wake* not only repeats the original language of Jesus but actually re-presents the presence of the divine in the human.[21]

> The language of the *Wake*, is not only human and divine at once, it is totally guilty and totally gracious at once, for our final epic language is a cosmic and historical Eucharist, a Eucharist centered in an apocalyptic and cosmic sacrifice of God. Now a primordial chaos and abyss is in-

distinguishable from Godhead, just as an original chaos has passed into the center of speech. But now, this ultimate chaos is fully and finally present, and present in and as this apocalyptic and liturgical text. [p. 234][22]

The eucharistic festival unleashed by devouring the antitext issues in a *missa jubilaea*—an all-inclusive Mass that encompasses the entire cosmos. "Therein and thereby the conjunction and coinherence of cosmos and chaos become actual and real, and actually and fully present in a *coincidentia oppositorum* wherein the opposites are real and opposing opposites even as they are united in a radically new and immediate *coincidentia*" (p. 223).

This "immediate coincidence" of opposites is the total presence of a universal humanity, which is at the same time fully divine, and an incarnate divinity, which is at the same time fully human. In the *missa jubilaea*, incarnation is crucifixion, which is resurrection, and resurrection is crucifixion, which is incarnation. In the end, three are one:

An actual end is an actual ending, a real ending of the voice of "I AM." That real ending is the silencing of "I AM," the self-silencing of "I AM," a self-silencing whereby "I AM" passes into "I am."[23]

The "I" that seemed to disappear before the beginning returns at the end not merely as itself but as the I AM of Being. At the end of history, the speaker who hears the Word discovers that his voice is the voice of God: I am I AM. The *missa jubilaea* is "a bacchanalian revel in which no member is sober."[24]

This new Dionysian redemptive way is nothing more and nothing less than the proclamation and the dance of Eternal Recurrence. Yet this is a uniquely modern or postmodern identity of eternal recurrence, for it reverses the archaic symbol of eternal return by both apprehending and creating an Eternity or "Being" which *is* the pure imminence of a present and actual moment. That pure imminence dawns only when the Eternity and the Being of our past have been wholly forgotten, only when God is dead. Then and only then is that center everywhere whereby and wherein: "Being begins in every Now." [p. 230]

In the total presence of Zarathustra's "Now," darkness becomes light:[25]

. . . midnight is also mid-day—
Grief is also a joy, curses are also blessings, night is also a sun—go away, or else learn: a sage is also a fool.
Did you ever say "Yes" to one joy? Oh my friends, then you also

said "Yes" to *all* pain. All things are entwined, enmeshed, enamoured –
– did you ever want once to be twice, did you ever say "I love you,
bliss – instant – flash –" then you wanted *everything* back.
    – Everything anew, everything forever, everything entwined,
enmeshed, enamoured – oh, thus you love the world –
    – you everlasting one, thus you love it forever and for all time;
even to pain you say: Refrain but – come again! *For joy accepts everlasting
flow!*[26]

Nat Now

After the end of the Book, questions remain. Has midday really arrived?
Has midnight struck? Does the midnight that is also midday ever come? Or is
it delayed, forever delayed? What if, as the author of *Le Dernier Homme* writes
elsewhere: "Midnight is precisely the hour that does not toll until after the
dice are thrown, the hour which has never come, which never comes, the
pure, ungraspable future, the hour eternally past"?[27] What if the sound of
Plurabelle is not "the pure sound (*le son pur*)" of speech but is the tolling of an
other bell, a bell(e) that echoes the writing of *Glas*? What does the writing of
the *Wake* "teach us about the essence of laughter if it recalls that laughter to
the limits of the calculable and the incalculable, when the whole of the
calculable is outplayed by a writing about which it is no longer possible to
decide if it still calculates, calculates better and more, or if it transcends the
very order of the calculable economy, or even of an incalculable or an
undecidable which would still be homogenous with the world of calculation?"
    Throughout the polyphony of *Finnegans Wake*, the foreign language
Joyce uses most frequently is Danish. Altizer notes that "the 'night' language
of the *Wake* in Danish is *nat* language, pronounced 'not language,' and the text
informs us in Nietzschean language that this night language is our origin: 'in
the Nichtian glossery which purveys aprioric, roots for aposteriorious tongues
this is nat language at any sinse of the word" (p. 239). What Altizer, who
neither speaks nor reads Danish, fails or refuses to recognize is that the
Danish *nat* calls into question the Nietzschean Now. To approach the *nat* that
"is'" Not or "is" not Now since Now always "is" Not, it is necessary to turn to
the most important writer in the history of the Danish language.
    In a prescript to what eventually becomes an unconcluding p. s.,
Kierkegaard reflects on the epic composed by Hegel and his followers: "In the
Hegelian school, the System is a fiction, similar to the one Schelling brought
to the world in 'the infinite epic,' which in its time was quite successful."[28] It is
precisely the *fictive* status of the epic of universal humanity that Hegel and
Hegelians do not acknowledge. This refusal transforms the epic of epics into
a comedy of tragic proportions.

In another fragmentary Journal entry, Kierkegaard explains: "If Hegel had written his whole logic and had written in the preface that it was only a thought-experiment [i.e., something like an imaginative fiction], in which at many points he still steered clear of some things, he undoubtedly would have been the greatest thinker who has ever lived. As it is he is comic."[29] This comedy can be met only with laughter—the laughter that "traverses the whole experience which refers us to *Finnegans Wake*." Such laughter is, in the words of one of Kierkegaard's first French translators, Georges Bataille, *le rire déchirant*. This lacerating laugh shatters Hegel's System and exposes the *impossibility* of apocalypse.

One might say of Altizer what Bataille says of Hegel: "He does not know to what extent he is right." Bataille sets the course for virtually all subsequent French readings of Hegel by insisting that the pivotal text in the entire Hegelian corpus can be found in the Preface to the *Phenomenology of Spirit*:

> But the life of Spirit is not the life that shrinks from death and keeps itself untouched by devastation, but rather the life that endures it and maintains itself in it. It wins its truth only when, in utter dismemberment (*déchirement*), it finds itself. It is this power, not as something positive, which closes its eyes to the negative, as when we say of something that it is nothing or is false, and then, having done with it, turn away and pass on to something else; on the contrary, Spirit is this power only by looking the negative in the face, and tarrying with it. This tarrying with the negative is the magical power that converts it into being.[30]

The "magical power" that transforms the negative into the positive is nothing other than the negative itself—the negative whose power lies in its duplicity. When negation is doubled, the negative is negated and the positive affirmed. In different terms, saying "No" to "No" is the "Yea *saying*" that says "Yes" to the total presence of the "Now." In the pure light of this "Now," neither "Not"nor *"nat"* is, or they are only as overcome.

For Bataille and many others, Hegel fails to appreciate the thoroughgoing radicality of the negative he discovers. Having recognized the importance of negativity, Hegel proceeds to undercut his own insight by insisting that negation is negated. In the Hegelian dialectic, a dialectic Altizer accepts virtually without revision, the negative always harbors a positive reserve that can be turned to profit. What neither Hegel nor Altizer can imagine is an "expenditure without return," a loss from which there is no recovery, a wound for which there is no cure. To entertain such an excessive loss, it is necessary to think what might be described as an "Hegelianism without reserve."

In an essay on Bataille entitled "From Restricted to General Economy:

A Hegelianism without Reserve," Derrida points out that "the blind spot of Hegelianism, *around* which can be organized the representation of meaning, is the *point* at which destruction, suppression, death, and sacrifice constitute so irreversible an expenditure, so radical a negativity—here we would have to say an expenditure and a negativity *without reserve*—that they can no longer be determined as negativity in a process or a system. In discourse (the unity of process and system), negativity is always the underside and accomplice of positivity. Negativity cannot be spoken of, nor has it ever been except in this fabric of meaning."[31] To *speak* the negative is to negate it. Radical negativity, therefore, is *unspeakable*. This unspeakable negativity is undeniably heterogeneous. Ungraspable, incomprehensible, and incalculable, the negative that cannot be negated is not simply unknown but is unknowable.

In *L'expérience intérieure*, Bataille attempts to explain the relation, or more accurately the nonrelation, between this nonknowledge and Hegel's System:

> The *Phenomenology of Spirit* comprises two essential movements completing a circle: it is the completion by degrees of the consciousness of self (of human *ipse*) and the becoming everything (*tout*) (the becoming God) of this *ipse* completing knowledge (and by this means destroying particularity within it, thus completing the negation of oneself, becoming absolute knowledge). But if in this way, as if by contagion and by mime, I accomplished myself in Hegel's circular movement, I define— beyond the limits attained—no longer an unknown, but an unknowable. Unknowable not on account of the insufficiency of reason, but by its nature.[32]

If confusion is to be avoided, it is important to recognize the peculiar character of the "unknowable (*inconnaissable*)" beyond, which, according to Bataille, exceeds the circular movement of Hegelian reflection. Bataille labels the radically negative *das ganz Andere*.[33] Such an other is neither the simple nor dialectical opposite of the same. The neither/nor of heterogeneity lies between the either/or of nondialectical understanding and the both/and of dialectical thought. The "domain" of this unknowable other is neither a transcendent beyond nor an immanent here and now. Never present, though not merely absent, the other remains "inside" as an exteriority interrupting all immediacy and dislocating every identity. The "nonabsent absence"[34] of the other forever defers apocalyptic presence.

When the other is approached in this way, it obviously eludes dialectical comprehension. Altizer cannot admit the possibility of such an other. His writings represent a sustained attack on every form of transcendence. The direction of his work, in part, has been set by the theological climate in which he began writing. It is clear that Altizer is engaged in a lifelong struggle with all forms of neoorthodoxy. He is convinced that Christendom's reversal of Jesus's faith comes to completion in Karl Barth's "Wholly Other" God. As early as his first book, Altizer describes this transcendent Other in terms of Blake's Urizen and Hegel's "Bad Infinite." The Other that is totally Other is the negation that must be negated—the God who must die if the total presence embodied in the speech of Jesus is to be recovered. The negation of negation is possible only if otherness is grasped dialectically. What Altizer *cannot* think is a nondialectical other.[35] The impossibility of entertaining the unspeakable other points to the impossibility of Altizer's theological project as a whole. Though Altizer is our most important death of God theologian, he has not thought the death of God radically enough.[36] To think the death of God in all its radicality is to confront the impossibility of presence and the inescapable absence of apocalypse. The impossibility to which the death of God points can be read in and as the eternal return of writing. Though radical altarity cannot be spoken, it might be possible to write it in a writing that is not secondary to, or has not "fallen" from, speech.

Perhaps the death of God can be *written* as: "HE WAR." But how is "HE WAR" to be read? Can "HE WAR" be spoken or can it only be written? In an important essay entitled "Joyce: The (r)use of writing," Hélène Cixous points out that when reading Joyce there are two possible courses of action:

> The first trusting to the known facts about Joyce's work, particularly his intensive use of symbols, and his obsessive and often explicit concern to control word-order, thus prejudging the book as a "full" text, governed by "the hypostasis of the signified," a text which conceals itself but which has something to conceal, which is findable. This reassuring position is in fact almost necessary, granted the conscious or unconscious fashion of pushing Joyce back into the theological world from which he wanted to escape, by squeezing him "through the back door" (cf. the versions of Joyce as a Catholic, Medieval Joyce, Irish Joyce, Joyce the Jesuit in reverse and hence the right way round as well, etc.). On the other hand, one can imagine a reading that would accept "discouragement," not in order to "recuperate" it by taking it as a metaphor for the Joycean occult . . . but rather by seeing in it that trap which confiscates signification the sign of the willed imposture that crosses and double-crosses the *whole* of Joyce's work, making that betrayal the very breath (the breathlessness) of the subject. Nothing will have been signified save the riddle.[37]

This riddle provokes the outbreak of *le rire déchirant*. Altizer reads Joyce in the first way, Derrida in the second way. To read Joyce with Altizer is to read in terms of speech; to read Joyce with Derrida is to read in terms of writing. If

Finnegans Wake is a writerly text rather than a speechly antitext, it becomes necessary to reread the epic of epics narrated in *History as Apocalypse* as fiction.

Writing "Two words for Joyce," Derrida explores the irreducible duplicity of Joyce's language by considering the not-so-simple phrase "HE WAR." Is this to be read as English, German, both English and German, or neither English nor German? Derrida argues:

> It *was* written *simultaneously* in both English and German. Two words in one (*war*), and thus a double noun, a double verb, a noun and a verb that are divided in the beginning. *War* is a noun in English, a verb in German, it resembles an adjective (*wahr*) in the same language, and the truth of this multiplicity returns, from the attributes (the verb is also an attribute) towards the subject, *he* who is divided by it right from the origin. In the beginning, difference, that's what happens, that's what has already taken place, that's what was when language was in act, and the tongue (*la langue*) writing. Where it was, *He* was."[38]

In the "beginning": difference; at the "origin": division. The duplicity of "HE WAR" involves a difference that cannot be translated into one language, or into the language of the One. As Derrida points out, precisely this duplicity is lost when writing is read as speech. To speak "HE WAR," it is necessary to speak one language. The sentence must be spoken in either English or German, for it is impossible to *speak* both at once. According to Derrida, speech always attempts to return difference to identity and other to same. This reduction, Derrida insists, is the essential gesture of theology:

> The infinite alterity of the divine substance does not interpose itself as an element of mediation or opacity in the transparence of self-relationship and the purity of auto-affection. God is the name and the element of that which makes possible an absolutely pure and absolutely self-present self-knowledge. From Descartes to Hegel [and beyond Hegel to Altizer] and in spite of all the differences that separate the different places and moments in the structure of that epoch, God's infinite understanding is the other name for the logos as self-presence. The logos can be infinite and self-present, it can be *produced as auto-affection*, only through the *voice*: an order of the signifier by which the subject takes from itself into itself, does not borrow outside of itself the signifier that it emits and that affects it at the same time. Such is at least the experience—or consciousness—of the voice: of hearing (understanding)-oneself-speak *(s'entendre-parler)*. That experience lives and proclaims itself as the exclusion of writing, that is to say of the invoking of an "exterior," "sensible," "spatial" signifier interrupting self-presence.[39]

To recover the "exteriority" of writing, which speech represses, it is necessary to read both "HE" and "WAR" otherwise.

The "HE" of "HE WAR" silences the narrational voice of *History as Apoclypse* by calling into question the "I" and the "We" that re-present the presence of "I AM" in the immediacy of the "Now." In contrast to "narrational voice," which is always an identifiable voice of presence, "narrative voice" approaches as a "radical exteriority" that can be neither represented nor recollected. This "voice" is the voice of the writer who does not speak in his own name. The narrative voice is never "I" or "we"; it is neither masculine nor feminine. Always neither/nor, it is neuter. Blanchot explains:

> The narrative voice is neuter. . . . For one thing, it says nothing, not only because it adds nothing to what there is to say (it does not know anything), but because it underlies this nothing—the "to silence," and the "to keep silent"—in which speech is here and now already engaged; thus it is not heard, first of all, and everything that gives it a distinct reality begins to betray it. Then again, being without its own existence, speaking from nowhere, suspended in the *récit* as a whole, it is not dissipated there either, as light is, which, though invisible itself, makes things visible: it is radically exterior, it comes from exteriority itself, the outside that is the special enigma of language in writing.[40]

This passage makes it clear that Blanchot's "neuter" must be distinguished from Altizer's "anonymity." While the anonymity of the narrational voice represents the total presence of speech itself, the neutrality of the narrative voice implies the nonabsent absence of writing. This nonabsent absence is the unspeakable other that renders language unavoidably enigmatic. Since this other is *never* present, it cannot be re-presented. The altarity that resounds in the narrative voice is the echo of the absent origin. The absence of the origin is written as "HE WAR." This "WAR" is a radical "was" that points toward an absolute past. This past eternally returns as the ever-absent future to disrupt the presence of every "Now." If "WAR" cannot be overcome, the Kingdom can never arrive. The darkness of the *nat* of "WAR" is not simply the absence *of* light or the dialectical opposite of the light of day. The night of the *"nat* now," which we recall is spoken "not now," is what Blanchot describes as "the night beyond night." In this night "midnight is precisely . . . the hour which has never yet come, which never comes, the pure ungraspable future, the hour eternally past."

In the night beyond night, another Thomas emerges—a Thomas who does not bear the good news of Apocalypse Now, but a Thomas who bears the obscure news of the impossibility of apocalypse. In a haunting *récit* entitled *Thomas the Obscure*, Blanchot writes:

Now, in this night I come forward bearing everything (*le tout*), toward that which infinitely exceeds the all. I progress beyond the totality which I nevertheless tightly embrace. I go on to the margins of the universe, boldly walking elsewhere than where I can be, and a little outside my steps. This slight extravagance, this deviation toward that which cannot be, is not my own movement leading me to a personal madness, but the movement of the reason that I bear within me. With me the laws gravitate outside the laws, the possible outside the possible. O night, now nothing will make me be, nothing will separate me from you . . . I lean over you, equal to you, offering you a mirror for your perfect nothingness.[41]

Bearing everything toward that which exceeds the all . . . beyond the totality . . . on the margins of the universe . . . slight extravagance . . . deviation toward that which cannot be . . . outside the laws . . . outside the possible . . . mirror of perfect nothingness. This "Now" is "Not"—*le pas au-delà*,[42] which is *nat*, the "night" of the "*nat* Now" that renders apocalypse impossible.

It is (un)finished
Amen
Sobeit
(p. s.)[43]

. . . p. s. . . . fin again. . . .

Far calls. Coming, far! End here. Us then, Finn, again![44]

6.

The Anachronism of A/theology

To inscribe the space of time, to devastate the discrete place of interiority, to solicit the abysmal silence of the crypt, the writer points to that "final" historical moment wherein God-who-is-All is effaced, allowing a return of sacred remains and attesting to the impossible ruins that open a radically altered nonspace for the religious imagination. To approach this space, which disallows every arrival, I begin (again) with a story – a story about an event or nonevent that might have taken place a terribly long time ago – a story that is, among other things, a story about our world, as well as a word.

Once upon a time (and my question will be: What time?), there were six brothers, known as the Titans, and six sisters, known as the Titanesses, who were the children of Uranus (Heaven) and Gaia (Mother Earth). The youngest of the Titans was named Cronos. Gaia, who, by herself, had given birth to Uranus, became angered when Uranus did not allow any of the children to see the light of day but kept them all entombed in the bowels of Mother Earth. Determined to free her children, Gaia asked them to exact vengeance for Uranus's actions. Only Cronus accepted the challenge. Gaia entrusted him with a sharp sickle. When Uranus came to lie with Gaia, Cronus cut off his father's testicles and threw them over his shoulder. The blood from Uranus's wound fertilized Mother Earth and she gave birth to the Giants, whose disastrous *Paysage foudroyé* we have already explored. Reflecting on this strange event, one might ask: Why is Cronus associated with cutting, or, more precisely, with castration?

Derrida recounts the story of Gaia and Cronos in *Glas*. His concern there, as elsewhere, is with the impossibility of absolute knowledge. Derrida repeatedly asks what Hegel's insistence on the possibility of attaining absolute knowledge leaves out or represses. He never answers this question directly but implies a response through various strategies of indirection. In an *aparté* inserted in the column (sometimes described as phallic) devoted to Gaia and Cronos, Derrida re-marks:

What would it mean not to comprehend (Hegel) the text of *Sa*? If it is a question of a finite failure, the failure is in advance included, comprehended in the text. If it is a question of an infinite fault or lack, one would have to say that *Sa* does not think itself, does not say itself, does not write itself, does not read itself, does not know itself, which no longer means anything by definition. *Sa* always ends by being full, heavy, pregnant with itself. The hypothesis of a bad reading has no place here. It has not even taken place. One must let it fall, in the margin or exergue, as a margin or exergue, as a remain(s) about which one does not *know* if it works, in view of or in the service of whom or what. Like such a note at the bottom of the page of *Concluding Unscientific Postscript to the Philosophical Fragments*, scraps of scraps under the last supper scene. . . . "It is presumably the witchery of this ever-continuing process that has inspired the misunderstanding that one must be a devil of a fellow in philosophy in order to emancipate himself from Hegel. But this is by no means the case. All that is needed is sound common sense, a fund of humor, and a little Greek ataraxy. Outside the *Logic*, and partly also with it, because of a certain ambiguous light that Hegel has not cared to exclude, Hegel and Hegelianism constitute an essay in the comic."[1]

That which is outside logic, the logic that is always paradigmatically Hegel's *Logic*, is, in the strict sense of the word, anachronistic. "The myth of Cronus," Joseph Shipley explains, "is confused; he was probably a pre-Hellenic god of time; from his name we have a number of words, such as *chronic, chronicle, chronological, crony, and anachronism.*"[2] Derived from the root *nebh* (mist, cloud, moist), "anachronism" (*ana*, against + *chronos*, time) means: "The representation of something as existing or happening at other than its proper or historical time; anything out of its proper time."[3] To think this anachronism, one must think anachronistically by thinking that which is outside "proper time" or "is" the outside "of" time proper. Such anachronism is what Western philosophy and theology have until recently left unthought.

Before proceeding to develop the implications of this unthought, I would like to return, for a moment, to the beginning–a beginning that is (as always) a story. I indicated that this story is, among other things, a story about our world and a story about a word. The word toward which the story points is "anachronism." The story associated with the curious origin of the word "anachronism" recounts something that is anachronistic–that is to say, something that took place, perhaps has always already taken place, outside proper time or time proper. The tear inflicted upon Father Heaven by Mother Earth through the agency of a Son named "Time" suggests a triangle that is less than triune. A nontriune triangle implies a nonsynthetic third that dislocates the binary or polar opposites between which theological thinking has been suspended. If the son who wounds the father is Cronus, perhaps we can figure the disruptive, nonsynthetic third by refiguring the anachronism of time. Though not immediately apparent, I would like to suggest that to think this mean is, in effect, to reexamine the *difference* between Hegel and Kierkegaard by rethinking Hegelian identity and Kierkegaardian altarity in and through Derridean *différance*.

The odd or not-so-odd couple of Hegel and Kierkegaard does not, I would insist, appear at this point simply because of my own preoccupations. Rather, Hegel and Kierkegaard represent the two poles between which the most creative philosophical and theological thinking throughout this century has oscillated. The longer I have wavered between Hegel and Kierkegaard, the less satisfactory the opposing extremes marked out by their contrasting viewpoints have become. In an effort to stake out a position *between* these two major figures, I have turned to the writings of Derrida. Derrida's work can be understood as an extended critique of Hegel. I am convinced that the margin of difference traced by Derrida—a margin that falls between Hegel and Kierkegaard—creates a seminal opening for contemporary religious reflection.

In order to indicate the direction such reflection might take, I would like to sketch in an admittedly oversimplified way the general thrust of leading tendencies in modern theology.

Having begun with the *"Nein"* proclaimed by Karl Barth in *The Epistle to the Romans*, twentieth-century theology has remained preoccupied with the correlative problems of transcendence and otherness. It would not be incorrect to insist that for most of this century (and not only for this century) theological reflection has been suspended, perhaps even hung up, between immanence and transcendence. Barth's "No" represents a rejection of every form of theological liberalism and all variations of cultural Protestantism in which divine presence is regarded as immanent in historical, social, and cultural processes:

> Religion, Barth argues, compels us to the perception that God is not to be found in religion. Religion makes us know that we are competent to advance no single step. Religion, as the final human possibility, commands us to halt. Religion brings us to the place where we must wait, in order that God may confront us—on the other side of the frontier of religion. The transformation of the "No" of religion into the divine "Yes" occurs in the dissolution of this last observable human thing.[4]

The historical situation in which Barth formulated his critique makes his suspicion of humankind's cultural constructs not only understandable but even persuasive. By saying "Yes" to a radically transcendent God, Barth says "No" to the culture that left Western Europe in ruins.

The force of the neoorthodox critique of culture and society has decreased as the distance from world wars has increased. The most significant index of this development is the death of God theology that emerged in the 1960s. The death of God theology remains one of the most significant theological movements of this century. I would even go so far as to argue that *modern* theology reaches a certain closure in the death of God theology. Thus any *postmodern* theological reflection that does not revert to premodern assumptions will have to pass through the "fiery brook" of the death of God. In this country, the most influential proponent of the death of God theology is Thomas J. J. Altizer. Altizer's program must be understood in the context of the neoorthodoxy that dominated theological discourse during the first half of this century. When Altizer declares (as he is still doing) the death of God, it is really the death of the Barthian God he proclaims. Altizer's "No" to Barth's "No" is at the same time a "Yes" to a radical immanence in which every vestige of transcendence is erased. In the Hegelian terms Altizer repeatedly invokes, the negation of negation issues in a total affirmation that overcomes every trace of unreconciled otherness. Within Altizer's apocalyptic vision, the death of God is the condition of the possibility of the arrival of the Parousia. When the Kingdom of God is at hand, authentic presence is totally realized *here and now*.

If one is to understand where Altizer departs from and remains bound to the presuppositions and conclusions of what Heidegger describes as "onto-theology," it is necessary to reformulate several crucial points in his position. By declaring the death of God, Altizer does not call into question the traditional understanding of Being in terms of presence. To the contrary, he insists that to be is to be present, and to be fully is to be present totally. Although never stated in these terms, Altizer's argument implies that the mistake of classical theism, of which Barthianism is but the most problematic variation, is not that it misunderstands Being as such, but that it identifies the locus of true Being as transcendent to, rather than immanent in, the world of space and time. From Altizer's perspective, the total presence of God in the incarnation marks the death of the otherness that inhibits the very possibility of enjoying presence in the present. To cling to the belief that the divine is in any way other or transcendent is to suffer the disappointment brought by the delay or deferral of the Parousia. Precisely this delay or deferral, Altizer argues, ends with the life and death of Jesus. Following Hegel, he maintains that what is implicit in Jesus becomes explicit in the course of the historical process. With the death of God, transcendent presence becomes totally present in space (here) and time (now). When the identity of the divine comes to completion in the identity of the human, difference—that is, unreconciled otherness—is overcome. In Altizer's own words:

Distance disappears in total presence, and so likewise does all actual otherness which is not the otherness of that presence itself. Difference can now be present only insofar as it is fully embodied in speech. When difference speaks, and fully speaks, it becomes present in speech, and wholly present in that speech. That speech is not simply the presence of difference, or the voice of difference. It is far rather the self-identity of difference, and its fully actualized self-identity, a self-identity in which difference embodies its otherness in the immediacy of a real and actual presence.[5]

With the incorporation of difference in identity, Altizer reinscribes the identity of identity and difference, which, as the Alpha and Omega of reflection, constitutes the very foundation of Hegel's System.

The question that remains after Hegel and after the theological reappropriation of his System is how to think otherwise than being by thinking a difference that is not reducible to identity. This is the task that Kierkegaard sets for himself in his philosophical fragments and unscientific postscripts. In our day, the question of difference has been taken up again by, among others, Derrida. Situating his own interrogation in relation to Hegel's System, Derrida maintains:

> As for what "begins" then – "beyond" absolute knowledge – *unheard-of* thoughts are required, sought for across the memory of old signs. . . . In the openness of this question *we no longer know.* This does not mean that we know nothing but that we are beyond absolute knowledge (and its ethical, aesthetic, or religious system), approaching that on the basis of which its closure is announced and decided. Such a question will legitimately be understood as *meaning* nothing, as no longer belonging to the system of meaning.[6]

To think beyond absolute knowledge (or, perhaps, to think the beyond "of" absolute knowledge) is to think after the end of Western metaphysics by thinking what the ontotheological tradition has not thought. In his influential essay "The End of Philosophy and the Task of Thinking," Heidegger explains: "What characterizes metaphysical thinking that grounds the ground for beings is the fact that metaphysical thinking departs from what is present in its presence, and thus represents it in terms of its ground as something grounded."[7] Heidegger insists that metaphysics or the ontotheological tradition "does not ask about Being as Being, that is, does not raise the question of how there can be presence as such."[8] The task of thinking, in the strict sense of the term, is to think the unthought of ontotheology that answers the question of how there can be presence as such.

One of the ways Heidegger characterizes this unthought is as "the *dif-*

ference between Being and beings," or more concisely, "difference *as* difference." This difference should not be confused with the presence of any specific difference. Heideggerian *Differenz*, which is the condition of the possibility of all presence and every present, is not a presence, and hence can never be properly present. Yet neither is it simply absent. What neither philosophy nor theology has thought (because neither can think such an "unheard-of" thought without ceasing to be itself) is that which lies *between* presence and absence, identity and difference, being and nonbeing. Neither representable in nor masterable by traditional philosophical and theological categories, this margin is the trace of a different difference and an other other.

No one has questioned this strange difference with greater rigor than Derrida. In the texts of Derrida, Heidegger's *Differenz* returns with a difference as *différance*. The neologism *différance,* which Derrida admits, "is neither a word nor a concept," trades on the duplicity of *différer,* which can mean both "to differ" and "to defer." Elaborating this important point, Derrida writes:

> The Latin *differre* is not simply a translation of the Greek *diapherein*, and this will not be without consequences for us, linking our discourse to a particular language, and to a language that passes as less philosophical, less originally philosophical than the other. For the distribution of meaning in the Greek *diapherein* does not comport one of the two motifs of the Latin *differre,* to wit, the action of putting off until later, of taking into account, of taking account of time and of the forces of an operation that implies an economical calculation, a detour, a delay, a relay, a reserve, a representation–concepts that I would summarize here in a word I have never used but that could be inscribed in this chain: *temporization. Différer* in this sense is to temporize, to take recourse, consciously or unconsciously, in the temporal and temporizing mediation of a detour that suspends the accomplishment or fulfillment of "desire" or "will", and equally effects this suspension in a mode that annuls or tempers its own effect. And we will see, later, how this temporization is also temporalization and spacing, the becoming-time of space and the becoming-space of time, the "originary constitution" of time and space, as metaphysics or transcendental phenomenology would say, to use the language that here is criticized and displaced.[9]

This admittedly difficult passage is nonetheless one of Derrida's clearest statements about the pivotal notion of *différance*. In this context, it is important to note the intersection of time and space in the play of *différance*. If *différance* involves the becoming-time of space and the becoming-space of time, then this curious nonconcept, this unheard-of thought, might point toward, which *is not* to say reveal, an anachronism that is always outside its proper time. Furthermore, to think the time of this difference and/or the difference of this time might open unheard-of spaces in which the a/theological imagination can err.

To glimpse the time-space of such erring, it is helpful to return to my all-too-schematic outline of twentieth-century theology. I have suggested that since at least 1918, theologians have wavered between emphasizing divine transcendence and divine immanence. While Barth attempts to reassert divine transcendence, which calls into question all human achievement, Altizer is concerned to reestablish divine immanence, which is supposed to overcome every form of alienated consciousness. When situated historically, it is possible to read Altizer's critique of Barth as a reversal of Kierkegaard's critique of Hegel. From this point of view, Altizer's "No" to Barth's "No" supplants Kierkegaard's dialectic of either/or with Hegel's dialectic of both/and. In the wake of this reversal of a reversal, one must ask: What have Barth and Altizer not thought? What does the alternative of transcendence and immanence leave out? Is there a nondialectical third that lies *between* the dialectic of either/or and both/and? Might this third be neither transcendent nor immanent? Does this neither/nor open the time-space of a different difference and an other other – a difference and an other that do not merely invert but actually subvert the polarities of Western philosophical and theological reflection?

Given the limitations of time and space, as well as the strictures of timing and spacing, I can only suggest the beginning of a response to such questions by proposing a return to Nietzsche, or more precisely, a return to Nietzsche's notion of the eternal return. In this context, such an approach might, at first glance, appear ill advised. After all, Altizer constructs his entire death of God theology around a Nietzschean rereading of Hegel or an Hegelian rereading of Nietzsche. In an article bearing the suggestive title "Eternal Recurrence and the Kingdom of God," Altizer explains:

> If the "glad tidings" are the announcement of the death of God, then living the "glad tidings" does lead to God. But it leads to that God who appears when all distance separating God and man disappears and is no more. True life is then found not in the life of God but in the death of God. Thereby life is not promised, it is here, it is *in you*, in you and me. For you and I have killed God, and we kill God when we pronounce His name, when we say life, and eternal life, and say it here and now. That life, that yes-saying, is not promised, it is found; and it is found in Christian *praxis*, in the immediate and total living of the "glad tidings" of the death of God.[10]

For Altizer, Nietzsche's notion of the eternal return is not an hypothesis about the nature of the cosmos but expresses a radical affirmation of the totality of experience in all its ambiguity. As such, this Yea-saying is the existential realization of a total presence in which past and future come together in a present that is completely actual. This is why Altizer contends that "all promise, all future hope and expectation, come to an end in the death of God."[11] This loss of hope does not lead to despair but is the occasion for a rejoicing that no longer looks beyond the present.

It is, however, possible to read Nietzsche's eternal return differently. This different reading involves a reading of difference that is inseparably bound to the rereading of time. In one of his most provocative works entitled *Le pas au-delà*, the too-little-known French writer-critic Maurice Blanchot proposes an interpretation of Nietzsche that stands in direct opposition to Altizer's reading of the eternal return:

> Nietzsche (if his name serves to name the law of the Eternal Return) and Hegel (if his name invites thought concerning presence as all and the all as presence) permit us to sketch out a mythology: Nietzsche can only come near Hegel, but it is always before and always after Hegel that he comes and comes again. Before: because, while thought of as absolute, presence has never reassembled within the accomplished totality of knowledge; presence knows itself to be absolute, but its knowledge remains a relative knowledge since it is not carried out in practice, and thus it knows itself only as a present that is not practically satisfied, not reconciled with presence as all: thus Hegel is still only a pseudo-Hegel. And Nietzsche always comes after, because the law that he bears presumes the accomplishment of time as present, and in this accomplishment, presumes its absolute destruction, so that thus the Eternal Return, affirming the future and the past as sole temporal instances and as identical, unrelated instances, freeing the future of all present and the past of all presence, shatters thought until this infinite affirmation will return infinitely in the future to that which under no form and in no time would know how to be present, just as that which, past and never having belonged in any form to the present, reverts infinitely to the past.[12]

Coming *after* Hegel, Nietzsche exposes the immemorial *before* that the System is constructed to recollect. This unrepresentable anachronism, which is always (the) outside of thought, is nonetheless thought in the "nonconceptualizable concept" of the eternal return. "The 're' of the return," Blanchot maintains, "inscribes the 'ex,' opening of all exteriority: as if the return, far from putting an end to it, marks exile, the commencement in its recommencement of exodus. To return, that would be to return again to ex-centering oneself, to erring."[13]

In contrast to Altizer's reading of Nietzsche, Blanchot's account of the eternal return is undeniably backwards. Blanchot does not interpret the future as a re-presentation of the present but reads the future in the past and the past in the future in order to approach the present by way of the detour through past and future. If return is eternal, not only will it never end, but it never began in the first place. In the absence of any true origin, nothing is original, which is not to imply that the origin is merely nothing. When nothing is original, all, as well as *the* all, is secondary. If, however, all is secondary, something is always missing and everything is always lacking. That which is always missing is a past that is "infinitely past" because it was never present in the first place. What has not been present cannot be re-presented. In this rereading of Nietzsche's eternal return, the "unrepresentable before" is what Blanchot describes as "the terrifyingly ancient." This radical past is not subject to Hegelian *Erinnerung,* either recollection or remembering. If the un-re-present-able time entails *le pas au-delà,* it is a Not that is different from both Barth's *"Nein"* and Altizer's "No" to Barth's "No." As the "outside of time in time," Blanchot's *pas* is anachronistic; it is always outside time proper. Inasmuch as this outside of time is "in" time and hence is not timeless, it is not eternal. The anachronism that a/theology struggles – yet always fails – to think is neither temporal nor eternal, present nor absent, immanent nor transcendent. This elusive mean, disruptive limen, odd third is what ontotheology is constructed *not* to think. The neither/nor solicited by a/theology is, in the strict sense of the term, unnameable. As unnameable, it (here we must note the inescapability of the neuter) cannot even be named the Unnameable. Every name must be erased as soon as it is articulated. It is precisely this play of inscription and erasure that insinuates the different difference and other other that solicits the errant thinker.

If all this remains obscure, it is only partly the result of my inability to explain the matter more clearly. In this case, precision necessarily entails a certain imprecision. In a final effort to render my imprecision more precise, I would like to try to situate the nonobject of a/theology in terms of what Paul Tillich describes as "The Two Types of Philosophy of Religion." I turn to Tillich not only because of the usefulness of the typology he outlines but also because his own theological position represents an appropriation of Heidegger that stands in marked contrast to the reading of Heidegger I am suggesting.

Tillich begins his well-known account of the two types of philosophy of religion by pointing out:

> One can distinguish two ways of approaching God: the way of overcoming estrangement and the way of meeting a stranger. In the first way man discovers *himself* when he discovers God: he discovers something that is identical with himself although it transcends him infinitely, something from which he is estranged, but from which he never has

been and never can be separated. In the second way man meets a *stranger* when he meets God. The meeting is accidental. Essentially they do not belong to each other. They may become friends on a tentative and conjectural basis. But there is no certainty about the stranger man has met.[14]

These two types of the philosophy of religion are embodied in contrasting arguments for the existence of God. According to Tillich, the three classic proofs of God's existence—the ontological, cosmological, and teleological arguments—really involve *two* alternative approaches. Inasmuch as both the cosmological and teleological proofs argue from effect to cause—the former from the actuality of the world to the necessity of a first cause, the latter from the order or design of the world to the necessity of a designer or an architect—they are merely variations of the same argument. The three proofs, therefore, constitute two types of the philosophy of religion: the ontological type, the way of overcoming estrangement, and the cosmological type, the way of meeting a stranger. Though any such typology inevitably distorts the complexities of various theological positions, it is remarkable how useful Tillich's schematism is for organizing contrasting theological options formulated throughout the Western tradition. While it is not possible to go into these matters in any detail in this context, a brief account of Tillich's two types serves to highlight certain features of the missing third that I am struggling to think.

"*Deus est esse*—God is Being." This claim, Tillich insists, is the basis of all philosophy of religion. Being, however, can be thought in different ways and different conceptualizations of Being issue in different philosophies of religion. Tillich defines the ontological principle in the philosophy of religion as follows: "*Man is immediately aware of something unconditional which is the prius of the separation and interaction of subject and object, theoretically as well as practically.*" As such, the ontological approach to God entails a transcendental argument in which one seeks the ground or condition of the possibility of knowledge and action. From this point of view, "*God is the presupposition of the question of God.*" Tillich's transcendental argument hinges on the identification of God and truth. God is truth and truth is presupposed in all rational discourse—even discourse that doubts the possibility of truth or knowledge. Accordingly, the ontological argument for the existence of God "is neither an argument, nor does it deal with the existence of God, although it often has been expressed in this form. It is the rational description of the relation of our mind to Being as such. Our mind implies *principia per se nota*, which have immediate evidence wherever they are noticed: the transcendentalia, *esse, verbum, bonum*. They constitute the Absolute in which the difference between knowing and being known is not actual. This Absolute as the principle of Being has absolute certainty. It is a necessary thought because it is the presupposition of all thought. 'The divine substance is known in such a way that it cannot be thought not to be.' "

The seeds of the dissolution of the ontological argument are already present in Anselm's classic formulation of the proof of God's existence. Anselm, Tillich points out, "transformed the *primum esse* into an *ens realissimum*, the principle into a universal being." In Heideggerian terms, the movement from the ontological to the cosmological type of the philosophy of religion involves a shift from conceiving God in terms of Being itself to understanding God as a being, albeit the highest being. When God is understood as *a* being, the divine-human relationship can no longer be regarded as immediate but now must be recognized as mediated. Different versions of the cosmological argument represent alternative efforts to approach God indirectly. According to Tillich, Thomas Aquinas begins a process of dissolution that comes to completion in the late medieval nominalism of William of Ockham. "God," Tillich writes, "ceases to be Being itself and becomes a particular being, who must be known, *cognitione particulari*. Ockham . . . calls God a *res singularissima*." For Tillich, the interpretation of God as *a* being rather than Being itself makes the atheism characteristic of modernity not only inevitable but understandable.

Tillich's entire theological enterprise is motivated by the desire to address twentieth-century anxiety, doubt, and despair through a reformulation of the ontological type of the philosophy of religion. Drawing on Heidegger's analysis of *Sein*, Tillich interprets God as the power of Being that is the ground of all beings. "This power of being," Tillich contends, "is the *prius* of everything that has being. It precedes every separation and makes every interaction possible, because it is the point of identity without which neither separation nor interaction can be thought." As the *prius* of every separation, the power of being is the condition of the possibility of all reunion. Because identity is primal, difference is secondary and thus penultimate. Though once having insisted on the importance of Schelling's late philosophy, by the time Tillich develops his mature theology, he is obsessed with something like the "point of indifference" for which Schelling was searching in his youthful *System of Transcendental Idealism*. By thinking God as the power of being, Tillich attempts to think "the God beyond God"—that is, the God beyond the God who is *a* being. When God is understood as the power of being, God is affirmed even in our most radical denials.

At this juncture, a seemingly simple question arises: Do Tillich's two types of the philosophy of religion exhaust the possibilities of the religious imagination? Perhaps not. Tillich remains committed to precisely the ontotheological tradition, which, as Heidegger insists, has reached closure. *If* theological reflection is to have a future—and this, like all else, remains uncertain—it must be not only *within* but also *beyond* ontotheology. To shift the focus of theology from beings or *a* being to Being or the power of Being actually changes nothing. Tillich, like most of his predecessors, fails to think the *difference* between Being and beings. Thus he does not think or try to think difference *as such*. This is not an accidental oversight, for the goal of on-totheological reflection is to heal the wound of difference by discovering or rediscovering the primal identity that is supposed to be always already *present*. This primal identity of the origin is reinscribed as the end in the total presence actualized by Altizer's apocalypse.

It is, however, possible to read the death of God otherwise. Instead of the condition of the *possibility* of presence, the death of God, which is always on its way, might be the condition of the *impossibility* of presence. The impossibility of presence, which is never simply absent, marks the erasure of all presence that can be faithfully represented. The trace of this erasure is the deferral of the Parousia—a deferral, which, as infinite, marks and remarks the timelessness of time itself. When time is thought radically, its gift is not a *present* but a *coup de don* that is the *coup de grâce*. The *coup* of this grace inflicts a wound as old as time itself.

I began with a story of un-re-membering—a story of the dis-memberment of a father/husband by a mother/wife through the agency of a son named Time. Why, I asked, is Cronus associated with cutting, or, more precisely, with castration? A possible answer to this question is beginning to emerge. Conception is not only an affair of knowledge. To conceive is to unite subject and object, self and other. After Hegel, the question that re-mains is the question of the remainder of conception. If conception leaves a remainder—something like a *smule*, a crumb or a fragment, a fragment that would have to be unphilosophical—if conception leaves a remainder, two are never one and the third that issues from incomplete union is less a synthesis than a limen—a hymen that not only joins but, just as importantly, separates. If this hymen cannot be broken, if the Other cannot be penetrated, theologians and philosophers are rendered impotent because conception is impossible.

In an effort to draw near an end, an end, which, in contrast to on-totheologians, I would insist is never totally present, I turn a final time (for we now suspect that time is final) to Blanchot:

> What is it that rings false in the system? What makes it limp? The ques-tion itself is lame and does not amount to a question. What exceeds the system is the impossibility of its failure, and likewise the impossibility of its success. Finally nothing can be said of it, and there is a way of keep-ing still (the lacunary silence of writing) that arrests the system, leaving it idle, unemployed, delivered to the seriousness of irony.[15]

The task of thinking at the end of theology is to think and rethink the tear of time. In this tear and as this tear we might be able to think the sacred anew. In the uncanny space of this time and time of this space, failure is success and success failure. If that which exceeds the system—Hegelian or otherwise—is the impossibility of its failure, the lacunary silence of writing will be heard, if at all, only in the possibility of a failure that echoes the impossibility of conception. "Finally nothing can be said of it." That is what I have been trying to say or not to say; but, of course, I have failed, for I have said it. So now *I* will not say it but will let another say it—another named Beckett, Samuel Beckett who, in *The Unnameable*, does not say but writes:

Is there really nothing new to try? I mentioned my hope, but it is not serious. If I could speak and yet say nothing, really nothing? Then I might escape being gnawed to death as by an old satiated rat, and my little tester-bed along with me, a cradle, or be gnawed to death not so fast, in my old cradle, and the torn flesh have time to knit, as in the Caucasus, before being torn again. But it seems impossible to speak and yet say nothing, you think you have succeeded, but you always overlook something.[16]

7.

Foiling Reflection

A mirror covered with flyspecks. Who will ever
tell of the kindness and perplexity of this aban-
doned pane?

Edmond Jabès

Memories of Hegel

The Tain of the Mirror is a *serious* book. But its seriousness *is not* the
seriousness of irony. Indeed, there is not a shred of irony in this *book*. This is
one of its problems and it is serious. It is no accident that one of Hegel's first
and most prescient critics began his interrogation of the System with a thesis,
which ironized theses, entitled *The Concept of Irony*. Kierkegaard realized that
to take Hegel seriously by approaching his System philosophically is to
become Hegelian. Rodolphe Gasché has not learned this lesson. By interpreting Derrida *philosophically*, Gasché presents what is, in effect, an Hegelian
reading of deconstruction.

Hegel is hard to forget . . . and hard to remember. More precisely,
Hegel is hard to forget because it is hard to remember in a non-Hegelian way.
The memory of Western philosophy is, in large measure, the memory of
Hegel. Insofar as Hegelian recollection (*Erinnerung*), understood as the process of representing the past in the present, defines memory as such, we implicitly remember Hegel whenever we remember anything. If we are to forget
Hegel, we must learn to remember differently by attempting to recall what
Hegel's System is constructed to forget. A different memory, a countermemory
that would be a memory of difference, would entail a recollection that is inseparably bound to a certain oblivion. This memory that is a forgetting and
forgetting that is a memory might displace Hegelianism and all it represents
by foiling reflection.

Nowhere is the memory of Hegel more haunting than in twentieth-
century French philosophy and literature. This memory can be traced to the

87

extraordinary influence of lectures Alexandre Kojève delivered at L'Ecole Pratique des Hautes Etudes. Subsequently published under the title *Introduction à la lecture de Hegel,* Kojève's reading of the *Phenomenology of Spirit* effectively sets the agenda for several generations of French intellectuals. Among those who, at one time or another, attended Kojève's lectures were Raymond Aron, Raymond Queneau, Georges Bataille, Maurice Merleau-Ponty, Jacques Lacan, and Jean-Paul Sartre. The center of the *Phenomenology* is, for Kojève, the master-slave relationship in which individuals engage in a seemingly senseless contest for recognition. History, which grows out of violent struggle, is a dialectical process in which irrational aspects of experience are overcome and opposites are reconciled in all-encompassing reason. According to Kojève, this reconciliation marks the end of both history and its subject—man.

Less often acknowledged but no less important than Kojève's lectures on Hegel is the work of Jean Hyppolite. While Hyppolite is best known for *Genèse et structure de la Phénoménologie de l'esprit de Hegel,* his brilliant commentary on the *Phenomenology,* it is a work that is virtually unknown outside France, *Logique et existence: essai sur la logique de Hegel,* that is more significant for later thinkers. In this study, Hyppolite contends that Hegel's speculative logic forms the *structural* foundation of his entire System. Hyppolite's account of Hegelian logic uncovers an unexpectedly close relationship between speculative philosophy and both phenomenology and structuralism. When read in the context of Hyppolite's Hegel, Husserlian phenomenology and all varieties of structuralism seem to be extensions of the theology and philosophy of the logos that undergirds Western reflection. From this point of view, Hegel appears to be a structuralist *avant la lettre* and structuralism seems little more than latter-day idealism. In light of this understanding of the complex interplay between Hegelianism and structuralism, it becomes possible to interpret poststructuralism as an extended critique of speculative philosophy.

In addition to establishing the relationship between idealism and structuralism, Hyppolite prepares the way for the poststructuralist critique of Hegelianism. Always resisting a one-sided reading of Hegel, Hyppolite exposes the return of the repressed in the System. In a characteristically seminal passage, he writes:

> Perhaps we touch here on the decisive point of Hegelianism, on this torsion of thought to think the unthinkable conceptually, on what makes Hegel at the same time the greatest irrationalist and the greatest rationalist who has ever existed. We are not able to escape the Logos, but the Logos departs from itself while remaining itself. As it is the indivisible self, the Absolute, the Logos thinks the unthought, thinks sense in relation to nonsense.[1]

To recognize the unthought that unsettles thought as well as the nonsense in the midst of sense is to discern the tear that rends Hegelianism. Derrida echoes Hyppolite, who was his colleague at L'Ecole Normale Supérieure, when he contends that inasmuch as Western philosophy reaches completion in Hegel's System, to reexamine Hegel is, in effect, to rethink philosophy as a whole. By approaching Hegel through the exploration of what he excludes or represses, it is possible to recall what Hegelianism wants to forget. This un-forgetting *(a-letheia)* of the repressed is not the erasure of oblivion but the recognition of the *impossibility* of overcoming forgetting. If forgetting is unavoidable and thus remembering is inevitably incomplete, the Hegelian text always exceeds its meaning. In his tattered and torn texts, Derrida struggles to write the excess of the Hegelian book.

Gasché's chief contribution in *The Tain of the Mirror* is his careful analysis of Derrida in relation to philosophy or, more specifically, to speculative philosophy. Gasché goes so far as to assert that "Derrida's thought can be adequately understood *only* if approached philosophically—that is, shown to be engaged in a constant debate with the major philosophical themes from a primarily philosophical perspective."[2] This account of deconstruction reflects a calculated resistance to the rhetorical reading that Derrida's texts demand. Gasché freely admits that his "emphasis on the philosophical dimensions of Derrida's work is clearly a function of his reception in this country, particularly by the proponents of what has come to be known as deconstructive criticism" (p. 2). He intends this book to be a corrective to purported misreadings of Derrida. Deconstructive literary criticism, which is devoted to demonstrating the *self*-deconstruction of texts, Gasché argues, is actually an extension of New Criticism. From this point of view, the principles implicitly informing both New Criticism and "New New Criticism" presuppose precisely the (speculative) notion of self-reflexivity that Derrida relentlessly interrogates. Gasché's effort to "save" Derrida from literary critics lends his argument a sharply polemical tone:

> My contention is that Derrida's marked interest in literature, an interest that began with his questioning of the particular ideality of literature, has in his thinking never led to anything remotely resembling literary criticism or to a valorization of what literary critics agree to call literature. [p. 255]

Having asserted an apparent antithesis between *Derrida's* deconstruction and "so-called deconstructive criticism," Gasché points toward a possible reconciliation of opposites that seems to hold out the promise of a critical practice true to basic Derridean principles. Explaining the implications of the foregoing passage, Gasché writes:

Such an observation does not mean, however, that Derrida's philosophy is without any relevance to literary criticism. Rather it implies that the importance of Derrida's thinking for the discipline of literary criticism is not immediately evident, and that any statement of its relevance to that discipline requires certain mediating steps beforehand. So-called deconstructive criticism, which, however important, is but an offspring of New Criticism, has not, to my knowledge, undertaken any of these preparatory steps and has done little more than apply what it takes to be a method for reading literary texts to the unproblematized horizon of its discipline. As a result, the genuine impact that Derrida's philosophy could have on literary criticism has not been, or at best has hardly been, noticed. [ibid.]

There can be little doubt that Derrida's rethinking of Western philosophy has led to problematic critical excesses on the part of *some* literary critics. The tendency to categorize and thematize "nonconcepts" like *"différance"* and "trace" creates the illusion of a method or technique that can be universally applied to disclose the identical aporetic structure in different texts. The styles and strategies of literary criticism that have emerged in response to Derrida's writings are, however, considerably more complex and diverse than Gasché acknowledges. Because Gasché never examines specific examples of so-called misguided deconstructive criticism, the targets of his attack often remain unclear. What is clear is that there are some literary critics who are every bit as sensitive as Gasché to the importance and implications of Derrida's critique of reflexivity. As will become apparent in what follows, Gasché's blanket condemnation of deconstructive literary criticism is inseparably bound to the seriousness of his philosophical agenda.

Before proceeding to a more detailed consideration of Gasché's argument, it is important to note that one of his most significant contributions is to have provided a helpful corrective to certain *philosophical* accounts of deconstruction that continue to exercise inordinate influence. Richard Rorty, for example, maintains that "Derrida is the latest and largest flower on the dialectical kudzu vine of which the *Phenomenology of Spirit* was the first tendril."[3] This understanding of deconstruction rests upon an idealistic misinterpretation of the claim that "there is nothing outside the text." Derrida contends that because the sign is always the sign of a sign, we are forever trapped in the prison house of language. Contrary to Rorty, this does not mean that deconstruction remains bound to the structure of reflexivity implied by the auto-telic nature of language. When Derrida insists that "there is nothing outside the text," he is claiming that "the outside" of the text neither is nor is not. Forever eluding the strictures of ontology, this *hors-texte* "is" the nothing that ontotheology leaves unthought and that Derrida strives to think. To think this unthought is to remember in a non-Hegelian way.

Gasché does not, however, always avoid the problems he so effectively detects in others. In attempting to counter a variety of misreadings, he constructs an analysis that employs a philosophical discourse that too often is blind to its own insight. As a result of his philosophical approach, Gasché unwittingly reinscribes many of the oppositions and hierarchies that Derrida tries to subvert. *The Tain of the Mirror* is a subtly Hegelian book about the most un-Hegelian of writers. The significance of Gasché's contribution is limited by his methodical repression of one of the most important lessons Derrida has taught us: philosophical analysis is undeniably rhetorical.

From Reflection to Reflexion

Hegel's System is inscribed between the extremes of a philosophy that emphasizes difference at the expense of identity, and a philosophy that privileges identity by reducing difference to mere appearance. The former Hegel describes as "the philosophy of reflection," represented by Kant; the latter he labels "identity philosophy," represented by Schelling. In formulating his System, Hegel seeks to articulate a mean that preserves *both* identity *and* difference.

For Hegel, reflection is not a term that refers to mental activity in general but denotes a specific cognitive function. "Reflection," he avers, "is the action that establishes oppositions and goes from one to the other, but without effecting their combination and realizing their thoroughgoing unity."[4] When interpreted in this way, reflection is the analytical activity by which one makes distinctions, posits oppositions, and establishes differences. From Hegel's point of view, this mental function is closely associated with understanding (*Verstand*). In contrast to the integrative activity of reason (*Vernunft*), understanding represents the capacity of the mind to dissolve concrete totalities into discrete parts and to identify the specific differences definitive of isolated particulars. Its guiding rules are abstract self-identity and the law of noncontradiction. According to these principles, "the determinations of thought are absolutely exclusive and different and remain unalterably independent in relation to each other."[5] This form of thought, which is rooted in the Cartesian opposition between the *res cogitans* and the *res extensa*, pervades Enlightenment philosophy from British empiricism to French materialism.

Hegel believes the most complete and provocative statement of this position is developed in Kant's critical philosophy. In matters theoretical, practical, and esthetic, Kantian philosophy remains suspended between fixed opposites reified by reflective understanding. Kant clearly defines the differences between intelligibility and sensibility, ideality and reality, infinite and finite, obligation and inclination, duty and desire, subjectivity and objectivity, and the like, but is unable to reconcile these opposites or synthesize these antitheses. There are, however, several points at which Kant glimpses the possibility of reuniting the differences he distinguishes. In his account of the transcendental unity of apperception in the *Critique of Pure Reason*, and his analyses of the beautiful, the poet, inner teleology, and the *intellectus archetypus* in the *Critique of Judgment*, Kant effectively describes what eventually becomes the structure of Hegel's speculative Idea. By insisting that these notions are merely regulative ideas, not constitutive of reality, Kant reasserts the oppositions he struggles to overcome. The failure of the philosophy of reflection to achieve a reintegration of opposites creates what Hegel describes as "the need of philosophy." In his early and important *Differenzschrift*, Hegel writes: "Division, disunity (*Entzweiung*) is the source of *the need of philosophy*. . . . When the might of union vanishes from the life of men and the oppositions lose their living relation and reciprocity and gain independence, the need of philosophy arises."[6] This need is directly or indirectly addressed by every major post-Kantian philosopher.

Hegel's speculative account of the aporias created by the philosophy of reflection is a response to the inadequacy of the solutions proposed by Fichte and Schelling. Though approaching the problem from opposite points of view, Fichte and Schelling both seek to overcome the estrangement (*Entzweiung*) perpetuated by Kant's critical philosophy. Extending the analysis of moral activity in the *Critique of Practical Reason*, Fichte reduces all objectivity (difference) to subjectivity (identity) by arguing that objects (the not-I) are posited by the creative subject (the I). Schelling, by contrast, elaborates Kant's esthetic interpretation of nature outlined in the Third Critique to develop a system of objective idealism in which the underlying identity of everything is original, and concrete differences are secondary. This primal identity, Schelling claims, can be apprehended through "intellectual intuition." Neither Fichte's subjective nor Schelling's objective idealism overcomes the impasse of critical philosophy. While Kant fails to secure the identity of differences, Fichte and Schelling are unable to maintain difference in relation to identity. Hegel addresses the inadequecies of these alternatives by trying to establish "the identity of identity and difference" or "the union of union and nonunion." "The Absolute," he asserts, "is the identity of identity and non-identity; being opposed and being one are both together in it."[7]

In order to develop a nonreductive mediation of opposites, Hegel tries to move beyond the philosophy of reflection to a speculative idealism that rests upon the structural foundation of self-reflexivity. If Hegel is to avoid reasserting the principle of opposition that plagues Kantianism, he cannot simply oppose the philosophy of reflection. Rather, he must formulate an *internal* critique of critical philosophy by exposing the unacknowledged presuppositions of reflection. In different terms, Hegel must think what Kant leaves unthought. What Kant never realizes or refuses to admit, Hegel argues, is that opposites presuppose unity. The antitheses articulated by the understanding are differentiated from an antecedent totality in which all opposites are co-implicated. In contrast to Schelling's "point of indifference" in which difference disappears, Hegel's primal whole *implicitly* preserves differences. To think this unthought (but not unthinkable) totality is to sublate (*aufheben*) the philosophy of reflection.

The totality that at once grounds and undercuts reflection becomes explicit when reflection turns back on itself and becomes absolute. When absolutized, reflection is reflexive.[8] Speculative reason surpasses the oppositions of understanding by re-cognizing the identity constitutive of difference and the difference ingredient in identity. As Gasché explains:

> Speculative thought is concerned with reconstituting the unity of what is diverse. . . . It has the boldness to conceive of opposites in their unity. Now, because the thought of such unity requires a beholding of what is opposite as such – that is, the being in opposition of the opposites as well as the mutual reflection by which these opposites become unified in the idea of the Spirit – speculative thought is grounded in this reflective mirroring of what is positively in opposition. . . . The mirroring that constitutes speculative thought articulates the diverse, and the contradictions that exist between its elements, in such a way as to exhibit the totality of which this diversity is a part. [p. 44]

The Hegelian Idea that grounds all reality is a structural totality in which everything becomes *itself* in and through *its own* other. Because otherness and difference are essential components of self-identity (or using linguistic terms, because identity is diacritical), relationship to otherness and difference is, in the final analysis, *self*-relationship.

If Hegelian reflexion is to heal the wounds left open by the philosophy of reflection, the speculative Idea must be all-inclusive. There can be no unassimilated excess or remainder, no exteriority or outside that is not interiorized, no fragment that is not re-membered or re-collected. The question that remains after the System reaches closure is whether Hegel, *malgré lui*, ends by privileging identity and repressing difference. While calling for a reconciliation of identity and difference, Hegel insists upon the *identity* of identity and difference. Within his speculative totality, difference is a transient (albeit necessary) moment. Derrida emphasizes the hierarchical relationship between identity and difference when he writes: " *'in seinem Anderen.'* The 'its other' is the very syntagm of the Hegelian proper; it constitutes negativity in the service of the proper, literal sense."[9] Inasmuch as identity always owns otherness, difference is inevitably repressed. As I have stressed, if we are to forget Hegel, we must learn to remember differently by attempting to recall what Hegel's System is constructed to forget. This non-Hegelian *mémoire*, which is thinking *sensu strictissimo*, solicits the (impossible) return of the repressed.

The Eternal Return of Difference

One of the ironies of this book is that its fundamental premise, suggested by the title, depends on a trope and yet when Gasché approaches his subject, he attempts to dispense with tropological readings. The tain of the mirror is the repressed underside of Hegelian speculation that both makes reflexion possible and renders it incomplete. Gasché argues:

> Deconstruction implies a breaking through of the tinfoils of the mirrors of reflection, demonstrating the uncertainty of the speculum. . . . To look through the mirror is to look at its reverse side, at the dull side doubling the mirror's specular play, in short, at the *tain* of the mirror. It is on this reverse side—on the tinfoil—that dissemination writes itself. . . . On this lining of the outside surface of reflection, one can read the "system" of the infrastructures that commands the mirror's play and determines the angles of reflection. [p. 238]

By pushing reflection beyond its limits, Derrida tries to "open thought . . . to a confrontation with Otherness that would no longer be *its own*. Indeed, such a possibility hinges on the inscription within thought of its structural limitations—limitations that do not result from the deficiencies of the cognizing subject as a finite being. Thought . . . would in this manner become able, perhaps for the first time, to think something other than itself, something other than itself in *its* Other, or itself in itself" (p. 101). This other is the "nonoriginal origin" of thought.

If understood in this way, it is clear that deconstruction represents a relentless critique of Hegel's System. When Derrida uses the word "philosophy," he means the philosophy of reflexion. The identification of philosophy with Hegelianism is not arbitrary but is the result of Derrida's acceptance of Heidegger's claim that the Western metaphysical tradition culminates in Hegel's speculative philosophy. From this point of view, to criticize Hegel is to criticize philosophy as such. In developing his critique of philosophy, Derrida does not simply attack Hegel from without. Rather, he pursues the fault in the System by miming Hegel's own dialectical analysis.

As Hegel seeks to move beyond Kant by thinking what the philosophy of reflection leaves unthought, so Derrida tries to move "beyond" Hegelianism by thinking what the philosophy of reflexion leaves unthought. While Hegel is convinced that Kant has not thought the identity that reconciles differences, Derrida insists that Hegel has not thought the difference that divides identities. In thinking the *identity* of identity and difference, Hegel leaves unthought the *difference* of identity and difference. Gasché correctly points out that "what distinguishes Heidegger's and Derrida's positions from that of idealist philosophy is primarily their inquiry into what may be called the difference between identity and difference, between the totality of what is and the difference that inhabits self-relation" (p. 87).

The difference that inhabits self-relation is the difference that displaces self-reflexion by interrupting the circuit of exchange between self and other. The structure of self-reflexion is fully realized in the perfect transparency of absolute self-consciousness. The subject becomes self-conscious by relating to itself in *its own* other. For Hegel, the division of self and other is a self-division that is the condition of the possibility of self-identity. For Derrida, the division of self and other, which is "original" and insurmountable, is the condition of the possibility *and* the impossibility of self-identity. The difference that both separates and joins identity and difference eludes the speculative economy it nonetheless makes possible. Presupposing that which it cannot contain, reflexivity is always incomplete and thus is never perfectly reflexive. The excess of reflexion shatters the mirror of speculation. Gasché maintains:

> The structure of auto-affection [i.e., the relation of the self to *itself* in and through otherness] requires a minimal division of the same in order for this same to constitute itself as itself. This minimal division takes on manifold shapes. It explains why auto-affection is possible only through an immediate exiting from interiority and why the same *as* the same, the retroflected same, must affect itself by Otherness. Thus the presence that is achieved in auto-affection is a supplement for a lack of self-presence, an absence that structurally haunts the self-affecting self. In short, "utterly irreducible hetero-affection inhabits – intrinsically – the most hermetic auto-affection." [p. 232][10]

The *herteros* infecting auto-affection is the unthought "ground" of all thinking. Ever since its origin in ancient Greece, philosophy has involved the ceaseless search for origins. Reading Derrida philosophically, Gasché concludes that deconstruction shares with the Western tradition "the goal of attaining the 'ultimate foundation' of concepts" (p. 120). The ultimate foundation that Derrida discerns is "more 'originary' . . . than any classical origin" (p. 152). This originary ground is, paradoxically, a "nonfundamental structure."[11] Neither an origin nor a ground in the traditional sense of these terms, Derrida's nonfundamental structure "simultaneously grounds and ungrounds" reflective and reflexive thought (p. 155). It is important to understand the im-

plications of this critical point. The nonfundamental structure that is the
"ultimate foundation" of thought is what Gasché names a "quasi-
transcendental." While a transcendental is the condition of the possibility of
something else, a quasi-transcendental is the condition of the possibility *and
the impossibility* of that which it "grounds." Derrida's deconstructive analysis of
philosophy does not simply negate reflexion. As he repeatedly states, we cannot escape logocentrism. What Derrida does claim is that what makes reflexion possible can never be thought as such. Philosophy presupposes that
which it cannot comprehend. To dream of complete knowledge is to repress
an other that can never be known.

Gasché describes the quasi-transcendental that grounds and ungrounds
thought as an "infrastructure." Just as the deconstructive "ground" is not exactly
a ground, and "foundation" is not precisely a foundation, so Derrida's "nonfundamental structure" is not quite a structure. Gasché argues:

> The infrastructure must be understood as the *medium of differentiation* in
> general of the heterogeneous possibilities, contradictory strata, lexicolo-
> gical disparities, and so on. This medium of all possible differentiation –
> the common element of all the oppositions, contradictions, and
> discrepancies – is not a medium that would precede, as an undifferen-
> tiated plenitude, the differences into which it fragments itself. The
> adverse terms are not liquefied or mixed within it. As the medium of
> differentiation in general, it precedes undifferentiated unity and the
> subsequently bipolar division. [p. 152]

This medium of differentiation must not be confused with the Hegelian
mean between identity and difference. While Hegel's *Mitte* is essentially synthetic, Derrida's *milieu* is nonsynthetic without being antithetical. This "between" (*entre-deux*), Derrida contends, has not even been thought by Heidegger.
While Heidegger clears the way for a critique of Western philosophy, he remains uncritically committed to many of the principles of ontotheology that
Derrida calls into question:

> What distinguishes the positions is that Heidegger's investigation is into
> difference *itself*, into the true *essence* of difference, not into difference
> that would simply be the same as the whole of Being . . . and that
> would unite what is set forth within it, whereas Derrida's inquiries are
> concerned with a difference that is no longer phenomenologizable, that
> has no "itself" to itself but that, in its irreducible plurality, ceaselessly
> differs from itself. In Derrida, this difference links identity based on
> self-relation to difference, each time in a different manner, in such a
> manner that what is held together does not form a whole. Within the
> network of relations of this difference, wholes can be set out, but

because they are inscribed within that difference, they remain forever incomplete. In other words, the difference Derrida is concerned with is a condition of possibility constituting unity and totality and, at the same time, their essential limits. [pp. 87–88]

Because the infrastructure possesses neither essence nor identity, it is never the same but always differs from itself. As the "ground" of being and nonbeing, which neither exists nor does not exist, the infrastructure "is" the eternal return of difference. If difference is to return eternally, it must always return differently. Consequently, "the" infrastructure is not unified but is comprised of irreducibly heterogeneous elements that are linked in associative chains. Gasché considers five such chains: *arche-trace, différance, supplementarity, iterability,* and *re-mark.* "By overlapping, replacing, and supplementing one another," these infrastructures "form a certain system" (p. 239). This "general system" is the liminal opening in which unification and totalization are determined.

When understood as the "heterological space" of inscription, the general system can be read as "the general text." No more philosophical than literary, the general text creates the space for philosophy, classical literature, and traditional literary criticism (even in its "deconstructive" form). As the originary ground ungrounds that which it nevertheless supports, so the general text limits what it makes possible. "By reinscribing the discourses of philosophy and literature into their margin, the general text unsettles their pretensions to authority and autonomy, and 'grounds' them in what they do not control" (p. 260). That which neither philosophy nor literature controls is the *difference* that establishes their identity and difference. As the interweaving of identity and difference, the general text (*textere,* to weave) is the "border itself" (p. 280). In its struggle for mastery, philosophy remains oblivious to this unmasterable margin. Deconstruction "forgets" Hegel by remembering what philosophy cannot re-member. This memory that is a forgetting and forgetting that is a memory is a disaster for philosophy.

"Already" or "always already" is the mark of the disaster, which is historically outside of history: before undergoing it, we (but who is not included in this we?) will undergo it—the trance as the passivity of the step beyond [*le pas au-delà*]. The disaster is the impropriety of its name and the disappearance of the proper name (Derrida); it is neither noun nor verb, but a remainder that would bar with invisibility and illegibility all that shows and is said—a remainder that is neither a result nor a balance. Patience again—the passive, when *Aufhebung* is arrested. Hegel: "Innocence alone is nonaction (the absence of operation)."[12]

Deconstruction strives but always fails to write this disaster.

Dis-course of Method

Gasché re-members deconstruction. However, in this monumental
work of remembering, he forgets "the seriousness of irony."

And if the "possibility" of writing is linked to the "possibility" of irony,
then we understand why the one and the other are always disappointing
and deceptive; it is impossible, not being able to lay claim to either;
both exclude all mastery (cf. Sylviane Agacinski).[13]

As I have noted, Kierkegaard remembers (without re-membering) what
Gasché forgets. In her brilliant book *Aparté: Conceptions et Morts de Sören
Kierkegaard*, Sylviane Agacinski points out that "with Kierkegaard, irony will
always be what escapes Hegelian sublation to the extent that irony . . . represents in an insurmountable way the point of view of the writer."[14]
Deconstruction helps us to realize that philosophers usually write to erase
writing. Efforts to the contrary notwithstanding, Gasché repeats this
philosophical gesture by reinscribing an Hegelianism without reserve. The
dis-course of this method is evident at several critical junctures in his argument.
    Gasché re-members Derrida by attempting to systematize his critique of
systems and to structure his criticism of structuralism. Philosophy, Gasché
points out, is "the demand for unity or totality" (p. 64). Approaching his subject philosophically, Gasché tries to discern the identity in the midst of Derrida's
different writings. This quest for unity culminates in chapter 9, which is entitled "A System beyond Being." The "system" that Gasché claims to have
discovered is, to be sure, no ordinary system. The network of infrastructures
does not constitute a unity or totality. Nevertheless, Gasché insists that the
infra-*structures* do form something like a system. "Derrida's intention," he
argues, "must thus be viewed as aiming at a more encompassing system which
inscribes the value of systematicity while criticizing that very value, but
without asserting the opposing (and contemporaneous) value of the fragment"
(p. 179). To read deconstruction as an alternative system—albeit a system
beyond being—it is necessary to bring together differences that Derrida per-
sistently holds apart. Derrida's texts resist Gasché's reappropriation as much
as Gasché resists their inappropriate rhetoric.
    Not only does Gasché try to reintegrate Derrida's scattered writings, he
also re-members deconstruction by situating it as the *third* moment in a
philosophical progression that begins with Kant. As I have maintained, Kant
attempts to overcome the oppositions of Enlightenment philosophy, which,
for the sake of brevity, can be described as empiricism and rationalism, by
formulating a transcendental philosophy that grounds both sense experience
and rational reflection. The failure to recognize that difference presupposes
unity renders the reconciliation Kant conceives ideal rather than real. Hegel

tries to resolve the tensions of Kantianism by thinking what Kant leaves un-thought. The ground of the philosophy of reflection, Hegel argues, is a complex unity in which both identities and differences are implicit. The complete articulation of this self-reflexive totality is the *telos* of the entire historical process. Within Gasché's scheme, Derrida's argument grows out of his conviction that neither Kant nor Hegel uncovers the ground of thought. To approach the "ultimate foundation" of reflection as well as reflexion, it is necessary to think what Hegel leaves unthought. To think this unthought is to think the nonoriginal origin that marks the "end" of philosophy from its very beginning.

In unfolding his implicitly dialectical analysis of Derrida, Gasché exposes another problematic aspect of his method. In the introduction, he explains:

> This book is based on almost the entirety of Derrida's writings up to *La vérité en peinture* (1979)—with the exception of *Glas*—as well as on a host of essays. Putting aside the delicate question of what is to be counted as more philosophical or more literarily playful, not to mention earlier or later, I have admittedly given greater prominence to the more philo-sophically discursive texts. [p. 4]

As always, the question most worth asking concerns what has been left out. Why does Gasché exclude Derrida's "more literarily playful" writings? And why, in a book on the relationship between deconstruction and the philosophy of "reflection," does Gasché refuse to consider *Glas*, which is Derrida's most extensive and important engagement with Hegel? The answer is clear: Gasché believes that Derrida's "nonphilosophical" texts are not really serious. The more "literarily playful" works merely re-present the ideas that are more adequately presented in the "philosophically discursive texts." "The difference between the more 'philosophical' and more 'literary' approach," Gasché maintains, "consists, primarily, in making philosophical arguments in a nondiscursive manner, on the level of the signifier, syntax, and textual organization" (p. 4). Signified/signifier, idea/ornament, serious/playful, philo-sophy/literature, philosophy/literary criticism. By privileging the former term in each binary, this "masterful" book reinscribes the hierarchical oppositions Derrida strives to subvert. The seriousness with which Gasché takes these *philosophical* oppositions leads to his unwarranted dismissal of all deconstruc-tive literary criticism. Gasché does not seem to see the irony of his method. This failure of vision is, in the words of Bataille (one of the first to translate Kierkegaard into French and an author about whom Gasché has written elsewhere with great sympathy and insight), "the blind spot of Hegelianism." As Kierkegaard knew but Gasché, at least for the moment, has forgotten, philosophers cannot afford to take ironists seriously, for ironic texts sound the disastrous *glas* of philosophy.

As an accomplished philosopher, Gasché *"does not believe in the disaster."*

One cannot believe in it, whether one lives or dies. No faith is commensurate with it, and at the same time a sort of disinterest, detached from the disaster. Night, white night—such is the disaster: the night lacking darkness, but brightened by no light."[15] In the white night, lacking darkness but brightened by no light, both reflection and reflexion are impossible. The impossiblity of reflection and reflexion points to the inescapability of writing. Even if *some* literary critics appear to have abused deconstruction, to respond by re-membering Derrida philosophically only repeats the error in reverse. Derrida's writings require a *different* reading—a reading that is *neither* philosophical *nor* literary. This neither/nor makes all philosophers edgy.

Apologies

The Tain of the Mirror is a "quasi"-apologetic book whose potential impact on critical discourse in America is difficult to anticipate. The defense of Derrida that Gasché offers constitutes a strange apology. Apologies usually are written on behalf of groups or movements whose viewpoints seem threatening to those in positions of social and political power. While apologists need not try to convert others, they must attempt to persuade critics to be tolerant of perspectives with which they do not agree. In his effort to gain a hearing from philosophers who dismiss Derrida because he does not seem to be a serious thinker, Gasché dismisses literary critics who are struggling more or less seriously to extend Derrida's insights. One need not condone everything done in the name of Derrida to recognize the strategic peril implicit in Gasché's approach. By insisting—but not arguing—that literary critics have misunderstood and thus misused Derrida's insights, Gasché's polemic might be construed by cultural and political conservatives as reinforcing their own rejection of critical departures that call into question traditional styles of analysis and forms of discourse. If literary critics cannot even understand the writings of Derrida and hence do not really know what they are doing, then what hope can there be for deconstruction? Gasché's answer seems to be that the only hope is to understand Derrida's writings *properly*. This response, which certainly should comfort both philosophers and traditional critics, should make very uneasy those who understand Derrida *improperly*.

There is, however, another, perhaps even more insidious, danger inherent in every apology. An apology is, in effect, an exercise in translation. Writers or speakers attempt to make the viewpoints they are defending comprehensible by translating them into the language of their critics. For example, the early Christian apologists attempted to defend themselves against persecution by demonstrating the way in which their theological beliefs represented the most important insights advanced by leading Greek philosophers. The problem with this *style* of argument—and it is important to stress that apology is a very specific style that explicitly depends upon sophisticated *rhetorical* strategies—is that the distinctive traits of the viewpoint being defended tend to be lost in translation. More precisely, apologists unwittingly facilitate assimilation of their viewpoint to the perspective of hostile critics. In this way, Christianity becomes Platonic or Neoplatonic. In other words, the price of toleration is domestication. The powers that *be* cannot bear transgression and thus must try to master aberrant discourse and praxis by depriving them of all offense. Reflecting on the furor released by his "offensive" texts, Kierkegaard wrote in his Journal:

> The concept "offense" or, as it is called, scandal, is the truth, is most often regarded as untruth. Thus if untruth has become entrenched in "an established order" and cozily settles down, and then the truth stirs, the latter is denounced as a scandal. When in the course of time literary infamy got the prescriptive right to exist, when such a thing was accepted instead of being a scandal every day it existed on such a disproportionate scale, absolutely no one dared say a word because all were afraid of arousing scandal. Well, thanks for that. And then when I said something many people thought and said: It's a scandal, a scandal he should have avoided . . . .
>
> It is the same in other situations. When a person has cozily settled down in the established order and has all possible profit from it, when the truth as such has become a kind of luxury and jumbling every possible point of view has become supreme wisdom, then to raise up the truth is a scandal.
>
> And if it is a professor against a professor—well, that's great—then it is a frightful scandal. But that the whole false peace and unity were the real scandal must not even be mentioned.[16]

As Kierkegaard knew better than most, it is precisely the unmentionable that the (ironic) critic is obliged to mention.

To mention the unmentionable is to raise questions that cannot easily be answered: Is the "peace and unity" between philosophy and deconstruction for which Gasché longs "false"? Are peace and unity always philosophical dreams from which we are called to awaken? Is every peace repressive and all unity exclusive? Does release from the dream of unity inevitably lead to violence or does freedom from the obsession with unity make it possible to forsake the violence that always seeks to master difference by totalizing otherness?

As an apologist for deconstruction, Gasché seeks to defend its insights against the misappropriations of its supporters and the misunderstandings of its detractors. This defense, however, is in the name of philosophy. Though aware of the way in which Derrida displaces the foundations of the Western philosophical tradition, Gasché attempts to render deconstruction tolerable, if not acceptable, by translating its "quasi concepts" into the language of philosophy. As I have suggested, the price of such translation is domestication. In contrast to Gasché, I would insist that this price is too high. Deconstruction disappears the moment the established order finds it tolerable.

In the wake of Derrida's undeniably offensive writings, the task that (always) lies ahead is not simply translation into philosophical discourse but is the repeated inscription of that which is untranslatable. If there is always an untranslatable remainder, translation inevitably fails. As Walter Benjamin points out:

> The transfer can never be total, but what reaches this region is that element in a translation which goes beyond transmittal of subject matter. This nucleus is best defined as the element that does not lend itself to translation. Even when all the surface content has been extracted and transmitted, the primary concern of the genuine translator remains elusive.[17]

To acknowledge the elusive limit of translation is to approach an other sometimes deemed sacred. This other, which is not and is not one, has always been and will always be a scandal for the philosopher, as well as for every reasonable person. Because writing presupposes an other that cannot be mastered, every text is haunted by that which it can neither contain nor express. Insofar as a text inscribes the inexpressible, it is *to a certain extent and in a certain way* "sacred" or "holy." In the course of his analysis of Benjamin's "The Task of the Translator," Derrida argues:

> The to-be-translated of the sacred text, its pure transferability that is what would give *at the limit* the ideal measure for all translation. The sacred text assigns the task to the translator, and it is sacred *inasmuch* as it announces itself as transferable, simply transferable, to-be-translated, which does not always mean immediately translatable, in the common sense that was dismissed from the start. Perhaps it is necessary to distinguish here between the transferable and the translatable. Transferability pure and simple is that of the sacred text in which meaning and literality are no longer discernible as they form the body of a unique, irreplaceable, and untransferable event, "materially the truth." Never are the call for translation, the debt, the task, the assignation, more imperious. Never is there anything more transferable, yet by reason of this indistinction of meaning and literality (*Wörtlichkeit*), the

pure transferable can announce itself, give itself, present itself, let itself be translated as untranslatable. From this limit, at once interior and exterior, the translator comes to receive all the signs of remoteness (*Entfernung*) which guide him on his infinite course, at the edge of the abyss, of madness and of silence.[18]

Derrida's errant texts graph an infinite course at the edge of the abyss, of madness and of silence. To think after deconstruction is to think the untranslatable by thinking the unavoidable failure of translation. This task is, of course, impossible. To undertake this impossible task *without apologies* would be to foil reflection differently than does *The Tain of the Mirror*.

8.

The Nonabsent Absence of the Holy

Was it a dark view through a gap or was it woods, was it a pool, or a house in which the people were already asleep, was it a church steeple or a ravine between the hills? Nobody must dare to go there, but who could restrain himself?

Franz Kafka

The era is defined by the failure of the gods to arrive, by the "default of God."

Martin Heidegger

A void in the universe: nothing that was visible, nothing that was invisible. I suppose the first reader foundered in this nonabsent absence, but without knowing anything about it, and there was no second reader because reading, from then on understood as the vision of an immediately visible, that is intelligible, presence was affirmed in order to render impossible this disappearance into *the absence of the book*.

Maurice Blanchot

In 1923, the year Martin Heidegger joined the faculty at the University of Marburg, Rudolf Otto, then professor of theology at Marburg, wrote in the Foreword to the first English translation of his now classic work *Das Heilige:*

In this book I have ventured to write of that which may be called "non-rational" or "supra-rational" in the depths of the divine nature. . . . This book, recognizing the profound import of the non-rational for metaphysics, makes a serious attempt to analyze all the more exactly the *feeling* which remains where the *concept* fails, and to introduce a terminology which is not any more loose or indeterminate for having necessarily to make use of *symbols*.[1]

The failure of "the concept" creates an opening for the return of what philosophy represses. Otto labels this repressed "the Holy." The Holy is Other–Wholly Other–*das ganz Andere*. Philosophy's exclusion of this Other is no accident; to the contrary, philosophy constitutes itself by *not* thinking the Other. *Das ganz Andere* is not only unthought; it is, more importantly, *unthinkable*. In *Das Heilige* Otto undertakes the impossible task of thinking this unthinkable Other by developing a phenomenological description of the experience of that which escapes all phenomenological description. Never present, without ever being absent, the Holy is, in Blanchot's apt phrase, a "nonabsent absence." As such, "the Holy" always implies a certain excess that is both theoretically and practically unmasterable. In an effort to distinguish the experience of the Holy (i.e., the religious) from moral experience (i.e., the ethical), Otto argues:

It is true that all this moral significance is contained in the word "Holy," but it includes in addition–as even we cannot but feel–a clear overplus, excess or surplus (*Überschuss*), and this it is now our task to specify. Nor is this merely a later or acquired matter; rather, "holy," or at least the equivalent words in Latin and Greek, in Semitic and other ancient languages, denoted first and foremost *only* this excess: if the ethical element were present at all, at any rate it was not original and never constituted the whole meaning of the word.[2]

One of Otto's most suggestive "names" for this unnameable excess or surplus of meaning is *das Ungeheuere*–"the monstrous." Explaining the difficulties involved in translating Sophocles's use of the word *deinos* in *Antigone*, Otto points out:

The German *ungeheuer* is not by derivation simply "huge," in quantity or quality;–this, its common meaning, is in fact a rationalizing interpretation of the real idea; it is that which is not *geheuer*, i.e., approximately, the *uncanny* [*das Unheimliche*] – in a word, the numinous. And it is just this element of the uncanny in man that Sophocles has in mind. If this, its fundamental meaning, be really and thoroughly felt in consciousness, then the word could be taken as a fairly exact expression for the numinous in its aspect of mystery, awefulness, majesty, augustness, and "energy"; nay, even the aspect of fascination is dimly felt in it.[3]

Recalling Freud's analysis of *das Unheimliche*, Otto maintains that "the uncanny" provokes an ambivalent response: *das Heilige* is both attractive and repulsive. It is precisely this ambiguity that drives the philosopher mad. In an effort to avoid madness, the philosopher struggles to erase surplus and excess by repressing the Holy in and through the reduction of difference to identity, and Other to same.

The repression of philosophy is inseparably bound to what Hölderlin describes as "the default of God" (*den Fehl Gottes*). This de-fault brings Night – the Night, which, according to Heidegger, is characteristic of our era:

Night is falling. Ever since the "united three" – Herakles, Dionysos, and Christ – have left the world, the evening of the world's age has been declining toward its night. The world's night is spreading its darkness. The era is defined by the god's failure to arrive, by the "default of God."[4]

In his later writings, Heidegger relentlessly explores the shadow cast by the approach of this awe-ful night. "Everyday opinion," he observes, "sees in the shadow only the lack of light, if not light's complete denial. In truth, however, the shadow is a manifest, though impenetrable, testimony to the concealed emitting of light. In keeping with this concept of shadow, we experience the incalculable as that which, withdrawn from representation, is nevertheless manifest in whatever is, pointing to Being, which remains concealed."[5] To think the obscurity of the shadow as such, it is necessary to "step back" from the Western ontotheological tradition and ask "what has always remained unasked throughout this history of thinking."[6] For Heidegger, as for Otto, what remains unasked in all metaphysics is the question of the Holy.

The struggle to think the unthought carries Heidegger to the limit of that which "conceals itself precisely where philosophy has brought its matter to absolute knowledge and to ultimate evidence." Different versions of metaphysics represent so many efforts to think the *ground* (*arche*) of what *is* in terms of *presence*. Heidegger is convinced that such reflection is insufficiently radical and thus does not go far enough. The metaphysician does not attempt to uncover the origin of presence. To ask what philosophy has left unasked since its beginnings in ancient Greece, it is necessary to think in a more "originary" way. Truly original thinking "strives to reach back into the essential ground from which thought concerning the truth of Being emerges. By initiating another inquiry, this thinking is already removed from the 'ontology' of metaphysics. . . . 'Ontology' itself, however, whether transcendental or precritical, is subject to criticism, not because it thinks the Being of beings and thereby reduces Being to a concept, but because it does not think the truth of Being and so fails to recognize that there is a thinking more rigorous than the conceptual."[7]

This more rigorous form of thinking cannot be described in terms of the traditional binary opposites that define conceptual thought. It is neither theoretical nor practical, neither metaphysical nor scientific, neither rational nor irrational. In contrast to the utilitarian calculations of science and technology, "such thinking has no result. It has no effect."[8] Its "value" is (the) incalculable. The "nonrepresentational thinking" that seeks to recover what metaphysics excludes and philosophy represses "directs our thinking to the realm that the key words of metaphysics – Being and beings, the ground and what is grounded – are no longer adequate to utter."[9] This is the liminal domain of *das ganz Andere*. While the Other always slips through structures imposed by conceptual reflection, the unthought *can* be evoked by means of the language of philosophy itself. The postphilosophical thinker must, therefore, strategically use language *against* language. "In order to make the attempt of thinking recognizable and at the same time understandable for existing philosophy," Heidegger explains, "it could at first be expressed only within the horizon of that existing philosophy and its use of current terms."[10]

Radical thinking actually has no object; nor is it merely subjective. "The matter of thinking," Heidegger insists, "is difference *as* difference" (*Differenz als Differenz*).[11] Neither subject nor object, difference is the condition of the possibility of all subjectivity and objectivity. To think "difference *as* difference" is, in the final analysis, to think "Being as difference."[12] By attempting to think the Being of beings in terms of the grounding presence of Being itself, traditional metaphysics leaves unthought the intermediate *difference* in and through which both Being and beings originate. Difference is "the between" (*zwischen*) that is "the essential origin" (*Wesensherkunft*)[13] of all identity and every difference. In other words, difference *delivers* the differences that constitute identity. Irreducible to the opposites it sustains, "the deliverance (*Austrag*) of that which grounds and that which is grounded, as such, not only holds the two apart, it holds them together."[14] The differential "between" that simultaneously joins and separates ground and grounded is the irreducible mean that founds the world and everything in it. In this way, difference originates by differentiating. Consequently, *Differenz* can be understood as *Unter-schied*.

In one of his richest explorations of the notion of difference, Heidegger writes:

> For world and things do not subsist alongside one another. They penetrate each other. Hence the two traverse a mean (*Mitte*). In it, they are at one. Thus at one, they are intimate. The mean of the two is inwardness. In our language, the mean of the two is called the between (*das Zwischen*). The Latin language uses *inter*. The corresponding German term is *unter*. The intimacy or inwardness of world and thing is not a fusion. Intimacy obtains only where the intimate–world and thing– divides itself cleanly and remains separated. In the midst of the two, in the between of world and thing, in the *inter*, division prevails: a *dif-ference* (*Unter-Schied*). The intimacy of world and thing is present in the boundary (*Schied:* border, limit, divide; case, sheath, vagina) of the between; it is present in the dif-ference. The word "difference" is now removed from its usual and customary usage. What it now names is not a species concept for various kinds of differences. It exists only as this single difference. It is unique. Of itself, it holds apart the mean in and through which the world and things are at one with each other. The intimacy of the difference is the unifying element of the *diaphora*, the carrying out that carries through. The dif-ference carries out world in its worlding, carries out things in their thinging. Thus carrying them out, it carries them toward one another. The dif-ference does not mediate after the fact by binding together world and things through a mean added on to them. Being the mean, it first determines world and things in their presence, i.e., in their being toward one another, whose unity it carries out.[15]

Heidegger's *Mitte* is not the Hegelian mean (*Mitte*) that mediates identity and difference by securing the *identity* of identity and difference. The delivery *of* difference is also the delivery *from* every form of all-inclusive identity that negates, reduces, absorbs, or swallows up otherness. As "the threshold" (*Schwelle*) of identity and difference, *dif-ference* is neither simply identical nor different. This distinctive *Unter-Schied* is what Heidegger labels "the same" (*das Selbe*). "The identical always moves toward the absence of difference, so that everything may be reduced to a common denominator. The same, by contrast, is the belonging together of what differs, through a gathering by way of the difference. We can say 'the same' only if we think difference."[16] The "sameness" (*Selbigkeit*) with which Heidegger tries to pass beyond Western

philosophy "approaches from further back than the kind of identity defined by
metaphysics in terms of Being as a characteristic of Being."[17] By taking a "step
back" from the ontotheological tradition, Heidegger attempts "to return to"
that which is "prior to thought."[18]

That which is prior to thought is never present as such. This irreducible
"before" marks the elusive time-space where "the event of appropriation" (*das
Er-eignis*) occurs. "Appropriation neither *is*, nor *is* appropriation *there*." To ask
what appropriation *is*, is to attempt to define appropriation in terms of Being,
whereas for Heidegger, Being must be understood in terms of the event of appropriation. Because it "is" not, or "is not there," appropriation "is, so to
speak, a '*neutrale tantum*.' "[19] By "oscillating within itself," this neutral *Es* gives
or sends Being as well as beings:

> To think Being itself explicitly requires us to relinquish Being (*Sein*) as
> the ground of beings (*des Seinden*) in favor of the giving that prevails
> concealed in unconcealment, that is, in favor of the It gives (*Es gibt*). As
> the gift (*Gabe*) of this It gives, Being belongs to giving. As a gift, Being
> is not expelled from giving. Being, presencing (*Anwesen*) is transmuted.
> As allowing-to-presence, it belongs to unconcealing, as the gift of un-
> concealing, it is retained in the giving. Being *is* not. There is, It gives
> Being as the unconcealing; as the gift of unconcealing it is retained in
> the giving. Being *is* not. There is, It gives Being as the unconcealing of
> presencing.[20]

That which sends Being and beings is not completely *revealed* in the
missionary act. The "It" that gives "holds back" (*epoche*) or "withdraws" in its
very donation. Though never properly present, the presencing of *Es gibt*,
which establishes all presence and constitutes every present, is not precisely
absent. The event of "sending" or "giving" Being and beings escapes the simple
alternative of presence and absence. The interplay of presence and
absence issues in the inseparability of concealment and unconcealment. In
different terms, the dis-closure of the origin of presence inevitably entails a
certain "dissemblance" (*Verstellung*).[21] As a result of this dissemblance, the
origin of presence harbors a "resevoir of the not-yet-uncovered, the un-
uncovered in the sense of concealment."[22] Always withdrawing in its very approach, "It" (*Es*) *remains*—remains as an unfathomable "abyss"(*Abgrund*). This
abyss is lost in oblivion.

Since presence and absence, as well as concealment and unconcealment, are inseparable, the revelation of difference is always at the same time
its reveiling. In the delivery of Being and beings, difference as such withdraws
and thereby reveils itself. Explaining a point upon which he and Hegel differ,
Heidegger writes:

In contrast to Hegel, this is not a traditional problem, already posed, but what has always remained unasked throughout the history of thinking. We speak of it, tentatively and unavoidably, in the language of tradition. We speak of the *difference* between Being and beings. The step back goes from what is unthought, from the difference as such, into what gives us thought. That is the *oblivion* of the difference. The oblivion here to be thought is the veiling of the difference as such, thought in terms of *léthé* (concealment); this veiling has in turn withdrawn itself from the beginning. The oblivion belongs to the difference because the difference belongs to the oblivion. The oblivion does not happen to the difference only afterward, in consequence of the forgetfulness of human thinking.[23]

Inasmuch as difference itself is never present, it cannot be re-presented. This nonrepresentable origin gives rise to conceptual and representational thought only insofar as it is forgotten, excluded, or repressed. As the nonrepresentable "before," which is always already "prior to thought," difference constitutes an "essential past" that can never be present-ed:

The criterion of what has not been thought does not lead to the inclusion of previous thought into a still higher development and systematization that surpass it. Rather, the criterion demands that traditional thinking be set free into its essential past that is still preserved (*sein noch aufgespartes Gewesenes*). This essential past prevails throughout the tradition in an originary way, is always in being in advance of it, and yet is never expressly thought in its own right and as the originary.[24]

The essential past that inevitably is repressed by conceptual reflection repeatedly returns to dislocate self-consciousness by disrupting all presence and every present. In this way, difference functions as something like an irreducible unconscious that simultaneously gives rise to and escapes consciousness. Ever reveiling itself, difference is a "surplus" or an "excess" (*Übermass*) that can never be contained, controlled, or mastered. Consciousness, therefore, is always incomplete, and transparent self-consciousness forever impossible.

Neither absent nor present, the repressed is, in the terms of Heidegger, later developed by Blanchot, "proximate" or "near" (*nahe*). The "proximate" (*Nähe*) is what is nearest yet farthest. Closer than anything present and farther than anything absent, the near cannot be re-presented:

We are too quick to believe that the mystery of what is to be thought always lies distant and deeply hidden under a hardly penetrable layer of strangeness. On the contrary, it has its essential abode in what is nearby, which approaches what is coming into presence and preserves what has drawn near. The presencing of the near is too close for our customary mode of representational thought—which exhausts itself in securing what is present—to experience the governance of the near, and without preparation to think it adequately. Presumably, the mystery that beckons in what is to be thought is nothing other than essentially what we have attempted to suggest in the name the "lighting."[25]

This "lighting" displays the shadow that "is a manifest, though impenetrable, testimony to the concealed emitting of light. In keeping with the concept of shadow, we experience the incalculable as that which, withdrawn from representation, is nevertheless manifest in whatever is, pointing to Being, which remains concealed." To approach the "obscurity" of this shadow, one "must first learn to exist in the nameless."[26] The neuter "It" of *Es gibt* always remains anonymous. "The area of the meaning meant by the It extends from the irrelevant to the demonic." And, I would add, beyond—to the Holy. The mystery of the Holy, however, "cannot be mediated cognitively, not even in terms of questions, but must be experienced."[27] The possibility of this experience opens with the origin of the work of art.

The site of the origin of the work of art is the temple. But what is a temple? "Temple" derives from the Latin *templum*, which, like *tempus* (time), comes from the Greek *temnos*. While *temnō* means "cut," *temnos* designates that which is "cut off." Accordingly , *templum* is a section torn away—a part cut off.[28] By extension, *templum* is "a space in the sky or on the earth marked out by the augur for the purpose of taking auspices; a consecrated piece of ground, especially a sanctuary or asylum; a place dedicated to a particular deity, a shrine."[29] While the locus of the origin of the work of art is the temple, the site of the temple, Heidegger suggests, is a cleft or cleavage. This cleavage is "a tear" (*Riss*, whence *zerissen* and *Zerissenheit*) that fissures what had seemed to be a solid foundation.

Exploring the origin of the work of art in *Holzwege*, Heidegger maintains: "A construction, a Greek temple, images nothing. It simply stands in the midst of a rock-cleft valley." The temple images nothing by holding open the differential *interval* of the between:

> Standing there, the construction rests on rocky ground. This resting of the work draws up out of the rock the obscurity (*Dunkel*, darkness, mystery) of the rock's monstrous yet spontaneous support. Standing there, the construction holds its ground against the storm raging above it and so makes the storm itself manifest in its violence. The luster and gleam of the stone, though itself apparently glowing by grace of the sun,

yet first bring to light the light of the day, the breadth of the sky, the darkness of the night. The secure tower makes visible the invisible space of air. The steadfastness of the work contrasts with the suge of the surf, and its own repose brings out the raging of the sea. Tree and grass, eagle and bull, snake and cricket first enter into their distinctive forms and thus come to appear as what they are.[30]

Neither eagle nor bull, tree nor grass, snake nor cricket is original. For Heidegger, each originates through the work of art. The origin *of* art is an "original" tear that makes possible all such paired opposites. Art works by opening this opening.

Heidegger opens his essay, "The Origin of the Work of Art," by asking: "Where and how does art occur?" "Art," he proceeds to argue, "breaks open an open place." This opening marks the boundary or limen where revealing and reveiling repeatedly intersect. This play of differences is "the essential strife" of "world"– that is, "the self-disclosing openness" and "earth"–that is, "the essentially self-secluding."[31] Artwork works by setting up world, which is the space-time where Being and beings emerge, and setting forth earth, which is the sheltering domain where they withdraw. The alternating strife of world and earth constitutes the "tear" (*Riss*) that lies in the midst of Being and beings:

> But as a world opens itself, the earth comes to rise up. It stands forth as that which bears all, as that which is sheltered in its own law and always self-secluding. World demands its decisiveness and its measure and lets beings extend into the open of their paths. Earth, bearing and jutting strives to keep itself closed and to entrust everything to its law. The strife is not a tear (*Riss*) as the gaping crack (*Aufreissen*) of a pure cleft (*Kluft*), but the strife is the intimacy with which combatants belong to each other. This tear pulls the opponents together in the origin of their unity by virtue of their common ground. It is a basic design (*Grundriss*), an outline sketch (*Aufriss*), that draws the basic features of the rise of the lighting of beings. This tear does not let the opponents burst apart; it brings the opposition of measure and boundary into their common outline (*Umriss*).[32]

The strife of the tear captures the duplicity of cleaving. To cleave is both to separate, divide, or split, and to adhere, cling, or stick. Tearing alternates between two rhythms—one centrifugal, the other centripetal. By holding open this alternating difference, the origin of the work of art simultaneously joins and separates. This separation that joins and joining that separates transforms the tear of cleaving into the tear of pain:

Pain, Heidegger explains, tears or rends (*reisst*). It is the tear or rift (*Riss*). But it does not tear apart into dispersive fragments. Pain indeed tears asunder, it separates, yet in such a way that it at the same time draws everything together to itself. Its rending, as a separating that gathers, is at the same time that drawing, which, like the predrawing (*Vorriss*) and sketch (*Aufriss*), draws and joins together what is held apart in separation. Pain is the jointing in the tearing/rending that divides and gathers (*schneidendsammelnden Reissen*). Pain is the joining or articulation of the rift. The joining is the threshold. It delivers the between, the mean of the two that are separated in it. Pain articulates the rift of the difference. Pain is dif-ference itself.[33]

The pain of dif-ference is the mark of truth.

Neither *certitudo* nor *adequatio*, truth, in Heidegger's well-known definition, is *aletheia*. *A-letheia* is the un-concealment that arises through un-forgetting. The history of Western metaphysics, I have stressed, is inseparably bound up with oblivion. Representational and conceptual thought originate by forgetting their origin. To think what philosophy represses, it is necessary to return to this origin through an act of un-forgetting. *A-letheia*, however, is not simply identical with re-collection or re-membering. The oblivion that obsesses Heidegger is not an accident that can be avoided. To the contrary, the in-evitability of oblivion reflects the necessity of concealment in all disclosure. To un-forget the origin is to remember *that* one has forgotten and to recognize that such forgetting is inescapable. Because the origin remains an inaccessible "abyss," remembering does not issue in the total recollection necessary for transparent self-consciousness. Remembering, therefore, can no more re-member than recollection can re-collect. The tear forever remains to rend the remembering subject. The truth "known" in the un-forgetting of *a-letheia* is a truth that always carries a shadow in the midst of its lighting:

> Truth occurs precisely as itself insofar as the concealing denial, as refusal, provides the constant source of all clearing or lighting, and yet, as dissembling, it metes out to all clearing, the unavoidable edge of diversion and confusion (*Beirrung*). Concealing denial is intended to denote that opposition in the essence of truth which persists between clearing or lighting and concealing. It is the opposition of the primal strife. The essence of truth is, in itself, the primal strife in which that open mean is sought within which that which is, stands, and from which it sets itself back into itself.[34]

As the primal strife of unconcealment and concealment, or light and darkness, truth is inseparable from error:

Being sets [beings] adrift in errancy (*Irre*). Beings come to pass in that errancy by which they circumvent Being and establish the realm of error (*Irrtum*) (in the sense of a prince's realm or the realm of poetry). Error is the space in which history unfolds. In error, what happens in history bypasses what is like Being. Therefore, whatever unfolds historically is necessarily misinterpreted. During the course of this misinterpretation, destiny awaits what will become of its seed. It brings those whom it concerns to the possibilities of the fateful and fatal. Man's destiny gropes toward its fate. Man's inability to see himself corresponds to the self-concealing of the lighting of Being. Without errancy there would be no connection from destiny to destiny: there would be no history.[35]

In contrast to the dream of the Western ontotheological tradition, Heidegger maintains that erring is endless. The prodigal son does not come home again – the seed once sown does not return to the father. Since the wound never heals and the tear never mends, the "kingdom of ends" never arrives; it is forever delayed.

The ceaseless deferral of the end reflects the infinite inaccessibility of the beginning. In rethinking the philosophical tradition, Heidegger discovers a difference that cannot be reduced to identity. This difference is an *Other* that can never be named properly:

> And yet – beyond what is, not away from it but before it, there is an Other (*ein Anderes*) that occurs. In the midst of beings as a whole, there is an open place. There is a clearing, a lighting. Thought of in relation to what is, to beings, this clearing is in a greater degree than are beings. This open center, therefore, is not surrounded by what is; rather, the lighting middle itself encircles all that is, like the nothing (*Nichts*) we hardly know.[36]

"The nothing we hardly know." This unnameable Other is not only "obscure" and "mysterious" but is "monstrous [*Ungeheuer*: huge, colossal, enormous, atrocious, frightful, shocking; *geheuer*: uncanny, haunting]."[37]

How can the unnameable be named – the unspeakable spoken? What "eye sees" difference as difference? What "ear hears" the other? What thought thinks the *Ungeheuer* that philosophy does not, indeed, cannot, think? The response Heidegger ventures to such questions is: "poetry." *Poiesis* discloses "how there can be presence as such." For Heidegger, "there is presence only when opening is dominant. Opening is named with *aletheia*, unconcealment, but not thought as such."[38] To think unconcealment, *aletheia* must be thought as *poiesis*. Instead of a specific artistic form, the poetry that allows opening to occur designates art itself:

All art, as the letting happen of the advent of the truth of what is, is, as such, *in essence poetry* (*Dichtung*). The essence of art, on which both the artwork and the artist depend, is the setting-itself-into-work of truth. It is due to the poetic essence of art that, in the midst of what is, art breaks open an open place, in whose openness everything is other (*anders*) than usual.[39]

So understood, poetry is the act of articulation that holds open the mean differentiating and thus identifying everything that is. The expression that renders existence articulate is "saying" (*Sagen*). "Poetry," Heidegger explains, "is the saying of the unconcealedness of what is. Actual language at any given moment is the happening of this saying, in which a people's world arises historically and the earth is preserved as that which remains closed. Saying sketchily (*das entwerfende Sagen*)[40] is saying which, in the prepartion of the sayable simultaneously brings the unsayable as such into the world."[41] Saying can no more be reduced to specific speech acts than poetry can be exhausted by particular poems. Through the analysis of poetry in terms of saying, Heidegger attempts to establish the linguisticality of Being itself.

While poetry is intrinsically linguistic, language is fundamentally poetic. Heidegger goes so far as to insist that "language (*Sprache*) itself is essentially poetry."[42] *Poiesis* means to make or create. Like Yahweh whose creative word brings form to formlessness by separating the primal waters, language is poetic insofar as it creates through the act of separation. Unlike the Old Testament narrative, however, the division of opposites that bestows determinate identity is not, according to Heidegger, secondary to a more original unity, but is a "*primal* strife." The creative origin of language is nothing other than the *temple* of Being:

> Being, as itself, spans its own precinct, which is cut off (*temnein, tempus*) by Being being in the word. Language is the precinct (*templum*), that is, the house of Being. The essence of language does not exhaust itself in meaning or signifying, nor is it merely something that has the character of sign or cipher. It is because language is the house of Being that we reach what is by constantly going through this house. When we go to the well, when we go through the woods, we are always already going through the word "well," through the word "woods," even if we do not speak the words and do not think of anything relating to language.[43]

Language, in this context, is not a means of communication by which decipherable messages are sent and received. Rather, language articulates the opening—the between—that makes possible all communication (*communicare*, to make common). In this way, language is always antecedent to and escapes from the communicative acts it enables to transpire. As the temple of Being, language exhibits the contrasting rhythms characteristic of all cleaving. The *poiesis* of language both joins and separates:

> The *hen panta* lets lie together before us in one presencing things that are usually separated from, and opposed to, one another, such as day and night, winter and summer, peace and war, waking and sleeping, Dionysos and Hades. Such opposites, borne along the farthest distance between presence and absence, *diapheromenon* let the laying that gathers lie before us in its full bearing. Its laying is itself that which carries things along by bearing them out. The *hen* is itself a carrying out.[44]

The mean that joins all extremes is the *logos*. The *logos* designates language in its capacity to gather, assemble, and unify. Heidegger suggests that "here our reflections reach a provocative juncture. Being becomes present as *Logos* in the sense of ground, of allowing to let lie before us. The same *Logos*, as the gathering of what unifies, is the *hen*. This *hen*, however, is twofold (*zweifaltig*)."[45]

The irreducible duplicity of language implies a rhythm that counters the unifying force of the *logos*. While language holds together opposites usually set apart, it also holds apart the opposites it brings together. In this way, language eternally returns to difference—the difference that is the origin of the work of art and the temple of everything that is:

> Language speaks (*die Sprache spricht*). It speaks by bidding the bidden, thing-world and world-thing, to come to the between of dif-ference. What is so bidden is commanded to arrive from out of the dif-ference in-to the difference. Here we are thinking of the old sense of command, which we recognize still in the phrase, "Commit thy way unto the Lord." In this way, the bidding of language commits the bidden thus to the bidding of the dif-ference. The dif-ference lets the thinging of the thing rest in the world. The dif-ference expropriates the repose of the fourfold.[46] Such expropriation does not diminish the thing. Only so is the thing exalted into its own, so that it stays world. To keep in repose is to still. The dif-ference stills the thing, as thing, into the world.[47]

I have already noted that the threshold between world ("self-disclosing openness") and earth ("the essentially self-secluding") marks the site at which Being and beings both emerge and withdraw. It now becomes clear that for Heidegger, this productive mean must be understood in terms of language.

As the elusive margin of unconcealment and concealment, the poetic language of dif-ference speaks the unspeakable that allows all saying to occur. In speaking the unspeakable, "language speaks as the tolling of stillness."[48] Movement and rest, saying and silence, meet at the threshold of language. To hear the stillness of this silence, one must do nothing. But how can one *do* nothing? How can nothing *be*—or *be done?* To do nothing, Heidegger responds, one must wait. More precisely, for nothing to be done, waiting must occur. When one waits *purposefully*, waiting does not take place. If waiting is not to be awaiting, it must be purposeless. Purposeless waiting, which, Heidegger insists, is "beyond the distinction between activity and passivity,"[49] displaces the purposeful striving of the constructive subject of modern philosophy. The release from masterful self-assertion is, in effect, a conversion that borders on the religious:

> Re-collection or re-inwardization (*Er-innerung*) converts that nature of ours that merely wills to impose, together with its objects, into the in-nermost invisible region of the heart's space. Here everything is inward: not only does it remain turned toward this proper inner of con-sciousness, but inside this inner, one thing turns, free of all bounds, into the other. The interiority of the inner-world-space unbars the open for us.[50]

Heidegger's *Er-innerung* recalls Hegel's use of the same word in the final paragraph of the *Phenomenology of Spirit*.[51] Unlike Hegelian *Er-Innerung*, Heideggerian re-collection does not completely overcome *Zerrissenheit* by closing every wound that rends and every tear that lacerates. Waiting releases one into a *Riss* that remains open. Instead of the security and certainty of self-possession, which is supposed to be produced by the mastery of otherness and the domination of difference, the converted subject discovers:

> The more venturesome risk produces no shelter. But it creates a safety or secureness for us. Secure, *securus, sine cure*, means: without care (*Sorge*). Here care has the character of purposeful self-assertion by the ways and means of unconditional production. We are without such care only when we do not establish our nature exclusively within the precinct of production and constitution—the useful and the defensible. We are secure only where we neither reckon with the defenseless nor count on a defense erected within willing. A security or certainty exists only out-side the objectifying turn away from the open, "outside all shelter or defense," outside the parting against the pure relation. That relation is the exorbitant middle (*unerhörte Mitte*) of all drawing that draws everything into the boundless, and covers it for the mean (*Mitte*). This mean is the "yonder" where the gravity of pure forces rules, weaves,

operates. Being secure or certain is the safe repose in the draw of the whole relation.[52]

Heidegger's "exorbitant mean" subverts every domestic economy founded upon the principle of profitable return. *Poiesis* simultaneously draws one away from purposeful striving and useful willing, and toward purposeless waiting and useless contemplation. To hear the silent tolling of the exorbitant middle, the careful subject, who avoids everything excessive, must undergo a conversion to care-less excess.

For those with ears to hear, the tolling of poetry is the "coming-into-the-nearness-of-distance." The "mysterious proximity" into which the words of the poet *draw* the waiting listener "is nothing human." By holding open the exorbitant middle, the word of the poet tolls "the trace of the holy" (*Spur des Heiligen*):

> "But they are, you say, like the wine-god's holy priests,
> Who fared from land to land in holy night."

Poets are the mortals who, singing earnestly of the wine-god, track the trace of the fugitive gods, stay on the gods' tracks, and so trace for their kindred mortals the way toward the turning. The ether, however, in which alone the gods are gods, is their godhead. The element of this ether, that within which even the godhead itself is still present, is the Holy. The element of the ether for the coming of the fugitive gods, the Holy, is the trace of the fugitive gods. But who has the power to track such a trace (*soche Spur zu spüren*)? Traces are often invisible and are always the legacy of a directive that is barely divined. To be a poet in a destitute time means: to attend, singing, to the trace of the fugitive gods. This is why the poet in the time of the world's night utters the Holy. This is why, in Hölderlin's language, the world's night is the Holy night.[53]

The trace of the fugitive gods is the nonabsent absence of the Holy. This trace is a different trace, the trace of difference itself, which can never be expressed directly, revealed totally, or known completely. It is ever elusive, evasive, excessive. Irreducibly ex-orbitant, the Holy eternally returns to interrupt the circulation of knowledge and to disrupt every form of reciprocal exchange. To hear the "inhuman," "anonymous," "uncanny" murmur of the Holy is to become open to that which cannot be conceived, grasped, mastered, or controlled. To be "released" or "drawn" into the un-dis-closable openness of this rending difference is to overcome nihilism by no longer "giving a negative reading to that which is." Released from the need to assert self by negating

other and incorporating difference, one is free "to read the word 'death'
without negation."[54] To walk in the shadow of this death is to linger in the
Night. Night . . . an other Night . . . Night of the Other . . . Other of the
Night . . . Holy Night . . . Night beyond Night . . . White Night . . . Vigil
Night . . . Waking Night . . . Night of the Wake:

> To wake is neutral. "I" do not wake: one wakes, night wakes, always
> and incessantly, hollowing out the night into the *other* night [*l'*autre *nuit*]
> where there can be no question of sleeping. One wakes only at night.
> Night is foreign to the vigilance that is exercised, carried out, and con-
> veys lucid reason toward what it must maintain in reflection–in the
> preservation of its identity. Wakefulness is estrangement: it does not
> waken, as if emerging from a sleep that would precede it, yet it
> *reawakens*: constant and incessant return to the immobility of the wake.
> Something wakes: something keeps watch without lying in wait or spying.
> The disaster wakes. When there is waking–when sleeping con-
> sciousness, opening into unconsciousness, lets the light of the dream
> play–then what wakes (the wake or the impossibility of sleep at the
> heart of sleep) does not illuminate with an increase of visibility, of
> reflecting brilliance. Who wakes? Precisely, the question is mistaken by
> the neutrality of the wake: no one wakes. Waking is not the power to
> wake in the first person; it is not a power but the stroke of the infinite
> without power, the exposure to the *other* of the night, where thought re-
> nounces the vigor of vigilance, gives up worldly clairvoyance, perspica-
> cious mastery, in order to be delivered to the limitless delay of insomnia,
> the wake that does not wake, the nocturnal intensity.[55]

In the dark light of this nocturnal intensity, the death of the
metaphysical subject announces the monstrous birth of an other–a (w)hol(l)y
Other that approaches as "the origin of that which has no origin":

> I force it to exist. O night, I am itself. Here it has drawn me into the trap
> of its creation. And now it is the one that forces me to exist. And I am
> the one who is its eternal prisoner. It creates me for itself alone. It
> makes me, nothing that I am, like unto nothingness. In a cowardly way,
> it delivers me joy.[56]

Through an ecstatic joy that issues in the tearing pain of difference,
openness to the night delivers that nothing in whose nonspace I am destined
to err. Nothing that I am . . . like unto nothingness: Nothing is Holy . . . Holy
Nothing . . . Nothing Holy but poetry . . . Poetry of Nothingness:

For the listener, who listens in the snow,
And, nothing himself, beholds
Nothing that is not there and the nothing that is.[57]

Nothing that is not there and the nothing that is . . . trace of fugitive gods . . . the nonabsent absence of the Holy.

9.

Paralectics

Rats and Rugs

The sewer . . . like all . . . "low and grotesque"
systems . . . could not entirely be closed off
from above. Passing between the sewer ("the
conscience of the town" which was now blocked
off) and the city . . . were the rats. . . . But
just as the meaning of the grotesque body was
transformed by its diacritical relation to the
emergent notion of the bourgeois body, so the
symbolic meaning of the rat was refashioned in
relation to the sanitary and medical developments of the nineteenth century. As the connections between physical and moral hygiene
were developed and redeployed, there was a
new attention to the purveyors of physical and
moral "dirt." The rat was no longer primarily an
economic liability (as the spoiler of grain, for in-
stance): it was the object of fear and loathing, a
threat to civilized life. . . . The rat, then, fur-
tively emerged from the city's underground
conscience as the demonized Other. But as it
transgressed the boundaries that separated the
city from the sewer, above from below, it was a
source of fascination as well as horror.[1]

The city rat invites the country rat onto
the Persian rug. They gnaw and chew leftover
bits of ortolan. Scraps, bits and pieces, left-
overs: their royal feast is only a meal after a

meal among the dirty dishes of a table that had
not been cleared. . . . It's nighttime, black.
What happens would be the obscure converse
of clear and conscious organization, happening
behind everyone's back, the dark side of the
system. But what do we call these nocturnal
processes? Are they destructive or constructive? Are they the exception or the genesis?
What happens at night on the rug covered with
crumbs? Is it a still active trace of (an) origin? Or
is it only a remaining margin (*marge restant*) of
missing suppressions? We can, undoubtedly,
decide the matter: the battle (*la bataille*) against
rats is already lost; there is no house, ship, or
place that does not have its share. There is no
system without parasites.[2]

Why do the rats, which, in the Western imagination, often figure "the
demonized Other," sit on a *Persian* rug? Is there any relationship between rats
and rugs—especially Persian rugs? Perhaps. Words sometimes tell strange and
surprising tales (if we are patient enough to listen). "Rat" derives from *an(e)*,
which means "breathe, breath; that which animates." Explaining the complex
origin of this Indo-European root, Joseph Shipley writes:

> Via Av, *prana*: breath of life. *ahura*: a good spirit. *asura*: first a good,
> then an evil spirit; *Vitrasura. Ahuramazda*: chief spirit; shortened to
> *Ormazd*: Zoroastrian god of good. *Mazdaism*: the religion, sometimes
> spelled *Mazdeism* by association with *deism*. The Parsi (name derived
> from *Persia*), the surviving Zoroastrians, in their morning prayer ask for
> three admirable things: good thoughts, good words, good deeds.[3]

Rats . . . evil spirits or good spirits? Are they destructive or constructive?
What *does* happen (or not happen) at night on the (Persian) rug?

In June of 1982, the PLO was expelled from Lebanon. One of the less reputable New York newspapers reported the exodus from Beirut under the headline:

RATS ON THE RUN

Why rats? Can we be so sure that running "rats" have been defeated? Can they ever be defeated? Or is "the battle against rats [always] already lost"?

The questions with which I would like to linger are posed by the discourse of the other. Does the other speak? Can I (the "I") hear/understand (*entends*) the other? Who or what is the other . . . the other that approaches (without arriving) as the not-same? Is the other who is my counterpart actually other or is he or she really identical in his or her difference? "Is" there another other that allows others to be other and differences to be different? How might such an other be (almost) thought? Does the other other make any difference . . . or every difference?

To linger with questions posed by the discourse of the other is to wrestle with the problem of translation. Can the other speak *my* language? Can I *make* the other speak *my* language? Can I speak an other or the other's language? Does translation allow the other to speak or does it silence the discourse of the other? Without translation, there is no conversation—no shared communication. And yet, can either *entretien* or *partager* be translated with certainty?

Entretien: conversation, talk, interview. *Entretenir*: to hold together, keep in good order; to maintain, support, feed; to converse or talk with, to entertain. *Entre*, between + *tenir*, to hold. *Entretien*: a holding-between.

Converse: French—*converser*, to pass one's life, to dwell with or in, to exchange words with; Latin—*conversari*, to turn oneself about, to move to and fro. Conversely. . . .
Converse: Latin—*conversus*, turned about, transformed. Turned round; opposite or contrary in direction; action, acting in reversed manner.[4]

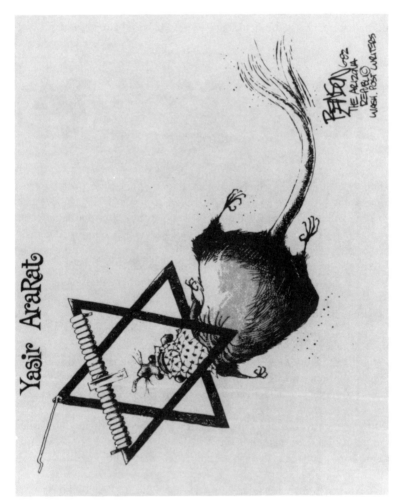

Figure 13. Yasir AraRat.

con verses
l'entretien infini

Partage: sharing, distribution, division; share, lot, portion, apportion-
ment. *Partager*: *diviser*; *démembrer, morceler; couper, fractionner, fragmenter*;
solidariser; participer. To divide, share out; to share, participate in.

> Share: the iron blade in a plough that cuts the ground at the bottom of
> the furrow. From *(s)ker*, scratch, cut, pluck, gather, dig, separate, sift; and
> *sek*, divide, cut, scrape.
> Share: a part or portion belonging to, distributed to, contributed by, or
> owned by a person or group; to divide, parcel out in shares; to appor-
> tion, participate in, use, or experience in common.

The word itself parts and divides by be(com)ing the converse of itself.

partager
la parole plurielle

Forever suspended *entre-deux, le partage des voix* marks the re-turn of *l'entretien
infini*.

Art of Conversation

> Granted that Derrida is the latest and largest flower on the dialectical
> kudzu vine of which the *Phenomenology of Spirit* was the first tendril,
> does that not merely show the need to uproot this creeping menace?
> Can we not now see all the better the need to strip the suckers of this
> parasitic climber from the still unfinished walls and roofs of the great
> Kantian edifice which it covers and conceals?[5]

In a series of articles and books written over the past decade, Richard
Rorty has been developing an interpretation of conversation – or more
precisely an interpretation of interpretation in terms of conversation – that has
become extremely influential. Because his central ideas are anything but new,
the impact of Rorty's work is somewhat puzzling. The excitement his texts
generate seems to be more a function of *who* is writing than the result of *what*
is written. To Rorty's erstwhile philosophical colleagues, the scandal seems to
be that one of the most respected members of their congregation has committed heresy by falling under the spell of illusions from which true believers
have long been free. When one recalls that contemporary Anglo-American
linguistic philosophy began as a reaction to the revival of Hegelianism in
England during the early decades of this century, the impact of Rorty's "fall"

Figure 14. Art Spiegelman, *Maus: A Survivor's Tale*.

becomes more understandable. In shedding his analytical skin, Rorty has had the audacity to argue that Hegel, if read in a certain way, was right.

To make matters worse, Rorty (mistakenly) maintains that the return to Hegel via Gadamer makes it possible to appropriate important insights from contemporary philosophers who have been anathematized by the high priests of the philosophical ecclesia. Rorty's errancy, however, is neither as extreme as his detractors insist nor as radical as his supporters believe. Acknowledging that he stands in the tradition of the *Phenomenology of Spirit*, Rorty suggests, albeit inadvertently, the way in which his philosophy extends the Western struggle to master difference. Instead of patiently listening to a discourse not his own, Rorty's "dialogue" ends as a monologue spoken/written to colonize the other. In the aftermath of this conversation, a persistent question remains: Is it ever possible to break the circle of domination by overcoming the domination of the (hermeneutical) circle?

As one skilled in the art of conversation, Rorty likes to tell stories. His reading of the story of modern philosophy has only two chapters, which are variously described as epistemology and hermeneutics or commensuration and conversation. As his use of the image of the parasitic kudzu vine suggests, Rorty traces these two types of philosophy back to Kant and Hegel, respectively. Though epistemology and hermeneutics differ significantly in assumptions and conclusions, the most important differences distinguishing them can best be seen in their alternative accounts of representation:

> The [Kantian] tradition thinks of truth as a vertical relationship between representation and what is represented. The [Hegelian] tradition thinks of truth horizontally—as the culminating reinterpretation of our predecessors's reinterpretation of their predecessors's reinterpretation. . . . This tradition does not ask how representations are related to nonrepresentations, but how representations can be seen as hanging together. The difference is not one between "correspondence" and "coherence" theories of truth. . . . Rather, it is the difference between regarding truth, goodness, and beauty as eternal objects which we try to locate and reveal, and regarding them as artifacts whose fundamental design we often have to alter.[6]

While "Kantianism" struggles to re-present primal presentations, "Hegelianism" acknowledges the inaccessibility of every thing-in-itself and admits that representations always refigure representations. In the absence of primal presentation, signs are signs of signs.

As I have noted, this (all too) neat-and-tidy philosophical tale makes sense *only* if Hegel is read in a certain way. It is significant that the tangled lines of Rorty's genealogy go back to the *Phenomenology of Spirit* rather than the System. For Rorty, there is a significant difference between the implications of the phenomenological and the systematic Hegel. In the *Encyclopedia of the Philosophical Sciences*, Hegel claims to have reached absolute knowledge by accurately representing the truth that had been gradually unfolding in nature and history from the beginning of time. The *Phenomenology*, by contrast, examines the experience of consciousness as it moves from subjective self-certainty to the truth that is purportedly (re)present(ed) in the System as a whole. Repeating (without acknowledging) insights advanced by earlier commentators, Rorty describes the *Phenomenology* as a *Bildungsroman* in which each chapter is, in effect, a rewriting of earlier chapters in the genesis of self-consciousness.[7] Over against Hegel, Rorty insists that the final chapter of the story cannot be written and thus a conclusive end is forever delayed. The deferral of absolute knowledge creates the possibility of an unending conversation that is essentially hermeneutical.

From this point of view, hermeneutics can be understood as something like Hegelianism without absolute knowledge. Rorty explains:

> Hermeneutics sees the relations between various discourses as those of strands in a possible conversation, a conversation which presupposes no disciplinary matrix which unites the speakers, but where the hope of agreement is never lost so long as the conversation lasts. This hope is not a hope for the discovery of antecedently existing common ground, but *simply* hope for agreement, or, at least, exciting and fruitful disagreement.[8]

Epistemology is an archeological search for secure foundations, but hermeneutics is a teleological quest for a certainty that never arrives. Rorty is persuaded that only when conversation gives up the dream of commensuration can it become edifying.

Though Hegel repeatedly asserts that philosophy can never edify, Rorty insists on "translating" Hegelian *Bildung* into hermeneutical *edification*.[9] Edification involves the process of building up oneself in and through the expansion of consciousness and self-consciousness brought about by "acculturation."[10] In Rorty's philosophical story, Gadamer emerges as a pivotal character. By successfully extricating the notion of *Bildung* from the most problematic metaphysical presuppositions of nineteenth-century idealism, Gadamer prepares the way for the recognition of the thoroughgoing historicity of human consciousness. Commenting on *Truth and Method*, Rorty writes:

> The importance of Gadamer's book is that he manages to separate off one of the three strands – the romantic notion of man as self-creative – in the philosophical notion of "spirit" from the other two strands with which it became entangled. Gadamer (like Heidegger, to whom some of his work is indebted) makes no concessions either to Cartesian dualism or to the notion of "transcendental constitution" (in any sense

which could be given an idealistic interpretation). He thus helps to reconcile the "naturalistic" point . . . that the "irreducibility of the *Geisteswissenschaften*" is not a matter of metaphysical dualism . . . with our "existentialist" intuition that redescribing ourselves is the most important thing we can do. He does this by substituting the notion of *Bildung* (education, self-formation) for that of "knowledge" as the goal of thinking. To say that we become different people, that we "remake" ourselves as we read more, talk more, and write more, is simply a dramatic way of saying that the sentences which become true of us by virtue of such activities are often more important to us than sentences which become true of us when we drink more, eat more, and so on.[11]

In Hegel's metanarrative, history is the process in which the absolute subject (*Geist*) becomes self-conscious through the emergence of total self-consciousness in individual subjects. With the disappearance of the absolute subject, history becomes completely anthropocentric. "Gadamer develops his notion of *wirkungsgeschichtliches Bewusstein* (the sort of consciousness of the past which changes us) to characterize an attitude interested not so much in what is out there in the world, or in what happened in history, as in what we can get out of nature and history for our own uses."[12]

When attempting to assess the implications of Rorty's account of *Bildung*, it is important not to overlook his use of phrases like "self-formation," "man as self-creative," "we 'remake' ourselves as we read more, talk more, and write more," "an attitude interested not so much in what is out there in the world, or in what happened in history, as in what we can get out of nature and history for our own uses." Firmly rooted in the Western humanist tradition, Gadamer declares that "like nature, *Bildung* has no goals outside itself."[13] So understood, *Bildung* is the auto-telic process in which selves perpetually remake themselves through ongoing interrelationships. Inasmuch as "the point of edifying philosophy is to keep the conversation going rather than to find objective truth," hermeneutics chooses "the infinite *striving for* truth over 'all of Truth.' "[14] The striving subject enters into conversation in order to build *itself* up through the search for truth. Thus persons who converse relate to *themselves* even when they seem to be relating to others. In one of his most revealing remarks about edification, Rorty explains: "For edifying discourse is *supposed* to be abnormal, to take us out of our old selves by the power of strangeness, to aid us in becoming new beings."[15] From this hermeneutical point of view, we enter relationships with "others" in order to become "new beings." The relation to the "other" is, therefore, a self-relation that is self-transforming. The "other" is not really other but is actually a *moment* in one's own self-becoming. The trick of conversation is to turn around (i.e., converse) in such a way that one rediscovers *self* in other.

Rorty is led to this understanding of hermeneutics by his acceptance of

Gadamer's claim that *play* provides the proper model for interpreting interpretation. The Gadamerian notion of play that Rorty appropriates exposes
the idealistic assumptions and conclusions that plague hermeneutics. In the
Preface to the *Phenomenology*, Hegel describes the life of the divine—which, it
is important to remember, is concretely incarnate in the life of each individual
subject—in terms of play:

> The life of God and divine cognition may well be spoken of as a play of
> love with itself (*ein Spielen der Liebe mit sich selbst*); but this idea sinks in-
> to edification (*Erbaulichkeit*), even insipidity, if it lacks the seriousness,
> the suffering, the patience, and the labor of the negative.[16]

Hegel's account of play extends the analysis advanced by Schiller in *On the
Aesthetic Education of Man* and elaborated by Kant in the interpretation of the
work of art presented in the *Critique of Judgment*.[17] The essential feature of
play for Hegel is its self-reflexivity. Inasmuch as play is always self-contained,
players actually never relate to anything or anyone other than themselves.

As Hegel emphasizes, it is a mistake to view play as simply lighthearted
or frivolous activity. Genuine play is impossible apart from what Hegel
describes as "the labor of the negative." Dialectical negativity is not merely
negative but is also positive. The negative becomes positive when it is doubled.
The structure of the Hegelian dialectic is double negation in which negation
first emerges and then is negated. Double negation reconciles what appears to
be merely negative (e.g., difference or otherness) by incorporating it within a
comprehensive totality that is essentially positive. In terms of the development of self-consciousness, Hegel maintains that to become itself, the subject
must enter into relation with others in such a way that their differences
become constitutive of the subject's own being. Because relation to other is
requisite for self-identity, the other is not simply other but is at the same time
also one's own self. Self-consciousness presupposes the recognition of self in
other. Hegel defines authentic subjectivity (i.e., *Geist*) as

> the doubling that sets up opposition, and then again the negation of this
> indifferent diversity and of its antithesis. Only this self-*restoring* identity,
> or this reflection in otherness within itself (*die Reflexion im Anderssein in
> sich selbst*)—not an *original* or *immediate* unity as such in the True. It is
> the process of becoming its own self, the circle that presupposes its end
> as its goal, having its end also as its beginning; and only by being worked
> out to its end, is it actual.[18]

In less convoluted terms, the relation to the other is a necessary moment in
the building up of the subject's own identity. Though Hegel rejects the term
"edification," his *Bildungsroman* anticipates Rorty's contention that we enter

into conversation with others "to aid us in becoming new beings."

The link joining Hegel's *Bildung* and Rorty's edification is Gadamer's esthetics of play. In *Truth and Method,* Gadamer argues that "the concept of play" is "the clue to the ontological explanation of the work of art and its hermeneutical significance." Indirectly recalling Kant's description of the work of art in terms of inner teleology, Gadamer approaches the esthetic object through the notion of *representation* implied in play. "Play," he argues, "is really limited to representing *itself*. Thus its mode of being is *self-representation*."[19] To say that play "is self-representation" is to say that play *must* be purposeless or, more precisely, must have no purpose outside itself. As soon as we play for a reason, we are not playing but working. Because play never points beyond itself, it represents nothing other than itself. For Gadamer, as for his precursors, play is essentially self-referential or self-reflexive.

Play, of course, becomes actual only through the activity of individual players. As Gadamer points out, "the self-representation of the game involves the player's achieving, as it were, his own self-representation by playing, i.e., representing something. Only because play is always representation is human play able to find the task of the game in representation itself."[20] Inasmuch as play is *self*-re-present-ation, its privileged time is the *present*, or, in Gadamer's terms, "a present time sui generis." Play re-presents itself in representative players. When play is satisfying, players become present to themselves in the act of re-presenting play itself. In this way, the self-representation of play creates the possibility of the self-presentation of players.

The self-presence of the player is not simple but is unavoidably complex. Having been taken up into the self-representation of play, players can become present to themselves only in and through another player. For this reason, Gadamer insists that "to be present is to share."[21] When sharing, one no longer seems bound up within oneself but appears to be integrally related to another person. If, as Gadamer avers, to be present is to share, then, "to be present, as a subjective act of a human attitude, has the character of being outside oneself.[22] Presence, in other words, is ecstasy (*ek-stasis*). The exteriority with which the subject that is "outside" itself is involved is not, however, radical but is a covert interiority waiting to be discovered. In Hegelian terms, true self-representation presupposes the negation of negation through which the universal realizes itself in the particular and the particular realizes itself in the universal. In theological terms, the self must lose itself to gain *itself*. Summarizing his analysis of play as the model for the hermeneutical significance of the ontology of the work of art, Gadamer explicitly invokes the theological language implicit in his entire argument:

> The spectator is set at an absolute distance which makes any practical, purposive share in it impossible. But the distance is, in the literal sense,

esthetic distance, for it is the distance from seeing that makes possible the proper and comprehensive sharing in what is represented before one. Thus to the ecstatic self-forgetfulness of the spectator there corresponds his continuity with himself. Precisely that in which he loses himself as a spectator requires his own continuity. It is the truth of his own world, the religious and moral world in which he lives, which presents itself to him and in which he recognizes himself. Just as the parousia, absolute presence, describes the ontological mode of esthetic being, and a work of art is the same whenever it becomes such a presence, so the absolute moment in which a spectator stands is at once self-forgetfulness and reconciliation with self. That which detaches him from everything also gives him back the whole of his being.[23]

Sharing is the redemptive *telos* of the hermeneutical enterprise. One enters into conversation or dialogue with an other—be that other historical—that is, a subject that was present in the past—or a contemporary—in order to establish a self-realizing communion/communication. The Parousia arrives (albeit momentarily) when horizons *fuse* to create (holy) communion:

> To reach an understanding with one's partner in a dialogue is not merely a matter of total self-expression and the successful assertion of one's own point of view, but a transformation into a communion, in which we do not remain what we were.[24]

When dialogue becomes "a communion, in which we do not remain what we were," conversation is truly edifying. Edifying discourse involves a sharing that unites rather than divides, joins rather than separates.

While acknowledging that conversation is *l'entretien infini*, hermeneutical interpretations of dialogue, like those developed by Gadamer and Rorty, entail a one-sided reading of *le partage des voix*.[25] As I have stressed, "to share" means not only to participate in, use, or experience in common, but also to divide and distribute. By reading *part* in *partage*, it becomes possible to hear the converse of hermeneutical conversation. Rorty (like Hegel and Gadamer before him) remains deaf to this alternative discourse. This deafness is not accidental but is "the blind spot" that, paradoxically, allows the hermeneutical philosopher to see. Why do hermeneuts, preoccupied with hearing and seeing, remain deaf and blind? Why can they neither see nor hear the other as other? Why does hermeneutical dialogue always turn into a complex monologue? The answer to these and related questions might be found in a different interpretation of play. Suppose play does not issue in presence or representation, but stages their impossibility.

In an extremely influential essay entitled "Structure, Sign, and Play,"

Derrida claims: "Play is the disruption of presence."[26] Rorty either does not hear or cannot understand the point Derrida is making. The reason for this failure lies in Rorty's insistence that "to understand Derrida, one must see his work as the latest development of this non-Kantian [i.e., Hegelian] tradition – the latest attempt of the dialecticians to shatter the Kantians' ingenuous image of themselves as accurately representing how things really are."[27]

While Hegel exposes the Kantian thing-in-itself as a covert concept, Derrida demonstrates that what seems to be outside any text is inescapably bound up in textual play. Derridean textualism is, according to Rorty, "the contemporary counterpart of idealism."[28] This is not to imply that Rorty believes that Derrida simply repeats Hegel. To the contrary:

> For Derrida, writing always leads to more writing, and more, and still more – just as history does not lead to Absolute Knowledge or to the Final Struggle, but to more history, and more, and still more. The *Phenomenology's* vision of truth as what you get by reinterpreting all the previous reinterpretations of reinterpretations still embodies the Platonic ideal of the Last Reinterpretation, the *right* interpretation at last. Derrida wants to keep the horizontal character of Hegel's notion of philosophy without its teleology, its sense of direction, its seriousness."[29]

Rorty claims that this "deconstructed" Hegel without teleology is virtually indistinguishable from the hermeneutical Hegel whose infinite striving never reaches the end. It is, of course, true that Derrida frequently asserts that absolute knowledge is forever delayed or deferred. Derridean deferral, however, differs significantly from hermeneutical postponement. Derrida's textualism entails a more radical critique of representation than either Gadamer's or Rorty's hermeneutics. Because he misreads Derrida as a dialectical thinker who, in spite of important differences, remains in the Hegelian tradition, Rorty fails to grasp the differences between the hermeneutical and the deconstructive critiques of representation. In both hermeneutics and deconstruction, reality as such or things-in-themselves can never be represented. From a deconstructive point of view, however, hermeneutics remains committed to a philosophy of presence that is repressive of difference and otherness. In self-referential dialogue and auto-telic conversation, the *structure* of representation persists as the self-reflexive process in which subjects become present to themselves in each other and remain identical with themselves in every difference. All dialogue/conversation is dialectical insofar as difference is negated and otherness sublated. The speaking subject, it seems, always *dictates*.

Hermeneutics, in other words, remains caught up in the circle of presence and plenitude. Though the *total* presence of (the) plenitude (of meaning) might forever be deferred, dialectical conversation always transpires within the horizon of presence and re-presentation. The absence of "the transcendental signified" is the condition of the *possibility* of hope in eschatological self-presence. By contrast, the "play" in "Structure, Sign and Play" announces a *"rupture"* with the entire economy of presence and representation. For Derrida, the "absence" (but this is a curious absence) of the transcendental signified is the condition of the *impossibility* of plenary self-presence in any temporal modality—past, present, or future. As the disruption of presence, "play is always play of absence and presence, but if it is to be thought radically, play must be conceived of before the alternative of presence and absence."[30] That which "is" before the alternative of presence and absence, and thus is properly neither present nor absent, opens the un-canny time-space for an other discourse, that might be the dis-course of the other:

> Here there is a kind of question, let us still call it historical, whose *con-ception, formation, gestation,* and *labor* we are only catching a glimpse of today. I employ these words, I admit, with a glance toward the opera-tions of childbearing—but also with a glance toward those who, in a society from which I do not exclude myself, turn their eyes away when faced by this as yet unnameable which is proclaiming itself and which can still do so, as is necessary whenever a birth is in the offing, only under the species of nonspecies, in the formless, mute, infant, and terri-fying form of monstrosity.[31]

The (always) as yet unnameable can be spoken/written, if at all, only "in"

Outlines

Must we always talk in circles . . . circles that tend to be hermeneutical? Are outlines impossible? Or do outlines sketch the im-possibility inscribed by the *Riss* of *Umriss?* Might the *Riss* rending *Umriss* imply "something that will not find itself in any text, the outside of the text (*hors texte*), the superfluous word, word too much (*le mot de trop*), in order that it not be wanting with respect to the completeness of complete Works, or to the contrary that it should always want"?[32] The *hors-texte . . . mot de trop* breaks the hermeneutical circle by interrupting every conversation:

> Behind discourse speaks the refusal to discourse, as behind philosophy would speak the refusal to philosophize: non-speaking speech (*la parole non parlante*), violent, concealing, saying nothing and suddenly crying.[33]

La parole non parlante is a word that divides as much as it unites, separates as well as joins. Neither simply binding nor unbinding, *le mot de trop* is always *entre-deux*–suspended (in the) between. Forever falling between the lines, *la parole non parlante* echoes in (empty) space or nonspace that cannot be represented but can, at best, be outlined. The dis-course of this strange word, which both haunts and eludes hermeneutical conversation, repeatedly returns to fragment Maurice Blanchot's extraordinary *L'entretien infini* and to disrupt Jean-Luc Nancy's provocative *Le partage des voix*. What Gadamer and Rorty struggle to repress, Blanchot and Nancy attempt to solicit.

Near the end of *Le partage des voix*, Nancy notes that somewhere Heidegger asks: "Is dialogue necessarily a dialectic and when?"[34] The task Nancy sets for himself is to reread Heidegger's interpretation of language and the hermeneutical circle through Blanchot's analysis of *l'entretien* so as to establish the possibility of nondialectical dialogue. Though Nancy never puts it in these terms, to entertain a nondialectical notion of dialogue, it is necessary to develop a nonlogocentric reading of language. While Heidegger remains caught in the logocentrism of the ontotheological tradition whose end he nonetheless tolls, some of his most interesting writings outline an account of language that points toward (but does not represent) that which escapes the hermeneutical circle. As we have seen, Heidegger develops an alternative account of language by rethinking language in terms of *Unterschied*–difference or distinction. In a text entitled *Unterwegs zur Sprache*, he writes:

> Language speaks (*die Sprache spricht*). It speaks by bidding the bidden, thing-world and world-thing, to come to the between of dif-ference (*zwischen der Unter-Schiedes*). What is so bidden is commanded to arrive from out of the dif-ference into the dif-ference. . . . The dif-ference gathers the two out of itself as it calls them into the rift (*in den Riss*) that is the dif-ference.[35]

From Heidegger's point of view, semantics and syntax, which usually are taken to be the essence of language, are secondary to a more originary play of differences that forever escapes nomination. In this context, language is not a means of communication by which decipherable messages are sent and received. Rather, language articulates the opening–the between–that makes possible all "comm-*uni*-cation" (*communicare*, to make common). As such, language is antecedent to and escapes from the communicative acts it enables to transpire. Because it entails a double rhythm, language is irreducibly duplicitous. While language holds together contraries usually set apart, it also holds apart the opposites it brings together. The mean that both joins and separates is dif-ference itself.

It is important not to confuse *Unter-Schied* with any particular difference. Heidegger's dif-ference articulates the differences that constitute language in the ordinary sense of the term. This marginal dif-ference is the tear that both enables and interrupts all discourse. Though the *Riss* of *Unter-Schied* creates the clearing in which the hermeneutical circle can be drawn, no circle can contain this *hors texte*.[36]

Nancy and Blanchot are obsessed with the tear of dif-ference. Heideggerian dif-ference, Nancy argues, forever eludes the (dialectical and binary) opposites it articulates. The *Riss* of *Unter-Schied* is a radical difference that can never be reduced to identity and a wholly other that cannot be returned to the same. While dialectical (i.e., hermeneutical) dialogue is either deaf to, or tries to silence, every such difference, nondialectical dialogue solicits an other it can neither contain nor express. In a footnote devoted to Heidegger's use of *Gespräch* (conversation, discourse, dialogue), Nancy underscores the inescapable duplicity of *partage:*

> Le *Gespräch* implies a *Ge-flecht* (netting, lattice, texture; *Flechte*, plait, tress; twist, braid; *flechten*, twist, interweave, intertwine) or is grasped in *Ge-flecht.* Perhaps it would be necessary to say that *Geflecht* is that which is given the regime or nature of the *Ge* of the *Gespräch:* that is to say, a "collective" (this is the ordinary nature of the *Ge-*), but with the function of a *between* (*entre-*) (interweaves [*entrelacement*], conversation [*entretien*]), and finally of a *dia-* that does not dialectise but that shares (*partage*). That which interweaves us divides us, that which divides us interweaves us.[37]

Inasmuch as conversation not only joins but also separates, *le partage des voix* "indicates the finitude of dialogue, that is to say, again, not the limited status of all actual dialogues, based on an infinite dialogue, but this – that the essence of dia-logue is in the infinite alteration of the other" (*l'altération infinie de l'autre*).[38] Paradoxically, dialogue is infinite precisely because it is finite.

The *infini* of *l'entretien infini* cannot be represented but can only be staged or performed *indirectly* – as if "in" outline(s). Language is never only itself but is always at the same time the discourse of the other, which, as *le mot de trop*, remains in a certain sense unspeakable. The converse of dialectical/ hermeneutical conversation repeatedly returns to interrupt the communication whose space it nonetheless clears.[39] Because the eternal return of the discourse of the other is inevitably differential, *la parole* is *la parole plurielle*.[40]

In an important section of *L'entretien infini* entitled *L'interruption*, Blanchot describes alternative approaches to (or of) interruption:

> Interruption is necessary to every sequence of words. Intermittence renders becoming possible; discontinuity assures continuity of understanding, from which there certainly would be much to infer. But for the moment I would like to show that this intermittence by which discourse becomes dialogue, that is to say dis-course, presents itself in two very different ways. In the first case, the arrest-interval (*l'arrêt-intervalle*) is

comparable to the ordinary pause that permits the "taking turns" of a conversation (*entretien*). Discontinuity, then, is essential, since it promises exchange; essential but relative: what it alludes to is, had it been late or never, and at the same time as early as today, the affirmation of unitary truth, where coherent discourse will no longer cease, and no longer ceasing, will confound itself with its silent inverse. From this perspective, rupture, even if it fragments, opposes, or disturbs common speech, still serves its interest. Not only does it confer meaning, but it disengages common meaning as horizon. It is the respiration of discourse. All forms that depend on a dialectical experience of existence and history—from quotidian babble to the highest moments of reason, struggle, and practice—would fall in this category. To interrupt oneself in order to understand onself/one another (*s'interrompre pour s'entendre*).

But there is another kind of interruption, more enigmatic and more critical (*grave*). It introduces the waiting that measures the distance between two interlocutors—no longer reducible distance, but the irreducible.[41]

The play of this *other* interruption—*l'étrangeté . . . l'autre . . . infiniment séparé . . . fissure . . . intervalle . . . en dehors de moi . . . altérité . . . l'inconnu dans son infinie distance*—is the play of altarity. In the strangeness of this interval, fissure, tear, *Riss*, Blanchot radically thinks play—"before the alternative of presence and absence."[42] This *jeu* is another play . . . a play that is the "monstrous" play of the other.

In the play of Blanchot's *entretien*, speech, the word says: "infinite distance and difference, distance that is attested in *la parole* itself and that holds it outside of all contestation, all parity and all commerce."[43] *L'entretien* maintains (*tient*) the between (*entre*) without which there can be no conversation and with which there can be neither unification nor communication:

> When I appeal to the Other, I respond to that which speaks to me from no place and am separated from it by a caesura such that the Other forms with me neither a duality nor a unity. It is this fissure—this relation with the other—which we have dared to characterize as an interruption of being, now adding: between man and man there is an interval that would be neither of being nor of non-being, carried by the Difference of speech, a difference that precedes everything different and everything unique.[44]

The "between" (*l'entre-deux*), which is neither positive nor negative, neither is nor is not, is a difference or an other that cannot be dialectically sublated through the duplicitous positivity of double negation. Repeatedly slipping away from the dialectical logic of both/and, as well as the antidialectical logic of either/or, the timely interval of *l'entretien* implies the paralogic of the neither/nor:

> *Between*: *between/ne(u)ter*. Play, play without the happiness of playing, with this residue of a letter that would appeal to the night with the lure of a negative presence. The night radiates the night as far as the neuter, where the night extinguishes itself.[45]

The paralogic of the neuter can be figured, if at all, only in paralectics. A paralectic parodies a dialectic by miming the communication of that which is incommunicable. As such, every paralectic is parasitic upon a dialectic. Conversely, each dialectic is parasitic upon a paralectic to which it must remain deaf if messages are to be sent and received. *Neither* both/and *nor* either/or, the paralogic of paralectics figures a neuter that simultaneously creates the space for dialogue and neutralizes the transparency of the signs exchanged:

> Something is at work on the part of the neuter, which is in the same instant the work of idleness *(désoeuvrement)*. There is an effect of the neuter, or a neuter effect—called the passivity of the neuter—which is not the effect *of* the neuter, not being the effect of a Neuter supposedly at work as cause or thing. There would not be therefore a labor of the neuter, as one says: labor of the negative. The Neuter, paradoxical name: it hardly speaks, mute word, simple, yet always veiling itself, always displacing itself outside of its meaning, operating invisibly on itself and not ceasing to uncoil itself, in the immobility of its position which repudiates depth. It neutralizes, neutralizes (itself), and thereby evokes (does nothing but evoke), the movement of *Aufhebung*; but if it suspends and retains, it retains only the movement of suspension, that is to say, the distance that it suscitates by the fact that, in occupying the terrain, it makes the distance disappear. The Neuter designates, then, the difference in indifference, the opacity in transparency, the negative scansion of the other which can only reproduce itself by the conjured—omitted—attraction of the one.[46]

In the absence of the *Un*, comm-*un*-ication seems to be impossible. In different terms (or in terms of difference), a paralectic creates static by constantly paraciting words that once seemed clear. *Le parasite* means not only "animal or vegetable organism that lives at the expense of an other (called the host), carrying detriment to it, but without destroying it." It also means "disturbances in the reception of radio-electric signals. *Parasites which impede listening to an emission.*"[47] Inasmuch as *le parasite* interferes with the emission and reception of messages (and of much else), the irreducibly paradoxical neuter faults the hermeneutical circle by interrupting interpretation. Within the nondialectical dialogue of paralectics, interpretation is always interrupreta-tion. While hermeneutical conversation tries to heal the tear and wipe away the tear of the *Riss, l'entretien infini* of paralectics "affirms interruption and rupture."[48] Within the paralogic of paralectics, the parasitical inter-play of dialogue and the discourse of the other issues in interruption, which, though unspeakable, makes speech possible. Neither inside nor outside, the *entre* of *l'entretien* is (impossibly) the condition of the possibility and the impossibility of communication.

In the first chapter ("Rats Meals") of the first part ("Interrupted Meals") of his book entitled *Le Parasite*, Michel Serres comments on the far-reaching implications of the conversation between two rats sitting on a Persian rug:

> Someone once compared the undertaking of Descartes to the action of a man who sets his house on fire in order to hear the noise the rats make in the attic at night. These noises of running, scurrying, chewing, and gnawing that interrupt his sleep. I want to sleep peacefully. Good-bye then. To hell with the building that the rats come to ruin. I want to think without an error, communicate without a parasite. . . . But at night, the rats return to the foundation. . . . The rats come back. They are, as the saying goes, always already there. Part of the building. The errors, trembling, confusion, obscurity are part of knowledge; noise is part of communication, part of the house.[49]

Rats, it seems, do make a difference. A difference that might be the rending *Riss* of *Unter-Schied*, a difference that is always different and an other that is forever other. "Maybe the radical origin of things is really that difference or fault, even though classical rationalism damned it to hell. In the beginning was the noise."[50] This noisy "beginning" is no ordinary beginning but "is" a begin-ning that makes all ending impossible, a beginning that marks the impossibility of ending. As that which never ends, the "beginning" of the neuter is the "before" of play—the before that is forever "before the alternative of presence and absence." A dialogue that does not incorporate difference and appropriate the other by becoming dialectical must repeatedly "speak" the outlines of the between.

Patience

The play of dialectical/hermeneutical conversation is always an impa-tient power play. "Imperative of the purge. Thus exclude the third, the Demon, prosopopoeia of noise. If we want peace, if we desire an agreement between object and subject, the object appearing at the moment of the agree-ment, at the Last Supper as well as in the laboratory, in the dialogue as on the

blackboard, we have to get together, assembling, reassembling, against
whoever troubles our relations, the water of our channel. He is on the other
bank [sometimes the Left, sometimes the West], the rival is. He is our common enemy. Our collective is the expulsion of the stranger, of the enemy, of
the parasite. The laws of hospitality become the laws of hostility. Whatever
the size of the group, from two on up to all humankind, the transcendental
condition of its constitution is the existence of the Demon."[51] "The
Demon" . . . "the demonized other" marks the return of the (repressed) rats.

     When fully developed, hermeneutics tends to become culturally im-
perialistic. "The attempt to edify (ourselves or others)," Rorty maintains,
"may consist in the hermeneutic activity of making connections between our
own culture and some exotic culture or historical period, or between our own
discipline and another discipline which seems to pursue incommensurable
aims in an incommensurable vocabulary."[52] As I have stressed, the par-
ticipants in dialectical/hermeneutical conversation move toward the other so
they can return to themselves enriched. The "exotic" edifies only when it is
first domesticated and then assimilated. The imperialistic implications of this
strategy of interpretation become clear in a remarkable statement that Rorty
makes in an essay entitled "Pragmatism, Relativism, Irrationalism." According to Rorty, the pragmatist "can only say, with Hegel, that truth and justice
lie in the direction marked by the successive stages of *European* thought."[53]
Bildung, it seems, is identified with the cultural tradition of the West. Other
cultural traditions are valued only insofar as they aid Westerners "in becoming
new beings."

     Though not immediately apparent, this cultural imperialism grows out of
the interpretation of the subject that emerges in modern European
philosophy. As we have seen, Rorty credits Gadamer with rescuing "the
romantic notion of man as self-creative" from the problematic metaphysical
framework of nineteenth-century idealism. Hermeneutics, however, remains
more metaphysical than most of its proponents are willing to admit. The self-
creative subject, which receives comprehensive expression in Hegel's
System, is essentially *constructive* and thus fundamentally impatient. In the
final analysis, the im-patient subject finds difference or otherness insufferable.
The end of dialogue is monologue and, as Blanchot insists, monologue tends
to be "imperious."[54]

     While dialectic issues in a dialogue that is a monologue, paralectic inter-
rupts monological discourse by allowing "impossibility" to be spoken:

> We have at first two important distinctions that correspond to a dialec-
> tical exigency and to a non-dialectical exigency of speech: the pause
> that permits exchange and the wait that measures infinite distance. But
> with waiting, it is not only the lofty rupture preparing the poetic act that
> affirms itself, but also, and at the same time, other forms of cessation,

very profound, very perverse, more and more perverse, and always such that if one distinguishes them, the distinction does not avert, but rather postulates, ambiguity. We have thus "distinguished" three forms: one where emptiness (*le vide*) makes itself work – the other where emptiness is fatigue, unhappiness – the other, the ultimate, the hyperbolic, where idleness (*désoeuvrement*) (perhaps thought) marks itself. To interrupt oneself in order to understand oneself/one another. To understand oneself/one another in order to speak. Finally, only speaking to interrupt oneself and to render possible the impossible interruption.[55]

Le partage des voix . . . l'attente qui mesure la distance infinie. L'attente: waiting, awaiting, expectation, hope. . . . Patience: *patior*, to suffer. The possibility of the im-possible (*in* + *possibilis* [*poti*-]) implies a certain impotence (*in* + *potens* [*poti*-]). In the play of paralectics, the dialectical struggle for mastery gives way to the patient suffering of the unmasterable dis-course of the other:

Passivity: we can evoke it only in a language that reverses itself. I have . . . referred to suffering: suffering such that I could not suffer it. If I had recourse to the thought of such suffering, it was so that this non-power (*non-pouvoir*), the I excluded from mastery and from its status as a subject (as first person) – the I destitute even of obligation – could lose itself as a self capable of undergoing suffering. . . . But the word "suffering" is too ambiguous. The ambiguity will never be dispelled, for, speaking of passivity, we cause it to appear, if only in the night where dispersion marks and unmarks it. . . . Passivity, the contrary of activity: such is the ever-restricted field of our reflections. We might coin a word for the absolute passiveness of total abjection – *le subissement*, which is (patterned on *subir*, "to undergo," but is also) simply a variation of *subitement* ("suddenly"), or the same word crushed; we might invent that term, *le subissement*, in an attempt to name the inert immobility of certain states said to be psychotic, the *patior* in passion, servile obedience, the nocturnal receptivity of mystics – dispossession, that is, the self wrested from itself, the detachment whereby one is detached from detachment, or again the fall (neither chosen nor accepted) outside of the self (*hors de soi*). Still, these situations, even if some are at the limit of the knowable and designate a hidden face of humanity, speak to us hardly at all of what we seek to understand by letting this characterless word be pronounced, *passivity*.[56]

. . . at the limit of the knowable . . . a hidden face of humanity. . . . To respond to the other, one must learn to be patient, or, more accurately, one must learn how to allow patience to arrive. The patient (subject) is always (already) passive before active. The suffering sub-ject receives itself as well as the other (sub-ject) from another other that is the tear of dif-ference "itself."

Rats are not always demons. Sometimes the other for which the rat is a vehicle can be a god:

> Gajasura had obtained the privilege of not being killed by a beast, a man, a god, or a demon. Pulliar (Ganesa) not being one of these, as he was half god, half elephant, was the only one who could deal with him victoriously. The giant broke off the god's right tusk, but Pulliar, using it as a javelin, transfixed Gajamukha Gajasura, who transformed himself into a rat and became the vehicle of the god.[57]

As the keeper of the gate, "Ganesa is sometimes called Vighnesa or lord (*isa*) of obstacles (*vighna*). The word *vighna* is itself a compound made up of the prefix *vi*, meaning 'away, asunder,' and *ghna*, a term appearing in compound that means 'striking with, destroying,' from the root *han*, 'strike, kill.' A *vighna* can be anything that prevents, interrupts, diverts, or impedes anything else. It is any kind of resistance." Ganesa, whose vehicle is a rat, seems to be something like a parasite that is a *pharmakon*—not only *Gift* but also gift. "By enlisting Ganesa's aid, the devotee acknowledges the inevitability of obstruction, one's own limited powers of control over the destiny of the action, and the necessity of including the power inherent in the resistance—that is, Vighnesa, the deity residing within the obstacle—as an ally in the undertaking."[58]

To meet a rat that is other than the demonized other of the West, it might be necessary to travel East—from middle to far—in search of an East that "is" different . . . different from a construction through which the West converses with itself while pretending to listen to someone/something other.

10.

The Eventuality of Texts

Questioning the point meant unflagging questioning of the question that had come up with it. Unassailable point, favorable and fatal to all thought—fighting with its own excess—for which it is the crest and base.

Edmond Jabès

The question is asked by one who, in his ignorance, does not even know what provided the occasion for his questioning in this way.

Søren Kierkegaard

Here is a painting I happened to drip red paint on. At first I was terribly upset, but then I started enjoying it. The trickle looked like a crack; it turned the building site into a battered old backdrop, a backdrop with a building site painted on it. I began playing with the crack, filling it out, wondering what might be visible behind it. And that's how I began my first cycle of paintings. I called it "Behind the Scenes." Of course, I couldn't show them to anybody. I'd have been kicked out of the Academy. On the surface, there was always an impeccably realistic world, but underneath, behind the backdrop's cracked canvas, lurked something different, something mysterious or abstract.

Milan Kundera

145

What's the Point?

What's the point? What's a point? Is there a point? Does the point exist? Can a point be thought? Or is the point (the) unthinkable? What's the point . . . of this text? Of any text? What's the point . . . of writing? And rewriting? Can the point be written? Might one write without a point?

> He
> spoke
> of
> the point
> and
> the one
> who
> was
> paying
> attention
> rubbed
> his
> eyes
> to cast out the night.[1]

Sabina was an artist whose paintings approached writing. By "playing with the crack," she glimpsed "something different." This something was nothing . . . the nothing that cast her into the night . . . the night in which she lost the point . . . by realizing that the point is always already lost:

After four years in Geneva, Sabina settled in Paris, but she could not escape her melancholy. If someone had asked her what had come over her, she would have been hard pressed to find words for it.

When we want to give expression to a dramatic situation in our lives, we tend to use metaphors of heaviness. We say that something has become a great burden to us. We either bear the burden or fail and go down with it, win or lose. And Sabina—what *had* come over her? Nothing. She had left a man because she felt like leaving him. Had he persecuted her? Had he tried to take revenge on her? No. Her drama was a drama not of heaviness but of lightness. What fell to her lot was not the burden but the unbearable lightness of being.

Until that time, her betrayals had filled her with excitement and joy, because they opened new paths to new adventures of betrayal. But what if the paths came to an end? One could betray one's parents, husband, country, love, but when parents, husband, country, and love were gone—what was left to betray?

Sabina felt emptiness all around her. What if that emptiness was the goal of her betrayals?[2]

What if the nothing that overcomes Sabina is the point? What if there is nothing left . . . nothing left to betray? What if nothing is what there is left to betray? What if betrayal "is" the point and the point cannot but be betrayed?

"Weight or lightness?" Milan Kundera asks. "The only certainty is: the lightness/weight opposition is the most mysterious, most ambiguous of all."[3] But what is weight and what is lightness? Kundera begins his exploration of the *difference* between weight and lightness by returning to Nietzsche:

> The idea of eternal return is a mysterious one, and Nietzsche has often perplexed other philosophers with it: to think that everything recurs as we once experienced it, and that the recurrence itself recurs ad infinitum! What does this mad myth mean?
>
> Putting it negatively, the myth of eternal return states that a life which disappears once and for all, which does not return, is like a shadow, without weight, dead in advance, and whether it was horrible, beautiful, or sublime, its horror, sublimity, and beauty mean nothing.[4]

The difference between weight and lightness is the difference between recurrence and nonrecurrence. What recurs is weighty; what does not is light:

> If every second of our lives recurs an infinite number of times, we are nailed to eternity as Jesus Christ was nailed to the cross. It is a terrifying prospect. In the world of eternal return the weight of unbearable responsibility lies heavy on every move we make. That is why Nietzsche called the idea of eternal return the heaviest of burdens (*das schwerste Gewicht*).[5]

The question of weight or lightness is not insignificant. To the contrary, it is the question of significance itself. Meaning presupposes iteration–what recurs is significant (weighty) and what does not is insignificant (immaterial). Weight/lightness, recurrence/nonrecurrence, significance/insignificance. (The) Difference is a matter of time. Meaning/absurdity: What's the point? The point of time?

Eventuating Structures

To question "the point . . . [the] unassailable point, favorable and fatal to all thought" is to ask about the relationship between time and interpretation. During the past several decades, no issue has stirred more heated debate among philosophers, theologians, literary and biblical critics than the problem of the significance or insignificance of temporality for interpretation. Competing interpretive strategies can be understood as different responses to the question(s) of time. In the following pages, I examine three forms of analysis that recently have influenced biblical criticism by considering their alternative accounts of temporality. In the movement from structuralism, through hermeneutics, to poststructuralism,[6] temporality is figured ever more radically.[7] As it twists and turns, time's point becomes more and more obscure.

The extraordinary impact of structuralism on biblical criticism is, at least in part, a function of the long-standing influence of historical-critical methods of analysis. Structuralism calls into question the philosophical assumptions that form the foundation of traditional historical criticism in all its guises. The historical critic looks *beyond* the text for meaning and significance. The point of the text, in other words, is always elsewhere. This "beyond" or "elsewhere" can take a variety of forms: the socio-cultural situation in which the text arose, actual historical events recounted in the narrative, the original words of the speaker, the intention of the author, or other writings and sayings from which the text is constructed. Though the assumptions and methods of each particular form of analysis vary considerably, all historical critics implicitly or explicitly agree that texts are representational and meaning is referential. It is commonly assumed that the text is a *sign* of something that is outside its bounds. This "exterior" referent functions as something like a "transcendental signified" that grounds the text. The task of the interpreter is to establish meaning by securing the relationship between textual signifier and extratextual signified.

The structuralist rejects this reading of the text. Instead of looking for meaning *beyond* the text, the structuralist searches for significant patterns *within* the text itself. Explaining the far-reaching implications of "the phonemic revolution in linguistics," Lévi-Strauss writes:

> Not only did it renew linguistic perspectives; a transformation of this magnitude is not limited to a single discipline. Structural linguistics will certainly play the same renovating role with respect to the social sciences that nuclear physics, for example, has played for the physical sciences. In what does this revolution consist, as we try to assess its broadest implication? N. Trubetzkoy, the illustrious founder of structural linguistics, himself furnished the answer to this question. In one programmatic statement, he reduced the structural method to four basic operations. First, structural linguistics shifts from the study of *conscious* linguistic phenomena to the study of their *unconscious* infrastructure; second, it does not treat *terms* as independent entities, taking instead as its basis of analysis the *relations* between terms; third, it introduces the concept of *system* – "Modern phonemics does not merely proclaim that

phonemes are always part of a system; it *shows* concrete phonemic systems and elucidates their structure"—finally, structural linguistics aims at discovering *general laws,* either by induction "or . . . by logical deduction, which would give them an absolute character."[8]

From this point of view, texts are not created by inventive individuals but are produced through the operation of general laws of which particular authors remain unaware. Taken together, the laws that govern textual production form a systematic totality. Within this syntactic whole, meaning is determined by the interrelation of terms rather than reference to something outside the structure of signifiers. As Paul Ricoeur points out in his important essay "Structure and Hermeneutics," which originally bore the title "Symbolique et temporalité," for the structuralist:

> Arrangements at an unconscious level are alone intelligible; understanding does not consist in taking up anew signifying intentions, reviving them through a historical act of interpretation which would itself be inscribed within a continuous tradition. Intelligibility is attributed to the code of transformations which assure correspondences and homology between arrangements belonging to different levels of social reality (clan organization, nomenclatures and classifications of animals and plants, myths and arts, etc.). I will characterize the method in one word: it is the choice of syntax over semantics.[9]

The structuralist interprets by decoding the text—be the text written, oral, or performative.[10] The point of the text is always *within* or, more precisely, *beneath* the play of signs. As one progresses from surface to depth, confusion yields to order. The transition from superficiality to depth marks the movement from lightness to weight.

We have discovered that the difference between lightness and weight is a matter of time. To choose syntax over semantics is, in effect, to privilege eternity over time. The structural unconscious that Lévi-Strauss claims to uncover is universal and thus unchanging:

> The unconscious . . . is always empty—or, more accurately, it is as alien to mental images as is the stomach to the foods that pass through it. As the organ of a specific function, the unconscious merely imposes structural laws upon inarticulated elements that originate elsewhere—impulses, emotions, representations, and memories. We might say, therefore, that the preconscious is the individual lexicon where each of us accumulates the vocabulary of his personal history, but that this vocabulary becomes significant for us and for others, only to the extent

that the unconscious structures it according to its laws and thus
transforms it into language. . . . If we add that these structures are not
only the same for everyone and for all areas to which the function ap-
plies, but that they are few in number, we shall understand why the
world of symbolism is infinitely varied in content, but always limited in
its laws. There are many languages, but very few structural laws valid
for all languages.[11]

Within the structuralist economy, signs are heavy with meaning because they
return eternally. Events, which, by definition, do not recur, are, by contrast,
insignificant. The debate between structuralism and hermeneutics revolves
around the closely related questions of time and history.

In his *Course in General Linguistics*, Ferdinand de Saussure explains that
while synchrony "is a relation between simultaneous elements, [diachrony is]
an event." Structural linguistics is "concerned with the logical and
psychological relations that bind together coexisting terms that form a system
in the collective mind of the speakers."[12] The preoccupation with synchronic
structure leads to the repression of diachronic events. Structuralism is consistently nongenetic and resolutely antihistorical. Temporal events become
intelligible only when incorporated within atemporal structures. "From this
point on," Ricoeur explains, "linguistics is synchronic first, and diachrony
itself is intelligible only as the comparison of states of anterior and posterior
systems; diachrony is comparative, and in this it depends on synchrony.
Finally, events are apprehended only when they have been realized in a
system, that is, by receiving from the system an aspect of regularity; the
diachronic datum is the innovation which arises from speech."[13]

Hermeneutics can be understood as an interpretive strategy that allows
the return of what structuralism represses. "The task [of hermeneutics] is," according to Ricoeur, "to reclaim for the understanding of language what the
structural model excluded and what perhaps is language itself as an *act* of
speech, as saying."[14] What structuralism excludes or represses is time and
history. Hermeneutics attempts to rehistoricize discourse by opening structures to the temporal events from which they emerge and through which they
develop. So understood, hermeneutics has as its goal the *eventuation* of structures. To eventuate structures is to fault closed systems. Discourse or saying,
sensu strictissimo, exposes the opening that creates the possibility of timely interpretation. Ricoeur writes: "The upsurge of saying into our speaking is the
very mystery of language. Saying is what I call the openness, or better, the
opening-out of language."[15]

For the structuralist, diacritical signs form a closed system that "has no
outside but only internal relations." In order to "break the closure of the sign,"
Ricoeur argues, it is necessary "to open the sign onto the other."[16] The

"other" that rends self-enclosed structures of signification emerges in *discourse*. In his account of discourse, Ricoeur returns to important aspects of Saussure's notion of speech (*la parole*). Drawing a distinction that is not unlike Husserl's contrast between ideal and empirical language, Saussure sets *la langue* over against *la parole*. *La langue* designates the socially constituted system of language, which, as the totality of formal structures, underlies and makes possible the actual speech events and concrete linguistic activity named *la parole*. Saussure explains that "in separating *langue* from *parole*, we are separating what is social from what is individual and what is essential from what is ancillary or accidental."[17] For the structuralist, *la parole* appears to be an expression of and thus reducible to *la langue*. While not dismissing the importance of *la langue*, Ricoeur insists that *la parole* is not insignificant.

Language, Ricoeur argues, is not a closed totality characterized by *internal* relations but is always open to dimensions of otherness that it does not contain and cannot exhaust:

> The experience we have of language reveals something of its mode of being which resists [the structuralist's] reduction. For us who speak, language is not an object but a mediation. Language is that through which, by means of which, we express ourselves and express things. Speaking is the act by which the speaker overcomes the closure of the universe of signs, in the intention of saying something about something to someone; speaking is the act by which language moves beyond itself as sign toward its reference and toward what it encounters.[18]

From this point of view, the "other" *of* language takes two forms: subjective and objective. Discourse is a temporal event in which *individual speakers* communicate by sending messages about *something* to *each other*. Ricoeur reintroduces intentionality and referentiality into the linguistic situation. "Whether we distinguish, with Frege, between *Sinn* and *Bedeutung* or, with Husserl, between *Bedeutung* and *Erfüllung*, what we thus articulate is a signifying intention that breaks the closure of the sign, which opens the sign onto the other, in brief, what constitutes language as a saying, a saying something about something."[19] Meaning is not merely the "empty" play of signifiers but is the expression of a subject to a subject about an object.

In his critique of structuralism, Ricoeur reinscribes a series of binary oppositions: atemporal/temporal, universal/individual, constraint/choice, institution/innovation, anonymity/allocution, and closure/reference. His aim, however, is not to dismiss structuralism by merely inverting its hierarchy of values. Rather, Ricoeur seeks to appropriate the insights of structuralism by establishing a thoroughly dialectical relationship between structure and event in which structures constrain events and events transform structures. Structures, in other words, become actual in events and events become comprehensible through structures. The point at which structure and event intersect is the *word:*

> Thus the word is, as it were, a trader between the system and the act, between the structure and the event. On the one hand, it relates to structure, as a differential value, but it is then only a semantic potentiality; on the other hand, it relates to the act and to the event in the fact that its semantic actuality is contemporaneous with the ephemeral actuality of the utterance . . . .The word . . . is less than the sentence in that its actuality of meaning is subject to that of the sentence. But it is more than the sentence from another point of view. The sentence . . . is an event; as such, its actuality is transitory, passing, ephemeral. But the word survives the sentence. As a displacable entity, it survives the transitory instance of discourse and holds itself available for new uses. Thus, *heavy* with a new use-value—as minute as this may be—it returns to the system. And, in returning to the system, it gives it a history.[20]

By eventuating structures, Ricoeur historicizes both particular words and frameworks of interpretation through which actual human beings make sense of their experiences. Hermeneutics is directed toward the recovery of meaning articulated in systems of symbols that have developed in the course of human history.

In an effort to redress the imbalance created by structuralism's concentration on syntax, Ricoeur focuses his investigation on the semantics of language. A symbol, he argues, is formed by the "excess" or "surplus of meaning." In his monumental study of Freud, Ricoeur offers his most complete definition of a symbol:

> A symbol exists . . . where linguistic expression lends itself by its double or multiple meanings to a work of interpretation. What gives rise to this work is an intentional structure which consists not in the relation of meaning to thing but in an architecture of meaning, in a relation of meaning to meaning, of second meaning to first meaning, regardless of whether that relation be one of analogy or not, or whether the first meaning disguises or reveals the second meaning. This texture is what makes interpretation possible, although the texture is first made evident only through the actual movement of interpretation.[21]

The relation of meaning to meaning constitutes the peculiar temporality of symbols. As a result of the dialectical interplay between linguistic events and interpretive structures, symbols as well as the systems they form change.

The temporal development of the structures of signification issues in a semantic sedimentation that renders signs and symbols "polysemous":

> The phenomenon of polysemy is incomprehensible if we do not introduce a dialectic between sign and use, between structure and event. In purely synchronic terms, polysemy signifies that at a given moment a word has more than one meaning, that its multiple meanings belong to the same state of the system. But this definition lacks the essential point, which concerns not the structure but the process. There is a process of naming, a history of usage, which has its synchronic projection in the form of polysemy. Now this process of the transfer of meaning— of metaphor—supposes that the word is a cumulative entity, capable of acquiring new dimensions of meaning without losing the old ones. It is this cumulative metaphorical process which is projected over the surface of the system as polysemy.[22]

When understood in this way, hermeneutics is an archeo-teleological activity in which the interpreter attempts to discover the intentionality of symbols by unearthing their covert meanings. The "semantic richness of the symbolic substratum appears only in diachrony." By extending his analysis from synchronic structures to diachronic processes, Ricoeur identifies what he describes as "the historicity of sense."[23]

The history of sense-making comprises a tradition. Every symbol harbors a "hidden time" that implies a "twofold historicity—of tradition, which transmits and sediments the interpretation, and of interpretation, which maintains and renews the tradition."[24] Always trying to *recover* meaning by *uncovering* the latent in the manifest, the hermeneut seeks to decipher the way in which the past is re-presented in the present and the future is implied in the past. While structuralism's insistence that every temporal event is "a purely contingent interference" results in the eclipse of history, the hermeneutical account of diachrony leads to a notion of tradition as "a series of interpreting recoveries that can no longer be considered the intervention of disorder in a system state."[25] To interpret diachronic processes of signification as the orderly transfer of meaning is to read history in terms of what Kundera calls "The Grand March." The question that must be asked of hermeneutics is whether the weight of tradition represses the unbearable lightness of "being."

The philosopher of The Grand March of history is Hegel. In Hegel's all-inclusive System, history achieves closure when it is perfectly comprehended in philosophical knowledge. Time is the concrete appearance of the *structural* totality that Hegel labels alternatively the Logos, logic, and the Idea. The identity (albeit within difference) of system and history expresses a "basic faith" that Kundera describes as "a *categorical agreement with being.*" For the true believer or the believer in truth, particular events become meaningful through inscription within systematic structure. Kierkegaard was the first to argue that by interpreting time as the necessary manifestation of an eternal logical process, Hegel renders historical development epiphenomenal and temporality illusory. "In spite of all that Hegel says about process," Kierkegaard avers, "he does not understand history from the point of view of becoming, but with the help of the illusion of pastness, understands it from the viewpoint of a finality that excludes all becoming."[26] As structures are constructed to repress events, so systems are built to master becoming. Kundera points to some of the unexpected implications of systematic belief:

> Behind all the European faiths, religious and political, we find the first chapter of Genesis, which tells us that the world was created properly, that human existence is good, and that we are therefore entitled to multiply. Let us call this basic faith a *categorical agreement with being.*
>
> The fact that until recently the word "shit" appeared in print as s— has nothing to do with moral considerations. You can't claim that shit is immoral, after all! The objection to shit is a metaphysical one. The daily defecation session is daily proof of the unacceptability of Creation. Either/or: either shit is acceptable (in which case don't lock yourself in the bathroom!) or we are created in an unacceptable manner.
>
> It follows, then, that the esthetic ideal of the categorical agreement with being is a world in which shit is denied and everyone acts as though it did not exist. This esthetic ideal is called *kitsch.*
>
> "Kitsch" is a German word born in the middle of the sentimental nineteenth century, and from German it entered all Western languages. Repeated use, however, has obliterated its original metaphysical meaning: kitsch is the absolute denial of shit, in both the literal and the figurative senses of the word; kitsch excludes everything from its purview which is essentially unacceptable in human existence.[27]

Systems and structures are kitsch. Shit is the trace of our mortality. The stench of shit is the aroma of our own decay. What is most unacceptable about human existence is that it ends. The repression of time is the denial of death. The systematic impulse so evident in "structuralists" as different as Hegel and Lévi-Strauss expresses the persistent desire for immortality. To try to incorporate history within the Idea or subordinate events to structure is, in effect, to attempt to translate the temporal into the atemporal. To give up the quest for totalizing systems and the search for abiding structures is to accept time and history for what they are—*final.*[28]

It is clear that Kierkegaard's encounter with Hegel anticipates many issues at stake in the debate between structuralism and hermeneutics. By attempting to bring philosophy back down to earth, Kierkegaard points toward the hermeneutical critique of structuralism's antihistorical tendencies. There seems to be a clear parallel between structuralism and Hegelian idealism on the one hand, and, on the other hand, hermeneutics and Kierkegaardian existentialism. This way of drawing lines of affiliation, however, is misleading. Appearances to the contrary notwithstanding, hermeneutics extends rather than subverts the fundamental assumptions of speculative philosophy. Consequently, hermeneutics fails to provide the radical reading of temporality that it promises. The reason for this failure is the refusal of those working within the hermeneutical tradition to give up some of the most basic philosophical assumptions that have grounded Western thought from its beginnings in ancient Greece to its closure in Hegel's System.

As we have seen, Hegel's speculative idealism is a philosophy of self-consciousness that rests upon the principle of reflexivity. Reflexivity is the structure of self-relation in which everything becomes itself in and through its *own* other. In the *Phenomenology of Spirit*, Hegel explains:

> That the True is actual only as system, or that substance is essentially subject, is expressed in the representation of the Absolute as *Spirit*–the most sublime notion and the one which belongs to the modern age and its religion. The spiritual alone is the *actual*; it is essence, or that which has *being in itself*; it is that which *relates to itself* and is *determinate*, it is *other-being* and *being-for-self*, and in this determinateness, or in its self-externality, abides within itself; in other words, it is *in and for itself*.[29]

Because the subject relates to *itself* in what appears to be other, all externality is really *self*-externality. Like the autotelic structure of linguists, the self-reflexive Logos of Hegel "has no outside but only internal relations." Exteriority is inwardized through a process of re-membering that turns everything outside in and inside out. In Hegelian *Er-innerung*, temporal dispersion is re-collected by re-cognition within the eternal Idea. The process of remembering, which brings history to a close, comes to completion in the absolute self-consciousness of the philosopher.

Contrary to expectation, Ricoeur explicitly subscribes to the most important tenets of Hegelian idealism. In the course of his critique of structuralism, Ricoeur discloses that hermeneutics remains a *philosophy of reflection* in which temporality and altarity are "essentially unacceptable." As a philosophy of reflection, hermeneutics presupposes the principle of reflexivity in which relation to other is mediate self-relation. For Ricoeur, as for Hegel, this self-relation emerges in the self-consciousness that is the product of historical development.

I have noted that for the structuralist, *conscious* linguistic phenomena emerge from and rest upon an *unconscious* infrastructure. From Ricoeur's point of view, this structural unconscious calls into question the very possibility of human understanding:

> An order posited as unconscious can never, to my mind, be more than a stage abstractly separated from an understanding of the self by itself; order in itself is thought located outside itself. Of course, "the day may come when all the available documentation on Australian tribes is transferred to punched cards, and with the help of a computer their entire techno-economic, social, and religious structures can be shown to be like a vast group of transformations" (*The Savage Mind*, p. 89). Indeed, this day may come, but on the condition that thought does not become alienated from itself in the objectivity of the codes. If the decoding is not the objective stage of the deciphering and the latter an existential—or *existentiell*—episode of the comprehension of self and of being, structural thought remains a thought that does not think itself.[30]

Hermeneutics, in other words, continues the *philosophical* search for the self-thinking thought that is supposed to complete self-consciousness. Structuralism's acknowledgment of the inescapability of unconscious operations renders this *telos* forever inaccessible. Hermeneutics emerges as a response to what Ricoeur regards as the structuralist's critique of reflection:[31]

> It is up to a reflective philosophy to understand itself as a hermeneutics, so as to create the receptive structure for a structural anthropology. In this respect, it is the function of hermeneutics to make the understanding of the other—and of his signs in various cultures—coincide with the understanding of the self and of being. Structural objectivity can then appear as an abstract moment—and validly abstract—of an appropriation and recognition through which abstract reflection becomes concrete reflection. At the limit, this appropriation and this recognition would consist in a total recapitulation of all the signifying contents in a knowledge of self and of being, as Hegel attempted—in a logic which would be that of contents, not that of syntaxes.[32]

The central claim advanced in this passage should be emphasized: hermeneutics seeks "to make the understanding of the other—and of his signs in various cultures—coincide with the understanding of the self and of being." Elsewhere Ricoeur underscores this point: "I seek to understand *myself* by taking up anew the meaning of the words of all men; it is on this plane that hidden time becomes the historicity of tradition and of interpretation."[33]

This is a *remarkable* conclusion. From the outset, Ricoeur defines the task of hermeneutics as the recovery of what structuralism represses:

> On the one hand, structural linguistics starts from a decision of an epistemological character, viz., to remain inside the closure of the universe of signs. By virtue of this decision, the system has no outside; it is an autonomous entity of internal dependencies. But this is a methodological decision which does violence to linguistic experience. The task is then, on the other hand, to reclaim for the understanding of language what the structural model excluded and what is perhaps language itself as act of speech, as saying.[34]

The excluded or repressed that structuralism finds "essentially unacceptable in human existence" assumes at least two closely related forms—time or history and otherness. As we have seen, Ricoeur argues that in order to tear open systematic structures, it is necessary to "break the closure of the sign" by "opening the sign onto the other." However, this "other" now appears to be a reflection of the inquiring subject. By making "the understanding of the other . . . coincide with the understanding of the self," Ricoeur negates the altarity of the other. Other returns to same in a structure of reflexion that negates difference. This negation of otherness and difference is tantamount to the negation of time and history. If the self discovers *itself* in every other, then the hermeneut inevitably understands not others but *himself* in "the words of all men." Within the hermeneutical circle, the past implies the present and future, and the present and future re-present the past. The time of the circle is the timeless time of the idyll:

> No one can give anyone else the gift of the idyll; only an animal can do so, because only animals were not expelled from Paradise. The love between dog and man is idyllic. It knows no conflicts, no hair-raising scenes; it knows no development. Karenin surrounded Tereza and Tomas with a life based on repetition, and he expected the same from them.
>
> If Karenin had been a person instead of a dog, he would surely have long since said to Tereza, "Look, I'm sick and tired of carrying that roll in my mouth every day. Can't you come up with something different?"
>
> And therein lies the whole of man's plight. Human time does not turn in a circle.[35]

Despite his best efforts, Ricoeur cannot "come up with something different." Attempting to bind the tears and wipe the tears that weigh on human existence, Ricoeur's philosophical hermeneutics ends by being heavy rather than light.

S B L

If the moment (*øieblikket*) is posited, the paradox is there, for in its most abbreviated form the paradox can be called the moment:[36]

Is there any answer to these questions?

And again he thought the thought we already know: Human life occurs only once, and the reason we cannot determine which of our decisions are good and which bad is that in a given situation we can make only one decision; we are not granted a second, third, or fourth life in which to compare various decisions.[37]

Perhaps the point – the point of time – has something to do with how one reads SBL or with how SBL reads.[38] Derrida begins a seminal essay on the poetry of Paul Celan by observing:

One time only: a circumcision takes place just once. So, at least, it would appear. We are going to circle around this appearance – I speak of an appearance and not a semblance – not so much in order to cir-cumscribe or circumvent some essence of circumcision as to let ourselves be approached by the resistance that "once" may offer to thought.[39]

Derrida's meditation on the resistance that "once" may offer to thought even-tually leads him to reflect on questions posed by possible readings of SBL:

Shibboleth is, if one may make use here of a word more common in French than in English, a word of *partage*: *partage* as difference, line of demarcation, parting of the waters, scission, caesura, border, dissocia-tion; but also as participation, as that which is divided because it is held in common, by virtue of partaking of the same. Fascinated by a resem-blance that is both semantic and formal and that nonetheless has no linguistico-historical explanation, I will hazard a comparison between *partage* as *shibboleth* and *partage* as *symbolon*. In both cases, we find S-B-L, in both a token transmitted to another . . . a word or piece of a word; the complementary part of an object divided in two comes to seal an alliance. This is the moment of engagement, of signing, of the pact or contract, of the gift, the promise, the ring.[40]

To read S-B-L as a symbol is to read hermeneutically; to read S-B-L as a shib-boleth is to read deconstructively.

"Symbol" derives from the Greek *sumbolon* (token for identification, by comparing with its counterpart) by way of the Latin *symbolum* (sign, token).

Sumbolon, in turn, derives from *sumballein,* to throw together: *sun-,* together + *ballein,* to throw. In ancient Greece, the symbol was the means by which communication was secured. When a messenger departed, he was given one half of a broken staff that was called a symbol. The message he bore upon his return was deemed trustworthy only if the messenger brought back with him the other half of the staff. When the two halves of the symbol were "thrown together," the circuit of communication was completed and the message transmitted. By extension, a symbol is that which bridges two realities by bringing them together. The two rhythms of the symbol are captured by the French word *partager,* which, as we have seen, means both share and divide or fragment.

For Ricoeur, I have stressed, a symbol is "an intentional structure that consists not in the relation of meaning to things but in an architecture of meaning, in a relation of meaning to meaning." The overdetermination of the symbol creates a surplus or excess of meaning that sets the process of interpretation in motion. The polysemy of the symbol constitutes a "hidden time" that creates the possibility of mediating the time of tradition and the time of interpretation. Ricoeur explains:

> I intend to look for a third temporality, a profound time which would be inscribed in the fullness of meaning and which would make the intersection of these two temporalities [i.e., of tradition and of interpretation] possible. This time would be the time of meaning itself; it would be like a temporal charge, initially carried by the advent of meaning. This temporal charge would allow for both a sedimentation in a deposit and a clarification in an interpretation; in short, it would permit the struggle between these two temporalities, one transmitting, the other renewing.[41]

The time of the symbol is the time of the transference of meaning. Within a symbolic economy, history is a metaphorical (*metapherein,* to transfer; *meta-* [involving change] + *pherein* [to bear]) process in which meaning is produced by translating past, present, and future into each other. To believe in meaning is to privilege weight over lightness.

A shibboleth is, of course, a catchword or password. *Shibboleth,* Derrida notes:

> Is found in a whole family of languages (Phoenician, Judeo-Aramaic, Syriac); apart from the multiplicity of meanings which are grafted on to it (river, stream, ear of grain, olive-twig), *Shibboleth* has the value of a password. It was used during or rather after the war, at the crossing of a border under watch. The word mattered less for its meaning than for

the way in which it was pronounced. The Ephraimites had been defeated by the army of Jephthah and in order to keep the soldiers from escaping across the river (*Shibboleth* also means river . . .), each person was required to say *"Shibboleth."* As the Ephraimites were known for their inability to pronounce correctly the *shi* sound, this was an "unpronounceable word" for them, so that they would say "sibboleth" and thus betray themselves to the sentientel at the risk of death.[42]

There is a critical difference between the S-B-L of the symbol and the S-B-L of the shibboleth. In the symbol, the relation of meaning to meaning makes communiction possible. A shibboleth, by contrast, is an unpronounceable word whose meaning is insignificant. By bringing together what it also holds apart, the symbol facilitates the sharing (*le partage*) of meaning; by holding apart what it also brings together, the shibboleth divides (*partage*) those who attempt to communicate. While the symbol facilitates metaphorical interpretation, the shibboleth resists translation by interrupting transference with a resistance that escapes the reducible ambiguity of polysemy:

> *Shibboleth* marks the multiplicity *within* language, insignificant difference as the condition of sense in language. And even if one speaks of a multiplicity *of* languages, it is proper to specify that Babelian untranslatability is connected not only with the difficult passage (*no parsán*) from one poetic language to another, but also with the aporia, the impasse beyond all possible transaction, which is connected with the multiplicity of languages within the uniqueness of a poetic inscription.[43]

As the *insignificant* difference that is forever untranslatable, the shibboleth is "the cipher of the cipher, the ciphered manifestation of the cipher as such." While the recovery of the lost half of a symbol makes it possible to decipher textual messages, possession of the shibboleth in no way "effaces the cipher, holds the key to the crypt, and guarantees the transparency of meaning. The crypt remains, the *Shibboleth* remains secret, and the poem unveils this secret as a secret that is withdrawn, beyond the reach of any hermeneutic exhaustion. The secret is not hermetic, but it remains, like a date heterogeneous to all hermeneutic totalization or radicalization. There is no one meaning, no single originary meaning, from the moment there is a date and a *Shibboleth*."[44]

Why are a shibboleth and a date associated with each other? Perhaps because a date is the "once" for which there is no "one" meaning, no "single" originary meaning. "Heterogeneous to all hermeneutic totalization," the date marks the "moment," which, as Kierkegaard observes, is "the paradox . . . in its most abbreviated form." This moment is the point of time that eludes not only structuralism but also hermeneutics. To struggle to think this unthinkable *Øieblik* is to approach a lightness that is nearly unbearable by confessing that the point of time is pointless.

To glimpse the pointlessness of the point of time, it is necessary to ask: "What is a date?" A date is the sign of an event. To ask: "What is a date?" is, therefore, to ask: "What is the sign of an event?" If an event is historical, it is unique—it takes place but *once*. If "once" resists thought, then can events be signed? Can there be a date? Does a date exist? "A date," Derrida argues, "is not something that *is there*, since it withdraws in order to appear, but perhaps *there are* (*gibt es*) dates."[45] Like a point that vanishes in order to appear and as such is the "appearance" of vanishing, the date *malgré lui* marks the appearance of disappearance. In one of the most difficult and important passages in his entire *oeuvre*, appended as a footnote in *The Concept of Anxiety*, Kierkegaard probes "the category of *the moment*" (*Øieblikket*) by considering Plato's account of the moment in *Parmenides:*

> *It is assumed both that the one* (*to hen*) is and that it is not, and then the consequences for it and for the rest are pointed out. As a result, the moment appears to be this strange entity (*atopon* [that which has no place], the Greek word is especially appropriate) that lies between motion and rest without occupying any time, and into this and out from this that which is in motion changes into rest, and that which is at rest changes into motion. Thus the moment becomes the category of transition (*metabolé*), for Plato shows in the same way that the moment is related to transition of the one to the many, of the many to the one, of likeness to unlikeness, etc. and that it is the moment in which there is neither *hen* [one] nor *polla* [many].[46]

The nonplace of the moment is the strange domain of the between (*mellum*): neither one nor many, neither likeness nor unlikeness, neither identity nor difference . . . This neither/nor not only is unsayable, but is unnameable and unthinkable.

Inasmuch as it is the inscription of that which cannot be named because it never returns, the date "is a structure of self-effacement (*d'auto-effacement*). Dates "mark only insofar as their readability enunciates the possibility of a recurrence, and the recurrence of that which precisely cannot return, the possibility, let us say then, of the spectral return of that which, unique in its occurrence, will never return. A date is a specter."[47] While Hegelian, structural, and hermeneutical interpretation tends to become specular, deconstuction's commemoration of events remains spectral. The momentary blindness that results from the mere blink of an eye forever cracks the mirror of reflexion:

A date marks itself and becomes readable only in freeing itself from the singularity that it nonetheless recalls. It carries forgetting into memory, but it is the memory of forgetting itself, the truth of forgetting; it annuls in the ring's annulation, in the same way that a month annually recalls and annuls a year, as it rounds on itself—by virtue of which a date is always a turnabout, a vicissitude, a "volta," and a revolt or revolution. It replaces itself in its vicissitudes. So that, commemorating what may always be forgotten in the absence of a witness, the date is exposed in its very essence or destination to annihilation, threatened in its very readability; it risks the annulment of what it saves. It may always become no one's and nothing's date, the essence without essence of ash in which one no longer even knows what one day, one time, under some proper name, was consumed. And the name itself shares this destiny of ash with the date. This does not happen by accident; it is incident to the date's erratic essence to become readable and commemorative only in effacing that which it was to date, in becoming no one's date.[48]

Risking the annihilation of what it saves, the date may always become no one's and nothing's date. That's the point . . . the point of the date . . . the point of the date that is the sign of the event that structuralism and hermeneutics try to repress. Deconstruction seeks to remember what structuralism and hermeneutics attempt to forget by carrying forgetting into memory as the memory of forgetting itself. To remember without remembering is to mourn—to mourn endlessly by mourning for what withdraws and can never return:

What withdraws from us draws us along by its very withdrawal, whether or not we become aware of it immediately, or at all. Once we are drawn into the withdrawal, we are, somewhat like migratory birds, but in an entirely different way, caught in the pull of what draws, attracts us by its withdrawal. And once we, being so attracted, are drawing toward what draws us, our essential being already bears the stamp of the "pull." As we are drawing toward what withdraws, we ourselves point toward it. We are who we are by pointing in that direction—not like an incidental adjunct but as follows: this "being in the pull of" is in itself an essential and therefore constant pointing toward what withdraws. To say "being in the pull of" is to say "pointing toward what withdraws."

To the extent that man *is* in this pull, he *points* toward what withdraws. *As* he is pointing that way, man *is* the pointer. Man here is not first of all man, and then also occasionally someone who points. No: drawn into what withdraws, pulled toward it and thus pointing into the withdrawal, man first *is* man. His essential being lies in being such a pointer. Something which in itself, by its essential being, is pointing, we call a sign. As he draws toward what withdraws, man is a sign. But since this sign points toward what draws *away*, it points not so much at *what* draws away as into the withdrawal. The sign remains without interpretation.[49]

In the withdrawal of the point, nothing leaves a trace . . . a trace that is almost nothing . . . a trace that is as light (and as dark) as *ash*:

> We can never know what to want, because, living only one life, we can neither compare it with our previous lives nor perfect it in our lives to come.
> Was it better to be with Tereza or to remain alone?
> There is no means of testing which decision is better, because there is no basis for comparison. We live everything as it comes, without warning, like an actor going on cold. And what can life be worth if the first rehearsal for life is life itself? That is why life is always like a sketch. No, "sketch" is not quite the word, because a sketch is an outline of something, the groundwork for a picture, whereas the sketch that is our life is a sketch for nothing, an outline with no picture.
> *Einmal ist keinmal,* says Tomas to himself. What happens but once, says the German adage, might as well not have happened at all. If we have only one life to live, we might as well not have lived at all.[50]

Life as a sketch . . . an outline . . . a *Grund-riss* . . . an *Um-riss* . . . of nothing . . . terrible tear . . . horrible tear . . . strange levity . . . the unbearable lightness . . . of pointlessness.

Nothing leaves a trace . . . a trace that is almost nothing . . . a trace that is as light (and as dark) as *ash*. The place or nonplace where ash remains is the crypt. "The date is also a sepulcher that gives rise to (*donne lieu á*) a work of mourning."[51]

> The crypt remains, the *Shibboleth* remains secret, and the poem unveils this secret as a secret that is withdrawn, beyond the reach of any hermeneutic exhaustion. The secret is not hermetic, but it remains, like a date, heterogeneous to all hermeneutic totalization or radicalization. There is no one meaning, no single originary meaning, from the moment that there is a date and a *Shibboleth*.

If the crypt remains and thus everything remains somewhat cryptic, how is one to read? How is one to read a simple sentence like: "Nothing leaves a trace"? Is this statement positive or negative? If reading, like writing, is an event, "there is no means of testing which decision is better because there is no basis for comparison."

S-B-L . . . S-B-L. Symbol or Shibboleth? Two testaments, one new and one old that bear witness to two readings of reading. The symbolic translation of messages presupposes the *presence* of the messenger. If the messenger does not arrive, is delayed, or is not recognized, the symbol remains broken . . . torn, rent, fissured. As the cipher of the cipher, the shibboleth testifies to the *absence* of the messenger who holds the key to all messages. The date is the sign of nonarrival. Though intended to represent a present, the date marks an absence. "Formally, at least, the affirmation of Judaism has the same structure as that of the date":

> The Jew is also the other, myself and the other; I am Jewish in saying: the Jew is the other who has no essence, who has nothing of his own or whose own essence is not to have one. Thus, at one and the same time, both the alleged universality of Jewish witness . . . and the incommunicable secret of the Judaic idiom, the singularity of its "unpronounceable name." . . . The Jew's "unpronounceable name" says so many things: it says *Shibboleth*, the word which is unpronounceable—which *can* not be pronounced—by one who does not partake of the covenant or alliance; it says the name of God which *must* not be pronounced; and it says also the name of the Jew which the non-Jew has *trouble* pronouncing and which he scorns or destroys for that very reason, which he expels as foreign and uncouth [*comme "un nom à coucher dehors,"* i.e., a long, unpronounceable name] . . . .Its unpronounceability keeps and destroys the name; it keeps it, like the name of God, or dooms it to annihilation. And these two possibilities are not simply different or contradictory. The Jew, the name Jew, is a *Shibboleth*; prior even to any use of the *Shibboleth*, prior to any communal or discriminatory division (*partage*), whether he is master or proscript, Jew and *Shibboleth* partake of each other: witness to the universal, but by virtue of absolute singularity, dated, marked, incised by virtue of and in the name of the other.[52]

The incision made by virtue and in the name of the other is an event that "takes place but once" . . . "one time only." "This event is circumcision. One may translate this word as 'reading-wound.' "[53] Circumcision is, among other things, a matter of language. The wound inflicted is the tear of the word. Inscribed in the name of one who remains unnameable, this word is the word of the other and as such is other than the word that is symbolic:

> Does one ever circumcise without circumcising a word, a name? And does one ever circumcise a name without something done to the body?

> If the word circumcision rarely appears, other than in connection with the circumcision of the word, by contrast the tropic of circumcision disposes cuts, caesurae, ciphered alliances, and rings throughout the text. The wound is also universal, a differential mark in language, precisely that which dates and sets turning the ring of recurrence. To say that "all the poets are Jews," is to state something that marks and annuls the mark of a circumcision. All those who deal or inhabit language as poets are Jews—but in a tropic sense. What the trope comes to is locating the Jew not only *as* a poet but also *in* every man circumcised by language or led to circumcise a language.[54]

To be inscribed in language is to be circumcised and to be circumcised is to be Jewish. If S-B-L is read as shibboleth rather than symbol, we are all Jews of a sort.

The wound of the word opens one to the other. The event of this opening occurs in a saying that is, in the final analysis, writing. We have seen that Ricoeur's philosophical hermeneutics is directed toward the recovery of an other that would rupture the closure of every system and all structures. This "other" emerges in "saying." "The upsurge of saying into our speaking is the very mystery of language. Saying is what I call the openness, or better, the opening-out, of language."

I have argued, however, that Ricoeur's abiding commitment to the principles of the philosophy of reflection leads to the failure of his hermeneutical project. Like idealism and structuralism, hermeneutics ends by reducing other to same. When the self discovers its own presence in every apparent other, altarity is repressed and time negated. If it is impossible *not* to discover one's self, then all interpretation is self-interpretation. Within the hermeneutical circle, texts remain insufficiently event-ual. Though sometimes delayed, messages eventually arrive.

But what if the messenger is delayed? What if the symbol's other half is still missing and might always be missing? In the absence of the messenger, texts themselves never arrive but remain *radically* eventual. This eventuality entails a saying other than that of hermeneutics.

A form of saying that is irreducibly eventual appears in Emmanuel Levinas's *Otherwise than Being or Beyond Essence*. EL's analysis rests upon a distinction between "saying" (*le dire*) and "the said" (*le dit*). The difference between saying and the said parallels the difference between structure and event as well as synchrony and diachrony. In its capacity as the said, language plays the role that Western ontotheology traditionally assigns the logos. Heidegger points out that "the word *Ho Logos* names that which gathers all present beings into presencing and lets them lie before us in it. *Ho Logos* names that in which the presencing of what is present comes to pass."[55] For EL, the "presencing of what is present comes to pass" through the logical process of de-sign-ating. To designate is to nominate or name what is or becomes present. Within the said, what *is* "can be conceived as a *system* of nouns identifying entities." *Le dit,* in other words, is a *systematic* structural totality that is the condition of the possibility of presentation:

> In a system, signification is due to the definition of terms by one another in the synchrony of a totality, where the whole is the finality of the elements. It is due to the system of the language on the verge of being spoken. It is in this situation that universal synchrony is effected. In the said, to have a meaning is for an element to be in such a way as to turn into references to other elements, and for the others to be evoked by it.[56]

It is clear that *le dit* is EL's version of Hegel's System, Saussure's *parole,* and Lévi-Strauss's structure. Within the bounds of the (always already) said, the last act has (always already) occurred. Since the Parousia has arrived, the logos is present and meaning can be truly communicated. By disclosing what is implicitly present in the beginning, the end assembles what appear to be dispersed temporal moments into a coherent narrative. In this narrative structure, only the present is: the past is a past present, and the future a future present. The Western ontotheological tradition culminates in the reading of this logos-ful story.

EL, however, insists that "the said and the non-said do not absorb all saying, which remains on this side of, or goes beyond the said." [57]EL's *dire* recalls Heidegger's *sagen,* which "in the presentation of the sayable brings the unsayable as such into the world."[58] Saying, according to EL, can say what remains unspoken in the said only through a "preoriginal saying." Such saying is "anterior to the verbal signs it conjugates, to the linguistic systems and the semantic glimmerings, a preface or foreword preceding languages, it is the proximity of the one to the other, the commitment of an approach, the one for the other, the very signifyingness of signification."[59] The preface or foreword to language (i.e., to the logos as the said) is the "anarchy" that the said seeks to exclude or repress in the very act of constituting itself. Anarchy is not merely disorder but is an *an-arche* that signals a "deep formerly" (*profond jadis*) that is not a " 'modification' of the present." Such anarchy faults systems and structures by exposing incurable wounds and irrepressible tears:

> This an-archy (*an-archie*)—this refusal to be assembled into a representation, has its own way to concern me: the *lapse.* But the lapse of time, irrecuperable in the temporalization of time, is not only negative like the immemorial.
>
> Temporalization as lapse, the loss of time, is neither an initiative of the ego, nor a movement toward some *telos* of action. The loss of

time is not the work of any subject. . . . Time passes. This synthesis that occurs *patiently*, called with profundity passive, is aging. It breaks out under the weight of years, and is irreversibly removed from the present, that is, from re-presentation. In self-consciousness, there is no longer a *presence* of self to self, but senescence. It is as senescence beyond the recuperation of memory that time, lost time that does not return, is a diachrony that concerns me.[60]

In contrast to the past that can be remembered, anarchy "is" a radical before that is "incommensurable with every present." Inasmuch as preoriginal anarchy is never present, this remote anteriority cannot be re-presented, but must be suffered—suffered passively:

> The passivity "more passive than all passivity" would consist of submitting—or more precisely in having already submitted in an irrepresentable past that was never present—an unassumable traumatism, wounded by the "*in*" of the infinite devastating presence and awakening subjectivity to the proximity of the other.[61]

This infinite is never inscribed *within* the text. Nor is it simply *outside* the text. The Other that cannot be reduced to the same is "inside" as an "outside" that renders every text irreducibly event-ual by sending it into exile from itself. From this "internal" exile there is no return. I repeat—only once—I repeat: From this "internal" exile there is no return. The exilic text is errant; its reader/writer a nomad:

> This way, preceded by no truth, and thus lacking the prescription of truth's rigor, is the way through the Desert. Writing is the moment of the desert as the moment of Separation . . . God no longer speaks to us; he has interrupted himself: we must take words upon ourselves. We must be separated from life and communities, and must entrust ourselves to traces, must become men of vision because we have ceased hearing the voice from within the immediate proximity of the garden. "*Sarah, Sarah with what does the world begin?—With speech?—With vision?*" Writing is displaced on the broken line between lost and promised speech. The *difference* between speech and writing is sin, the anger of God emerging from itself, lost immediacy, work outside the garden. "*The garden is speech, the desert writing.*"[62]

Sarah . . . Sarah who . . . which Sarah? Sarah, the woman who laughs, the woman whose previous name, Sarai, means mockery, the woman who bore a son named "He laughed"? Does Sarah's laughter provoke *Fear and Trembling* by tolling the unbearable lightness of being?

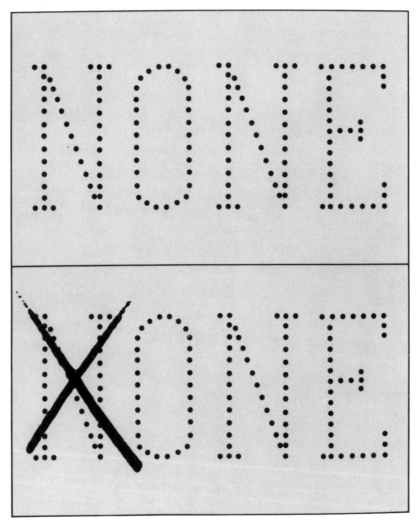

Figure 15. (above and opposite) Edmond Jabès, *El, or The Last Book*.

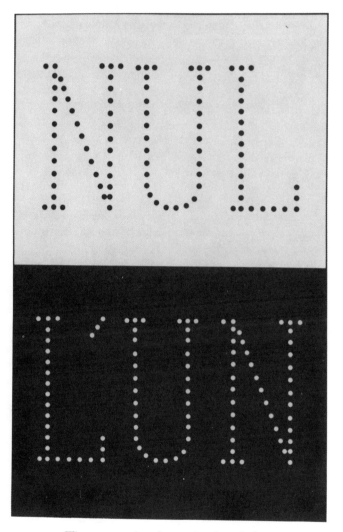

The most pointed question is pointless

.
.
.

Pointless Point

For the writing of circumcision that the intercessor asks of him is a *writing of Nothing*. It performs its operation on Nothing, it consists in inscribing Nothing in the flesh, in the word, in the flesh of the circumcised word.[63]

"One time only: a circumcision takes place just once."

Once
One
Ein
Ein Sof

"God refused image and language in order to be himself the point. He is image in the absence of images, language in the absence of language, point in the absence of points, he said."

tsimtsum

"Questioning the point meant unflagging questioning of the question that had come up with it. Unassailable point, favorable and fatal to all thought—fighting with its own excess—for which it is crest and base."

øieblikket

". . . the most abbreviated form of the paradox can be called the moment."

"Absolute Paradox."
"The Absurd."
"Impossible to read."
"Reading is impossible."
"Absurd book."

What's the point? What's a point? Is there a point? Does the point exist? Can a point be thought? Or is the point (the) unthinkable? What's the point . . . of this text? Of any text? What's the point . . . of writing? And rewriting? Can the point be written? Might one write without a point? Is writing pointless?

After EL . . . in the wake of *EL, or The Last Book*, a single question remains: How is one to (be) read?[64]

11.

Secretions

When Amor leaves Psyche, he says to her: You will bear a child who will be divine if you remain silent but will be human if you betray the secret.

Søren Kierkegaard

It is in the soul itself that the leap is accomplished, in the soul that the abyss, which no thought, no act can jump over, is hollowed out. The beyond is in us in a manner that forever separates us from ourselves and our nobility is that this secret makes us have to reject ourselves absolutely in order to find ourselves absolutely. What is there in man? That, man cannot know. ("No one knows what the innermost soul is," says Meister Eckhart.)

Maurice Blanchot

Secret(e)s

Betrayal: I am going to tell you a secret. A secret about Kierkegaard. A secret about Kierkegaard that might be the secret of secrets. A secret of secrets that allows secrets to secrete. Listen carefully, for secrets have a way of slipping by . . . unnoticed.

How can I avoid betraying a secret? I am going to tell you a secret. A secret about secrets. Or, perhaps, so it will have seemed. I am not sure I can tell you a secret. Can a secret be told—told in such a way that it remains—remains (a) secret? In telling, does a secret remain? Or must a secret be told in order to be a secret? Would a secret that no one knows be a secret? Is the secret that

171

remains in telling the remains that always remains, the remainder that is always to be told? Is the secret telling rather than told? Telling as the always yet-to-be-told? What might this telling toll—toll for philosophy?

I am going to betray Kierkegaard by telling you a secret. A secret about Kierkegaard that might be the secret of secrets that secretes the texts written in "his own" name and in the name of others or an Other. Secrets: What is a secret and what does it mean to secrete?

Words sometimes (perhaps always) harbor secrets. A secret is, of course, that which is "kept from knowledge or observation; hidden, concealed." When used of a place, secret means "retired, remote, lonely, secluded, solitary."[1] The word "secret" derives from the Latin *secretus* (separate, out of the way), which, in turn, comes from the past participle of *secernere* (to put apart, separate). Joseph Shipley lists three roots for secret: *ker*, scratch, cut, pluck, gather, dig, separate, sift; *sek*, cut, scrape, separate, sift; and *sue, se*, personal relations, one's own; his, hers, its. "*Se*, by oneself, came to mean apart, without; in this sense it is an English prefix to innumerable words, as *secret, secrete*; secure (whence *sure*); *seduce*: lead astray; *segregate*: part from the herd; *separate, sever*; *several*: existing apart; *sex*, cut apart, as Eve from Adam."[2] For reasons that will become apparent as we proceed, it is not insignificant that script and scripture also derive from *ker* and *sek*.

The Danish word for secret is *hemmelighed*. *Hemmelighed* carries the trace of *hjem*, which means "home." That which is secret is separate, cut off, private; something that is inside or interior, as if restricted to and by the family hearth. There is, however, something strange about *hemmelighed*. When pushed too far, its domestic connotations are reversed. *Hemmelighedsfuld* means mysterious or uncanny. The other Danish word used to designate that which is uncanny is *uhyggelig*. *Hyggelig*, an extremely important word in Danish language and culture, has no precise English equivalent. It connotes coziness, comfortableness, and homeyness. Forever returning to disturb the *hygglig* feeling of the home, *u-hyggelig* suggests something that can never be domesticated.

The implications of the associations among *hjem, hemmelighed, hemmelighedsfuld*, and *uhyggelig* can be clarified by considering their German equivalents. The German word for secret is *Geheim*, which, like the Danish *hemmelighed*, is associated with the home: *die Heim*. *Geheim* and *Heim* bear an unexpected relationship to the uncanny—*unheimlich*. Freud begins his famous essay on "The Uncanny" with a long etymological excursus in which he explores the interplay of *unheimlich, Heim*, and *Geheim*:

> What interests us most in this long extract is to find that, among its different shades of meaning the word *heimlich* exhibits, one which is identical with its opposite, *unheimlich*. . . . In general we are reminded that the word *heimlich* is not unambiguous, but belongs to two sets of ideas,

which without being contradictory are yet very different: on the one hand, it means that which is familiar and congenial, and on the other, that which is concealed and kept out of sight. The word *unheimlich* is only used customarily, we are told, as the contrary of the first signification, and not of the second. . . . On the other hand, we notice that Schelling says something that throws quite a new light on the concept of the "uncanny," one which we had certainly not awaited. According to him everything is uncanny that ought to have remained hidden and secret, and yet comes to light.

Some of the doubts that have thus arisen are removed if we consult Grimm's dictionary.

We read:

Heimlich; adj. and adv. *vernaculus, occultus*; MHG. heîmelich, hemilîch. . . .

4. *From the idea of "homelike," "belonging to the house," the further idea is developed of something withdrawn from the eyes of others, something concealed, secret, and this idea is expanded in many ways.* . . .

Heimlich in a different sense, as withdrawn from knowledge, unconscious: . . . *Heimlich* also has the meaning of that which is obscure, inaccessible to knowledge. . . .

9. *The notion of something hidden and dangerous, which is expressed in the last paragraph, is still further developed, so that "heimlich" comes to have the meaning usually ascribed to unheimlich.*

Thus *heimlich* is a word the meaning of which develops towards an ambivalence, until it finally coincides with its opposite, *unheimlich*.[3]

In order to develop the ambiguities associated with the uncanny, Freud turns to a children's story by E. T. A. Hoffmann entitled "The Sand-Man." Freud reads this "fantastic tale" in terms of the struggle between the father and his children. The uncanny effect of the Sand-Man (i.e., the effect of the character in the tale on the children, and of the story on the reader) can best be understood, Freud argues, in terms of the return of the repressed castration complex. The Sand-Man, "who tears out children's eyes," figures the act of castration by which the (word of the) father forever separates the son from the bosom (*le sein*) of mother.

Kierkegaard cites Hoffmann ten times in his Journals. In the most suggestive reference, he records (in German and without comment) a passage from Hoffmann's *Meister Floh*. The text concerns a secret that both joins and separates father and son:

How did a man who searched out the most secret thoughts (*die geheimsten Gedanken*) of his brethren speak to himself? Does not this fatal gift bring over him that frightful condition that came over the eternal

Jew, who wandered through the bright tumult of the world without hope, without pain, in apathetic indifference which is the *caput mortuum* of despair, as if through an uncomfortable, comfortless wasteland?[4]

Does the secret of the Father become the secret of the Son? Is this the secret that Søren's writings betray by *not* telling?

Northerly T(r)opics

Writing is at the North: cold, necessitous, reasoning, turned toward death, to be sure, but by that *tour de force*, by that detour of force that forces it to hold on to life. In fact, the more a language is articulated, the more articulation extends its domain, and thus gains in rigor and in vigor, the more it yields to writing, the more it calls writing forth.[5]

The question of the secret is, at least in part, the question of a strange place or nonplace that implies a certain displacement. If there is a secret—something that is always questionable—what is its place or nonplace . . . its *topos* or *atopos*? Might northerly writing *always* be indirect—forever turning and returning . . . repeatedly troping? Secretive topics to ponder: *topos, atopos, tropos,* trop-ics, trop-es . . . twists and turns displacing each other until it all becomes *trop—de trop*.

I begin (again) indirectly with three northmen: a Norwegian, a Swede, and a Dane; a painter, a cinematographer, and a writer.

In 1929 Edvard Munch wrote to Rangar Hoppe, a Swedish art historian who was preparing a catalogue for a major Munch exhibit:

I am glad to hear you describe [my work] as exemplary of "Nordic spiritual life." People are always trying to shove me down to Germany. But we do after all have Strindberg, Ibsen, Søren Kierkegaard, and Hans Jæger up here, and Dostoevsky in Russia. Only during the last year did I become familiar with Kierkegaard, and there certainly are remarkable parallels between him and me. Now I understand why it has so often been said that a similarity exists between his world and mine.[6]

What Kierkegaard writes, Munch paints (and vice versa).

Nowhere is the intersection of Kierkegaard's and Munch's preoccupations more evident than in Munch's well-known work *The Scream* (Fig. 16). In this haunting study, a skeletal figure, whose sex is uncertain, stands on a bridge above the sea. The wavy lines of the land/seascape increase the sense of vertigo suggested by the height of the bridge. What is most striking about the work is the apparent futility of the scream. Though there are two other

Figure 16. Edvard Munch, *The Scream*, courtesy of The Sarah G. and Lionel C. Epstein Collection.

figures on the bridge, neither seems to hear the cry. Even when s/he is with others, the individual appears to be separate, cut off, isolated, alone. Wo/man screams, always screams, into a void.

The Scream is best known as a lithograph completed in 1895. This version of the work, however, is the result of a long process of evolution. The earliest trace of *The Scream* (1893) is a simple pastel drawing on cardboard; in its final form it is a striking oil painting (ca. 1909 or 1915–18). To appreciate the multiple nuances of this work or series of works, *The Scream* must be placed in the context of other drawings and paintings that Munch completed during the 1890s. *The Scream* reworks themes initially presented in a painting entitled *Despair* (Fig. 17; 1892) and anticipates the dark mood of *Angst* (Fig. 18; 1894). *The Scream*, it seems, breaks out between *Despair* and *Dread*. As we know from Kierkegaard, despair is "The Sickness Unto Death" and *Angest* is the way in which every individual experiences the primordial guilt associated with original sin.

What critics have failed to notice is that *The Scream* also points toward an etching that bears the title *The Dead Mother and Her Child* (Fig. 19; 1901). The child, standing in front of the mother on her deathbed, repeats the deadly figure who is screaming on the bridge. Edvard was five years old when his mother died of tuberculosis. If we read *The Scream* in terms of the sketches from which it came and the paintings to which it led, we discover a fascinating chain of signs: Despair . . . The Scream . . . Anxiety . . . The Dead Mother. When this sequence is read backward, the impossible "source" of *The Scream* becomes *The Dead Mother and Her Child*.

# # # #

. . .

Ingmar Bergman, to my knowledge, never mentions Kierkegaard. And yet no sinematographer is more Kierkegaardian. What Kierkegaard writes and Munch paints, Bergman films. Bergman's most Kierkegaardian film is *Persona*. The film reaches its climax in the penultimate scene.

> *Alma stops, sees herself for a brief moment, this is Alma, this is Elisabeth and herself. She can no longer distinguish, nor does it matter. Elisabeth laughs, shortly, coarsely.*
> —Try to listen. (*Whispers Alma.*) Please. Can't you hear what I'm saying? Try to answer now.
> *Elisabeth lifts her face from her hands. It is naked, sweating. She nods, slowly.*
> —Nothing, nothing, no, nothing.
> —Nothing.
> —It'll be alright. That's how it must be.[7]

Figure 17. Edvard Munch, *Despair*, courtesy of Munch Museet.

The "Nothing" of Elisabeth and/or Alma (we cannot be sure who is who) recalls not only Munch's *Angst* but also Kierkegaard's *Begrebet Angest*. Commenting on the innocence that is always already lost through original sin, Kierkegaard writes:

> In this state [of innocence] there is peace and repose, but there is simultaneously something other (*noget Andet*) that is not contention and strife, for there is indeed nothing against which to strive. What, then, is it? Nothing (*Intet*). But what effect does nothing have? It begets dread.[8]

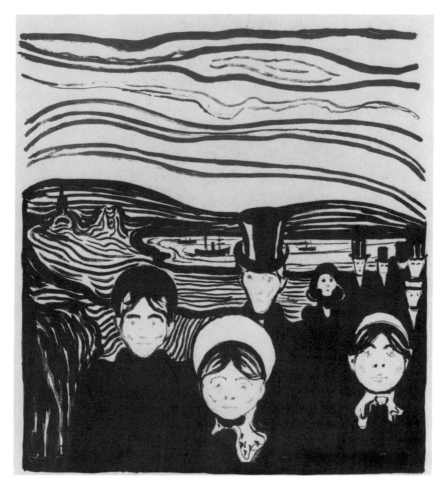

Figure 18. Edvard Munch, *Anxiety*, courtesy of The Sarah G. and Lionel C. Epstein Collection.

The dread of nothing renders Elisabeth dumb. Throughout most of the film she does not speak. While Munch's *Scream* is silent, Bergman's silence screams. Elisabeth's silence breaks out suddenly while she is on stage. The character she is portraying, the persona she is wearing is Electra.

Electra is, of course, the daughter of Agamemnon and Clytemnestra, who returns with her brother, Orestes, to avenge the death of her father by murdering his murderers—her mother and her mother's lover Aegisthus. In 1913, while Munch was redrawing *The Scream*, Jung introduced the notion of the "Electra complex" into psychoanalytic discourse. Freud immediately rejected (or repressed) Jung's reinterpretation of the mother and her death.[9]

These apparently free associations point to another intriguing sequence of signs: Bergman . . . El-izabeth . . . El-ectra. If we read this sequence backward, questions emerge about the impossible "source" of *Persona*. Is Bergman's persona Elizabeth's persona? Does this *Persona*/persona refigure *The Dead Mother and Her Child*? Who or what is El(le)?

# # # #

. . .

Kierkegaard has a secret—a secret he never tells or tells repeatedly by not telling:

> After my death no one will find in my papers the slightest information (this is my consolation) about what really has filled my life; no one will find the inscription [*den Skrift* (*Sk-rift*); cf. German *der Riss*, rift, rent, cleft, fissure, gap, break, flaw, rupture] in my innermost being that interprets everything and that often turns into events of prodigious (*uhyre*) importance to me that which the world would call bagatelles and which I regard as significant if I remove the secret note (*hemmelige Note*) that interprets them.[10]

In the absence of this secret note, how can Kierkegaard's texts be read? *Can* they be read or are they unreadable? Does the tolling of this uncanny note hollow out Kierkegaard's texts as if from within? Is this note the echo of *le glas* that sounds the death of the mother? Does Kierkegaard write or does something Other secrete "his" texts? Does this Other render all his names—even Søren Aabye Kierkegaard—pseudonyms or personae? Why did Kierkegaard forever defer writing the modern version of Antigone he promised? These questions (and others) return repeatedly to disrupt every proposed reading. The *atopos* of this displacement remains (the) secret.

Unthinkable Thoughts that Wound from Behind

> . . . my whole huge literary work had just one idea: to wound from behind.[11]

> . . . she stared at me from the depths of an extreme past, a wild place, towards an extreme future, a desert place.[12]

Figure 19. Edvard Munch, *The Dead Mother and Her Child*, courtesy of The Sarah G. and Lionel C. Epstein Collection.

If I always arrive late (and I do), if I am always secondary (and I am), then I am *always* already in debt. To be in debt always is to be in debt from the beginning and without end. This catastrophic debt cannot be repaid. Books, therefore, never balance. Forever accountable for this impossible imbalance, which I/the "I" did not create but which in a certain sense creates me/the "I," my debt is my guilt. *Meine Schuld ist meine Schuld.* My guilt, which is not exactly "mine," is "original"–original because it is without origin. This abysmal guilt raises an unanswerable question: To whom or what am I, to whom or what is the "I" in debt? I do not know . . . the "I" cannot know. Not knowing to whom or what I am in debt, I am in debt to that which is unknown. In other words, the nonoriginal origin of my guilt is (the) unknown. "What, then, is the unknown?"

The question is not my own; it is the question of an other – Kierkegaard's pseudonym, Johannes Climacus:

> What, then, is the unknown (*Ubekjendte*)? It is the boundary (*Grændsen*) that is continually arrived at, and therefore when the determination of motion is replaced by the determination of rest it is the different, the absolutely different (*det absolut Forskjellige*). But it is the absolutely different in which there is no distinguishing mark. Defined as the absolute-different (*det Absolut-Forskjellige*), it seems on the verge of being disclosed, but not so, because the understanding cannot even think the absolutely different; it cannot absolutely negate itself but uses itself for that purpose and consequently thinks the difference in itself, which thinks it by itself. It cannot absolutely transcend itself and therefore thinks as above itself only the sublimity that it thinks by itself. If the unknown (the God) is not solely the boundary, then the one thought about the different is confused with the many thoughts about the different. The unknown is then in [dispersion], and the understanding has an attractive selection from among what is available and what fantasy can think of (the prodigious, the ridiculous, etc.).[13]

The unknown, Kierkegaard through the persona of Johannes Climacus (whose improper name I abbreviate J. C.) argues, is the boundary, border, frontier, or limit that is not merely different but is *absolutely* different. What, one might ask, is the difference between difference and absolute difference? Absolute difference "is" the difference of the between that creates the time and space for specific differences to emerge and pass away. If absolute difference were not always differing from itself, it might be called difference as such. When difference is radical, it is, in terms Kierkegaard uses elsewhere, "infinitely and qualitatively different" or "qualitative heterogeneity" (*qvalitative*

Ueensartethed).[14] That which is infinitely and qualitatively different is Other–wholly Other. This other difference or eternally differing Other "is" the difference that makes possible all difference and every difference.

So understood, *det Absolut-Forskjellige* can also be named "God." "God" is the sign of the unknown to which I am always already in debt. This sign is, however, strange. Appearances to the contrary notwithstanding, "God" is never a proper name but is the pseudonym of the unknown that is un-nameable. Implicitly repeating J. C.'s insight, Blanchot explains:

> The name God signifies not only that what is named by this name does not belong to the language in which this name intervenes, but that this name, in a manner difficult to determine, would still be a part of it [i.e., language] even if this were set aside. The idolatry of the name or simply the reverence that makes it unpronounceable (sacred) is related to this disappearance of the *name* that the name itself makes appear, and which forces language to rise up where it conceals itself until forbidding it. Far from lifting us to all the lofty significations that theology authorizes, it gives rise to nothing that would be proper to it: a pure name that does not name, but is rather always about to name, the name as name, but, in that way, not at all a name, without nominative powers, hung on language as if by chance and thus passing on to it its (devastating) power of nondesignation that relates it to itself.[15]

Since understanding operates by reducing difference to identity and returning otherness to same, it cannot think the pure name that does not name. In attempting to conceive *det Absolut-Forskjellige*, understanding gives birth only to itself. J. C. concludes:

> If a human being is truly to come to know something about the unknown (the God), he must first come to know that it is different from him, absolutely different from him. The understanding cannot come to know this by itself . . . ; if it is going to come to know this, it must come to know this from the God, and if it does come to know this, it cannot understand this and consequently cannot come to know this, for how could it understand the absolutely different?[16]

Unable to conceive absolute difference in and by itself, awareness of the Other must come from without–from an outside that is irreducibly exterior. Forever approaching from elsewhere, the Other bears an unbearable gift that is *ein Gift, un don* that is *un coup, un coup de don* that is *un coup de grâce*.

This unthinkable *coup*, which, having always already been suffered, inevitably approaches from behind, inflicts a mortal wound upon the understanding. The mark of this wound is a paradox. As the sign of the absolutely different, this paradox is itself absolute. The Absolute Paradox is the impossible *conicidentia oppositorum* that emerges when the wholly Other draws near in and through a likeness from which it nonetheless remains totally different. In a draft for *Philosophical Fragments*, Kierkegaard explains:

> First he must know the difference, but this he cannot know by himself. The difference that he himself provides is identical with likeness, because he cannot get outside himself. If, then, he comes to know the difference, he comes to know it absolutely and comes to know the absolute difference, and this is the first paradox. Now follows the second, that in spite of this absolute difference, the God must be identical with man, and not with humanity but with this individual human being. But the moment he comes to know that the God is absolutely different from him, he also comes to know that he himself is absolutely different from the God.[17]

The "disclosure" of the absolutely different always results in an unresolvable contradiction. Revelation is at the same time concealment. The totally Other repeatedly approaches by withdrawing and withdraws by approaching. Never present as such and yet not precisely absent, the Other remains forever "incognito." The incognito of the God is not a fanciful disguise or playful pseudonym but is the inescapable persona of the Other that can never communicate directly.

The paradox, which as J. C. (whose initials now become suggestive) insists, "specifically unites the contradictories, is the eternalizing of the historical and the historicizing of the eternal."[18] As the site or nonsite of the intersection of differences, the Absolute Paradox inscribes a certain boundary, border, margin, limen, or threshold. This threshold that escapes understanding is something like a shibboleth, which, we have discovered, permits passage but resists translation. The untranslatable shibboleth "is the cipher of the cipher, the ciphered manifestation of the cipher as such. And when a cipher manifests itself as what it is, that is to say, in encrypting itself, it does not say to us 'I am a cipher.' It may still conceal from us, without even wanting to, the secret that it shelters in its very readability. It moves, touches, fascinates, or seduces us all the more. The ellipsis and caesura of discretion inhabit it, there is nothing it can do about it, it is a passion before it becomes a calculated risk, before it risks a strategy of encryptment, or a poetics of ciphering intended, as with Joyce [and Kierkegaard], to keep the professors [and priests] busy for generations."[19]

The indecipherable secret encrypted in the Absolute Paradox constitutes the passion of understanding that discloses understanding's impotence:

But one must not think ill of the paradox, for the paradox is the passion of thought, and the thinker without passion is like the lover without passion: a mediocre fellow. But the ultimate potentiation of every passion is always to will its own downfall, and so it is also the ultimate passion of the understanding to will the collision, although in one way or another the collision must become its own downfall. This, then, is the ultimate paradox of thought: to want to discover something that thought itself cannot think.[20]

The paradox of thought is that understanding both *must* and *cannot* think the unthinkable or know the unknowable. Understanding must struggle to discover something that thought itself cannot think, for only in pushing itself to its limit can understanding constitute itself by establishing the legitimate bounds of its activity. And yet this very border that is constitutive of understanding also marks the uncrossable threshold that forever faults its activity. Understanding, in other words, presupposes that which it cannot contain, express, grasp, or domesticate. J. C. implies that understanding inevitably harbors what Blanchot describes as the "(devastating) power of nondesignation." The power of nondesignation is inscribed as *det Absolut-Forskjellighed*, which (impossibly) cannot be designated. This "nonsignifying difference" is, in a certain sense, "insignificant." Paradoxically, this strangely insignificant difference is "the condition of sense in language." Absolute Difference "is untranslatable, not because of some inaccessibility of its meaning to transference, not simply because of some semantic secret, but by virtue of that in it that forms the cut of a non-signifying difference in the body of the (written or oral) mark."[21]

The untranslatability of Absolute Difference is, at least in part, a function of its uniqueness or once-and-for-allness. Over against Hegel, J. C. argues that the Absolute Paradox does not re-present a universal truth that is present in all places at all times. To the contrary, the Absolute Paradox is the sign of a *unique* and *unrepeatable* event. It is the uniqueness of the event to which Kierkegaard points when he contends that "the God must be identical with man, and not with humanity but with this individual human being." If, however, an event is unique, *can* it really be dated? Or *must* an event be unique to be dated?

On the one hand, uniqueness, which, by definition, is unrepeatable, is the condition of the possibility *and* the impossibility of the date. On the other hand, repetition, which by definition, is not unique, is the condition of the possibility *and* the impossibility of the once-and-for-allness of the date. Dating, in other words, presupposes a repetition that the singularity of every event makes possible and interrupts. The repetition that dating presupposes erases the very uniqueness of the event the date is supposed to mark. The date, therefore, commemorates that which cannot be dated. The signs through which one attempts to date actually designate by de-sign-ating. "These coded marks all involve the same shift: while assigning or consigning the singularity of an event to a particular place and time, they must, at the same time, in the possibility of commemoration, mark themselves off from themselves. In effect, they mark only insofar as their readability enunciates the possibility of a recurrence, and the recurrence of that which precisely cannot return, the possibility, let us say then, of a spectral return of that which, unique in its occurrence, will never return. A date is a specter."[22]

This specter of the date, which we have previously encountered in another context, implies an Other from which everything has always already been sent. When this message from the Other is an Absolute Paradox, it can be read as the Word. A "nonsignifying difference," the undatable Word is an unreadable paradox inscribed in sacred scripture. Derrida points out:

> What comes to pass in a sacred text is the occurrence of a *pas de sens*. And this event is also the one starting from which it is possible to think the poetic or literary text that tries to redeem the lost sacred and there translates itself as its model. *Pas de sens* – that does not signify poverty of meaning but no meaning that would be itself, meaning, beyond any "literality." And right there is the sacred. The sacred surrenders itself to translation, which devotes itself to the sacred. The sacred would be nothing without translation, and translation would not take place without the sacred; the one and the other are inseparable. It is the absolute text because in its event it communicates nothing, it says nothing that would make sense beyond the event itself.[23]

The Absolute Paradox, written in the absolute text, leaves an unanswerable question for the reader: How can one communicate nothing? Perhaps by (the) not telling (*ne pas le dire*) (of) a secret – as when Abraham speaks by remaining silent or remains silent by speaking. "First and foremost," Johannes de Silentio observes, Abraham "does not say anything, and in that form he says what he has to say."[24]

Crypts

> What is a crypt? No crypt presents itself. The grounds are so disposed as to disguise and to hide: something, always a body in some way. But also to disguise the act of hiding and to hide the disguise: the crypt hides as it holds. Carved out of nature, sometimes making use of probability or facts, these grounds are not natural. A crypt is never natural through and through, and if, as is well known, *physis* has a tendency to

encrypt (itself), that is because it overflows its own bounds and encloses, naturally, its other, all others. The crypt is thus not a natural place, but the striking history of an artifice, an *architecture*, an artifact: of a place *comprehended* within another but rigorously separated from it, isolated from general space by partitions, an enclosure, an enclave. So as to purloin *the thing* from the rest. Constructing a system of partitions, with their inner and outer surfaces, the cryptic enclave produces a cleft (*un clivage*) in space, in the assembled system of various places, in the architectonics of the open square within space, itself delimited by a generalized closure, in the *forum*. Within this forum, a place where the free circulation and exchange of objects and speeches can occur, the crypt constructs another, more inward forum like a closed rostrum or speakers box, a *safe*: sealed, and thus internal to itself, a secret interior within the public square, but, by the same token outside it, external to the interior.[25]

There is something *hemmelighedsfuld, uhyggelig, unheimlich* about Abraham. This uncanniness seems to have something to do with the cutting edge of secrecy. Abraham cuts and is cut . . . cuts off and is cut off. He is cut off from others by the Other—the Other he cannot name but nevertheless (impossibly) names "God . . . God, the Father." The gift of the Father is the *coup* that separates one from others as well as from oneself. This separation (*secretus*) creates a secret that *cannot* be told.

Though not immediately apparent, Johannes de Silentio (J. S. for short) is deeply concerned about the issue of translation. More precisely, Johannes is preoccupied with the implications of the inevitability of mistranslation. Throughout his meditation on Abraham, he is concerned with the painful collision between rational reflection and ethical obligation, on the one hand, and, on the other, the absurdity of religious claims and demands. According to J. S., the ethical and the rational are inseparable: the ethical is rational and the rational is ethical. For the rational ethicist and ethical rationalist, translation (*trans*: across + *latus:* carried) involves something like a metaphorical process. Metaphor is "the figure of speech in which a name or descriptive term is transferred to some object different from but analogous to that to which it is 'properly' applicable." In this transference process, something is supposed to appear in and through something else. The vehicle delivers the tenor. The aim of transference is the safe arrival (after a momentary delay) of what is transported. The goal of translation, in other words, is readability. A "good" translation should be lucid, leaving as little ambiguity as possible.

The rational-ethical is first and foremost *universal*—that is, all-encompassing and comprehensive. Within any such inclusive totality, there is supposed to be no outside or exterior that is not actually incorporated or potentially assimilable. For the rational person, J. S. explains, there ought to be "no residual incommensurability" (*der intet Incommensurabelt bliver*). Senseless remains defer rational comprehension and remaining sensuousness frustrates the accomplishment of duty. Everything that differs from the universal must be sublated. For the thinker devoted to reason and the actor dedicated to morality, what "wisdom amounts to is the beautiful proposition that basically everything is the same" (*at i Grunden er Alt der Samme*).[26] The law of the rational-ethical is "the law of the same." Within the regime of ethics, there is nothing or no one who is outside the law. When every outside is inwardized and every exterior recollected, the rational-ethical becomes "a perfect, self-contained sphere."

The realization of this comprehensive and comprehensible sphere presupposes the effective translation of difference to same and the actual transference of particular to universal. The interplay of particular and universal renders both of them metaphorical. At one moment, the particular is the vehicle and the universal the tenor, and at another, the universal is the vehicle and the particular the tenor. When one becomes transparent in and through the other, the metaphor is properly comprehended. Successful translation insures the perfect readability that is the goal of reason and ethics. The person who is both reasonable and ethical – ethical because reasonable and reasonable because ethical:

> Knows that it is beautiful and beneficial to be the single individual who translates himself into the universal (*der oversætte sig selv i det Alt*), the one who, so to speak, personally produces a trim, clean, and, as far as possible faultless (*feilfri*) edition of himself, readable for all (*læselig for Alle*). He knows that it is refreshing to become understandable to himself in the universal in such a way that he understands it, and every individual who understands him in turn understands the universal in him, and both rejoice in the security of the universal. He knows it is beautiful to be born as the single individual who has his home (*har sit Hjem*) in the universal, his friendly abode, which immediately receives him with open arms if he wants to remain in it.[27]

For a translation to be perfectly readable, there cannot be anything that remains hidden, concealed, or cryptic. Rational-ethical translation demands not only the carrying over of the particular into the universal and the universal into the particular; it also requires the transference of the inner to the outer:

> The ethical as such is the universal; as the universal it is, in turn, the disclosed, the revealed (*Aabenbar*). The single individual, qualified as immediate, sensate, and psychical, is hidden, concealed, disguised (*Skjulte*). Thus his ethical task is to work himself out of hiddenness and to become disclosed in the universal. Every time he desires to remain

hidden, he trespasses and is immersed in temptation from which he can only emerge by revealing himself.[28]

What the rationalist-ethicist refuses to acknowledge is that such transgression might be inescapable and guilt therefore unavoidable. Translation, after all, might be impossible. Something might always be missed in translation. Transference might inevitably leave something out. The untranslated could be untranslatable. What slips between the lines and thus is not said might remain unsaid because it is unsayable. Perhaps some secrets cannot be told. Perhaps (un)certain interiors are irreducibly cryptic. Abraham seems to think so, but he is not speaking.

Abraham is a "knight of faith" who responds to an Other he cannot understand. He believes – "by virtue of the absurd." "The absurd," J. S. explains, "does not belong to the differences (*Differentser*) that lie within the proper (*eget*) domain of understanding."[29] The faithful response to the Other that exceeds the differences constitutive of understanding singles out the individual from all other individuals. The relationship to the absolutely different differentiates absolutely. Faith is the "paradox that the single individual is higher than the universal." The singularity of the believer is a remainder that *cannot* be comprehended by reason and *cannot* be assimilated by morality. This breach renders Abraham guilty and strikes him dumb. Abraham's silence is no ordinary silence. It is the profound silence of difference itself, the difference that is "the Absolute-Difference":

Abraham remains silent – but he *cannot* speak. Therein lies the distress and anxiety. Even though I go on talking day and night without interruption, if I cannot make myself understood when I speak, then I am not speaking. This is the case with Abraham. He can say it all (*Han kan sige Alt*), but one thing he cannot say, and if he cannot say that – that is, in such a way that the other understands it – then he is not speaking. The relief provided by speaking is that it translates me (*oversætter mig*) into the universal. Now, Abraham can describe his love for Isaac in the most beautiful words to be found in any language. But this is not what is on his mind; it is something deeper, that he is going to sacrifice him because it is a trial. No one can understand the latter, and thus everyone can only misunderstand the former.[30]

Even when Abraham tries to speak, language inevitably fails. "Speak he cannot; he speaks no human language. And even if he understood all languages in the world, even if those he loved also understood them, he still could not speak – he speaks a divine language, he speaks in tongues."[31]

This silence faults language and deepens the paradox surrounding the singular individual. From the rational-ethical perspective, *"das Äussere (die*

Entäusserung) is higher than *das Innere.* " The outer that is higher than the inner is the revelation of an outwardness that is, paradoxically, the result of the "interiorizing" (*Er-innerung, Er-rindring*) of all exteriority. For Abraham, by contrast, "interiority (*Inderlinghed*) is higher than exteriority (*Yderlighed*)." "The paradox of faith," according to J. S., "is that there is an interiority that is incommensurable with exteriority, an interiority that is not identical, please note, with the first but is a new interiority."[32] This "new interiority" is an extraordinary inwardness. Not simply an inner that is the opposite of an outer, this interiority somehow remains exterior. "The inside of the soul," Blanchot avers, "coincides absolutely with the inside of the divinity; the most secret interiority opens on the Other."[33] The secret interior that exposes one to the Other eliminates all closure and faults every identity. The hollowing out of identity through the process of elimination forms an invaginated crypt that cannot be opened. This inaccessible tomb haunts language by leaving it forever open. Language that is always open to and opened by an Other is irreducibly cryptic.

Communicatio Interruptus: S/Tex(t)ual Secretions

Secrets secrete secretions. To secrete (*secretio*, from *secernere*) is to separate. "In an animal or vegetable body," secretion is "the action of a gland or some analogous organ in extracting certain matters from the blood or sap and elaborating from them a particular substance, either to fulfill some function within the body or to undergo excretion as waste." From the perspective of the body proper, secretions are not merely improper but are actually disgusting:

> Disgust from an item of food, a piece of filth, waste, or dung. Spasms and vomiting protect me. Repulsion, the retching that thrusts me to the side and turns me away from defilement, sewage, and impurity. The shame of compromise, of *l'entre-deux*, of betrayal. The fascinated start that leads me toward and separates me from them.
> Food disgust is perhaps the most elementary and most archaic form of abjection. When the eyes see or the lips touch that skin or surface of milk—harmless, thin as a sheet of cigarette paper, pitiful as a nail pairing—I experience a gagging sensation and, still farther down, spasms in the stomach, the belly; and all the organs shrivel up the body, provoke tears and bile, increase heartbeat, cause forehead and hands to perspire. With the vertigo that confuses sight, *nausea* makes me balk at that milk cream, separates me from mother and father who present it to me. "I" want none of that element, sign of their desire; "I" want to know nothing of it, "I" do not assimilate it, "I" expel it. But since the food is not an "other" for "me," who am only in their desire, I expel *myself*, I spit

myself out, I abject *myself* within the same motion through which "I" pretend to pose myself. That detail, perhaps insignificant, but one that they ferret out, emphasize, evaluate, that trifle turns me inside out like a glove, guts sprawling; it is thus that *they* see that "I" am in the process of becoming an other (*un autre*) at the expense of my own death.[34]

Secretions, it seems, are always *entre-deux*. While a secret is an outside that is inside, a secretion is an inside that is outside. Who or what secretes? If not I or the "I," then perhaps an Other, perhaps the Other that "I" am in the process of becoming at the expense of my own death.

Though often white, secretions can also be black; though often sexual, secretions can also be textual. Who or what secretes textual remainders . . . remainders that are indigestible *smuler*: crumbs, scraps, fragments?

Kierkegaard is something of a ventriloquist. The ventriloquist spills his or her guts by speaking from the belly (*tolku*, talk + *udero*, belly). Ventriloquists, of course, do not speak directly. They speak indirectly by speaking through an other who cannot speak and who is, therefore, a dummy. Kierkegaard's dummies are his pseudonyms. By assuming various personae, Kierkegaard attempts to communicate indirectly. Indirect communication "says" by not saying. The not-saying of the pseudonyms betrays a secret that cannot be told. The task of the writer, Kierkegaard indirectly suggests, is to *write* in order not to *say*. "First and foremost," the writer "does not say anything, and in that form he says what he has to say." Not to say anything might be to write nothing.

Kierkegaard does not, however, write only pseudonymous texts. Sometimes he sheds his personae and speaks in "his own" name. But do the texts signed by Søren Aabye Kierkegaard really leave ventriloquism behind? Or do they imply that the speaker/author is a dummy who speaks for an Other? In the posthumously published *The Point of View for My Work as an Author*, Kierkegaard, speaking in "his own" name, claims that he never speaks in his own name but always speaks for an Other:

> From the very beginning I have been as it were under arrest and every instant I have sensed the fact that it was not I that played the part of the master, but that an other (*en Anden*) was master. I have sensed this with fear and trembling when he let me feel his omnipotence and my nothingness (*Intethed*); I have sensed it with indescribable bliss when I turned to him and did my work in unconditional obedience.[35]

The *Anden* that Kierkegaard names "God" is the same Other that J. C. names *det Absolut-Forskjellige*—the Absolute-Difference. This different difference, we have discovered, "is" the difference of the between . . . *la différence de l'entre-deux*. Never able to speak directly, the Other always speaks through others. Søren Aabye Kierkegaard, author of authors, is himself a ventriloquist's dummy for an Other he can never know. Appearances to the contrary notwithstanding, Kierkegaard *never* speaks in "his own" name; his works always bear witnesses to an Other. "Kierkegaard's" discourse (is) in other words, is always the discourse of the Other.

While always remaining secret, the discourse of the Other nonetheless secretes by separating the self from itself and isolating the self from others. When secrets cannot be told, discourse becomes dis-course. Dis-course interrupts the com-uni-cation it also makes possible. In a brief essay entitled "Interruptions," Blanchot writes:

> Interruption is necessary for any sequence of words. The gap makes becoming possible. Discontinuity assures continuity of understanding. . . . But there is another kind of interruption, more mysterious and more important. It introduces waiting, which measures the distance between two speakers, and not the reducible distance, but the irreducible. . . . This time, there is no unifying effort. . . . Now, what is at stake is the strangeness between us, and not only that obscure part that escapes our mutual knowledge and is nothing but the obscurity of being within the "I"—the singularity of the singular "I"—a strangeness that is still relative (an "I" is always close to another "I", even in difference, competition, desire, and need). What is at stake now and has to be accounted for is all that separates me from the other, that is to say, the other insofar as I am infinitely separate from him: separation, cleft, gap that leaves him infinitely outside me, but also claims to found my relation with him on this very interruption that is an interruption of being—otherness through which he is, I must repeat, for me neither I, nor another existence . . . but the unknown in its infinite distance.[36]

The unknown in its infinite distance haunts Kierkegaard and everything "he" writes. Never speaking only for himself, Kierkegaard's name is improper rather than proper. Who or what is (a) *Kierkegaard*? When used as a common rather than a proper noun, *kierkegaard* means cemetery:[37]

> The Self: a cemetery guard. The crypt is enclosed within the self, but as a strange, foreign place, prohibited, excluded. The self is not the proprietor of what he guards. He makes the rounds like a proprietor, but only the rounds. He turns around and around, and in particular he uses all his knowledge of the grounds to turn visitors away. "He stands there firmly, keeping an eye on the comings and goings of the nearest of kin

who claim – under various titles – to have the right to approach the
tomb. If he agrees to let in the curious, the injured parties, the detectives, it will only be to serve them with false traces and fake tombs."[38]

Mor(e) Crypts

> But then the understanding stands still, as did Socrates, for now the
> understanding's paradoxical passion that wills the collision awakens
> and, without really understanding itself, wills its own downfall. It is the
> same with the paradox of erotic love. A person lives undisturbed in
> himself, and then awakens the paradox of self-love as love for an Other,
> for one missing or lacking (*en Anden, til en Savnet*).[39]

> Thus, the cryptic place is also a sepulcher. The topography has taught
> us to take a certain nonplace into consideration. The sepulchral func-
> tion in turn can signify something other than simply death. A crypt,
> people believe, always hides something dead. But to guard it from
> what? Against what does one keep a corpse intact, safe both from life
> and from death, which could both come in from the outside to touch it?
> And to allow death to take no place in life? . . . The inhabitant of a
> crypt is always a living dead, a dead entity we are perfectly willing to
> keep alive, but *as* dead, one we are willing to keep, as long as we keep
> it, within us, intact in any way save as living.[40]

Mor(e) crypts: I am going to betray Kierkegaard by telling you a secret.
A secret about Kierkegaard that might be the secret of secrets that secretes
the texts written in "his own" name and in the name of others or an Other.
The secret of secrets is that the secret is a crypt and the crypt is the *atopos* of
death. But whose crypt? Whose death?

Exploring the uncanny "*atopos* of death," Derrida contends that "cryptic
incorporation always marks an effect of impossible or refused mourning."[41] It
is possible that the infamous melancholy of Kierkegaard has something to do
with such mourning. Freud, author of the well-known essay "Mourning and
Melancholy," concludes the section of his study of "The Uncanny," which
opens with his analysis of Hoffmann's story of "The Sand-Man," by observing:

> To conclude this collection of examples, which is certainly not com-
> plete, I will relate an instance taken from psychoanalytic experience; it
> furnishes a beautiful confirmation of our theory of the uncanny. It often
> happens that male patients declare that they feel there is something un-
> canny about the female genital organs. This *unheimlich* place, however,
> is the entrance to the former *heim* (home) of all human beings, to the

place where everyone dwelt once upon a time and in the beginning. There is a humorous saying: "Love is home-sickness"; and whenever a man dreams of a place or a country and says to himself, still in the dream, "this place is familiar to me, I have been there before," we may interpret the place as being his mother's genitals or her body. In this case, too, the *umheimlich* is what was once *heimisch*, homelike, familiar; the prefix "un" is the token of repression.[42]

To re-cite a question apparently forgotten: Does the *hemmelige Note* that Kierkegaard "removes" from his writings echo *le glas* that sounds the death of the mother? Is the secret inhabitant of Kierkegaard's strange texts the mother who is a living dead—a dead entity he is perfectly willing to keep alive, but *as* dead? Does *mor*(e) crypt—always crypt? The Danish word *mor*, which is pronounced like the English word "more," means mother. Is this the *mor* encrypted in *la mor-t* commemorated by the cryptic writings of Kierkegaard?

The mother is absent—totally absent—from Kierkegaard's writings. The father, by contrast, is present—ever-present. Nowhere is the father more present than in the passage from Hoffmann's writings, which, I have noted, Kierkegaard cites in a foreign language:

Wie sprach er zu sich selbst ein Mensch, der die geheimsten Gedanken seiner Bruder erforscht, bringt über den diese verhängnisvoll Gabe nicht jenes entsetzliches Verhältnitz, welches den ewigen Juden traf, der durch das bunteste Gewühl der Welt, ohne Freude, ohne Hoffnung, ohne Schmerz, in dumpfer Gleichgültigkeit, die das caput mortuum der Verzweiflung ist, wie durch eine unwirthbare trostlose Einöde wandelte?

The one harboring *die geheimsten Gedanken* becomes an exile who, like Abraham, roams, wanders, and errs endlessly. Whose secret condemns one to such unsettling exile? For Kierkegaard, as for Abraham, it is the secret of the Father.

From one point of view, Kierkegaard's entire corpus can be read as a prolonged struggle not to tell the secret of the father. The question that remains after the *oeuvre* achieves closure is whether his silence nevertheless betrays this secret. If betrayal takes place, it would be through what is *not* written. Of the many works Kierkegaard did not write, one is of particular interest. Kierkegaard promises to write a modern version of *Antigone*. Though the promise is never completely fulfilled, he provides several hints about the play that might have been. One of his most tantalizing clues appears in an essay entitled "The Ancient Tragic Reflected in the Modern Tragic: An Essay in the Fragmentary." The title page of the essay indicates that it was originally a lecture read before a meeting of the *Symparanekromenoi. Symparanekromenoi* is an impossible word that Kierkegaard coins. The translators of *Either-Or* suggest that this Greek term can best be rendered as "the fellowship of buried lives." The unnamed author seems to imagine himself addressing a society comprised of persons "who for one cause or another, are living lives which are spiritually or mentally entombed and isolated."[43] In the course of his address, the speaker proposes a new reading of Antigone:

> Labdakos's family is, then, the object of the indignation of the angry Gods. Oedipus has slain the sphinx, liberated Thebes; he has murdered his father, married his mother, and Antigone is the fruit of this marriage. Thus goes the Greek tragedy. Here I diverge from the Greek. All the relationships are the same in mine, and everything is different. That he has slain the sphinx and liberated Thebes is known to everyone, and Oedipus lives honored and admired, happy in his marriage with Jocasta. The rest is hidden from the eyes of men, and no suspicion has ever called this terrifying nightmare into actuality. Only Antigone knows it. How she has come to know it lies outside the tragic interest, and everyone is free to work out his own explanation in regard to it. At an early age, before she was fully developed, dim suspicions of this dreadful secret (*denne rædsomme Hemmelighed*) had at times gripped her soul, until certainty with a single blow cast her into the arms of anxiety.[44]

Having realized the transgression of the father, Antigone devotes her whole life to guarding his secret. The secret of the father becomes the secret of the child:

> Proud she is of her secret (*sin Hemmelighed*), proud that she has been selected in a singular manner to save the honor and renown of the house of Oedipus; and when the grateful people acclaim Oedipus with praise and gratitude, then she feels her own importance, and her secret sinks even deeper into her soul, still more inaccessible to every living being. She feels how much responsibility is placed in her hands, and this gives her a supernatural greatness (*overnaturlige Størrelse*), which is necessary if she is to engage our attention as tragic.[45]

The secret of the father is, of course, the violation of the mother. This is the unspeakable crime Antigone cannot betray.

This modern-day Antigone is another persona through which Kierkegaard attempts to speak indirectly. The identification of author and mask is explicit in a Journal entry dated November 20, 1842:

> No doubt I could bring my Antigone to an end if I let her be a man. He forsook his beloved because he could not keep her together with his

private agony. In order to do it right, he had to turn his whole love into a deception against her, for otherwise she would have participated in his suffering in an utterly unjustifiable way.[46]

The beloved is Regina, the woman Kierkegaard always loved but could not marry. Though he never told her directly, Kierkegaard repeatedly insists throughout his writings and Journals that his religious vocation makes it impossible for him to wed her or anyone else. Kierkegaard's individual, private relation to the Father who is Other—wholly Other—interrupts his life by cutting him off from all others. As J. S.'s account of Abraham makes clear, the relation to the Father is a secret that cannot be told. But questions still remain: Who is the father of the Father? And what is *his* secret? Answers are not clear. In what remains the best biography of Kierkegaard, Josiah Thompson offers an engaging vignette of Søren's aging father. After returning from a brief shopping trip, the old man sinks into his favorite chair to read a book on theology:

> As on so many occasions recently, he couldn't keep his mind on the text. Perhaps it was just that he was getting older. No. It was something else, something more foreboding, as if the past held some secret which, if he could just remember it properly, would explain everything. But try as he might, he couldn't make it out.[47]

Couldn't or *wouldn't* remember?

Michael Pederson Kierkegaard was a man whose life was interrupted by death: the death of two wives and the death of five of his seven children. The demands of his highly successful textile business prevented him from marrying until he was in his late thirties. In 1794 Michael married Kirstine Røyen, the sister of his business partner, Mads Røyen. Two years later she died, leaving Michael childless. On April 27, 1797, before the year of mourning had expired, Michael married Ane Sørensdatter Lund, who had been Kirstine's maid. Less than five months after the marriage, the couple's first child, Maren Kirstine, was born. To say that Michael was ambivalent about the marriage would be an understatement. His marriage contract included the following clause: "should the unexpected happen, that the temperaments cannot be united, it must be permitted us to live separate from table and bed, in which case my future wife will take her body linens and clothes, in addition to which I will give her once and for all 300 rigsdaler yearly as long as she lives."[48] In spite of such uncertainty, the marriage survived. In the years that followed, Ane bore six more children, the youngest of whom, Søren Aabye was born on May 5, 1813, when Ane was forty-five and Michael was fifty-six. Having buried three of her seven children, Ane died on July 31, 1834.

Michael's relation to Søren was no less ambivalent than his relation to Ane. On February 2, 1797 – less than three months after his fortieth birthday – Michael signed over his flourishing business to M. A. Kierkegaard and Christian Agerskov, and completely withdrew from the world of business and commerce to devote himself to theological reading and religious reflection. The date of *la retraite* is of critical importance. Michael and Ane, I have noted, married on April 27, 1797, and Maren Kirstine was born in September 1797. Maren must have been conceived in December 1796. It is probable that Michael learned of the likelihood of Ane's pregnancy late in January 1797. Within a matter of weeks or even days he gave up his business and turned away from public life.

The theology that preoccupied Michael reflects the Protestant pietism that was then sweeping Denmark. One of the chief tenets of this religious outlook is the thoroughgoing sinfulness of human nature. Sin is inextricably bound up with sensuality in general and sexuality in particular. In the years following his retirement, Michael became increasingly obsessed with his guilt and need for redemption. He saw in his youngest son the possibility for the salvation he so ardently desired. Søren was to be Michael's Isaac – the son sacrificed in the name of the Father. Toward that end, Michael subjected Søren to an extraordinarily rigorous religious upbringing. The relationship to the father left an indelible impression on the son. Looking back on his youth, Søren remarks:

> It's terrible when I think, even for a single moment, over the dark background that from earliest time was part of my life. The dread with which my father filled my soul, his own awful melancholy, the many things in this respect I can't write down.[49]

What can't Kierkegaard write about the father?

Though always passionately devoted to Michael, Søren became increasingly anxious about the inheritance of guilt his father had left him. This anxiety eventually led to a conflict between father and son. In 1838, several months before the death of the father (August 8, 1893), Kierkegaard records in his Journal what he describes as "the great earthquake":

> Then it was that the great earthquake (*den store Jordrystelse*) occurred, the frightful upheaval that suddenly drove me to a new and infallible principle for interpreting all the phenomena. Then I surmised that my father's old-age was not a divine blessing, but rather a curse, that our family's exceptional intellectual capacities were only for mutually harrowing one another; then I felt the stillness of death deepen around me, when I saw in my father an unhappy man who would survive us all, a

memorial cross on the grave of all his personal hopes. A guilt must rest on the entire family, a punishment of God must be upon it: it was supposed to disappear, obliterated by the mighty hand of God, erased like a mistake, and only at times did I find a little relief in the thought that my father had been given the heavy duty of reassuring us all with the consolation of religion, telling us that a better world stands open for us even if we lost this one, even if the punishment the Jews always called down on their enemies should strike us: that remembrance of us would be completely *obliterated*, that there would be no trace of us.[50]

Kierkegaard never explains what precipitated this "earthquake." This strange event seems to be *det hemmelige Note* that he "removes" from all his writings.

Or *almost* removes. Seven years *après coup* Kierkegaard offers a possible clue in the most "autobiographical" of his pseudonymous writings, " 'Guilty?'/'Not Guilty?': A Passion Narrative, A Psychological Experiment by *Frater Taciturnus*," published on April 30, 1845, as the third part of *Stages on Life's Way*. This diary, purportedly written by a "certain" Quidam, recounts the painful process by which a young man breaks his engagement because of what he believes to be his religious obligation. The story is repeatedly interrupted by entries dated midnight on the fifth of every month that have nothing to do with the events Quidam records.[51] Though not immediately apparent, these entries are allegorical accounts of Kierkegaard's personal life. In the present context, the most important allegory is entitled "Solomon's Dream." In this *aparté*, Quidam or Frater Taciturnus or Kierkegaard or an Other (it remains unclear who the author is) writes:

Thus Solomon lived happily with the prophet Nathan. The father's strength and the father's achievement did not inspire him to deeds of valor, for in fact no occasion was left for that, but it inspired him to admiration, and admiration made him a poet. But if the poet was almost jealous of his hero, the son was blissful in his devotion to the father.

Then one day the son visited his royal father. In the night he awoke at hearing movement where the father slept. Terror seizes him, he fears it is a villain who would murder David. He steals nearer–he beholds David with a crushed and contrite heart, he hears a scream [*Skrig*–perhaps an anticipation of *The Scream*] of despair from the repentant soul.

Faint, powerless, impotent (*Afmægtig*) at the sight, he returns to his couch, he falls asleep, but he does not rest, he dreams, he dreams that David is an ungodly man, rejected by God, that the royal majesty is the sign of God's wrath upon him, that he must wear the purple as a punishment, that he is condemned to rule, condemned to hear the people's benediction, whereas the Lord's righteousness secretly and hiddenly (*skjult og forborgent*) pronounces judgment upon the guilty one; and the dream suggests the suspicion that God is not the God of the pious but of the ungodly, and that one must be an ungodly man to be God's elect— and the terror of the dream is this contradiction.

While David lay upon the ground with shattered and contrite heart, Solomon arose from his couch, but his understanding was shattered. Terror seized him when he thought of what it was to be God's elect. He suspected that holy intimacy with God, the sincerity of the pure man before the Lord, was not the explanation, but that a secret guilt (*lønlig Skyld*) was the secret (*den Hemmelighed*) that explained everything.

And Solomon became wise, but he did not become a hero; and he became a thinker, but he did not become a man of prayer; and he became a preacher, but he did not become a believer; and he was able to help many, but he was not able to help himself. . . . There was a split or rift in his nature (*Der var sat Splid i hans Væsen*), and Solomon was like the paralytic who is unable to support his own body.[52]

The secret of the father splits the son. The son, in other words, is (always already) a split subject. Solomon's relation to his father, David, points to the nonoriginal origin of this split or rift.

Secret(ions)

At the turn of the year, when kings take the field, David sent Joab out with his other officers and all the Israelite forces, and they ravaged Ammon and laid seige to Rabbah, while David remained in Jerusalem. One evening David got up from his couch and, as he walked about on the roof of the palace, he saw from there a woman bathing, and she was very beautiful. He sent to inquire who she was, and the answer came, "It must be Bathsheba daughter of Eliam and wife of Uriah the Hittite." So he sent messengers to fetch her, and when she came to him, he had intercourse with her, though she was still being purified after her period, and then she went home. She conceived, and sent word to David that she was pregnant. [2 Samuel 11:1–5]

Upon receiving word of Bathsheba's pregnancy, David ordered Joab to "Put Uriah opposite the enemy where the fighting is fiercest and then fall back, and leave him to meet his death" (2 Samuel 11:15). Uriah was killed and the most powerful king of ancient Israel married the wife of his victim. The son of David and Bathsheba was Solomon.

Søren is Solomon; Michael is David; Ane is Bathsheba. The story of Solomon is the story of the violation of the mother by the father. Because the son (Søren) identifies with the father (Michael), the son bears the guilt of the father's sin. The guilt of the father visited upon the son is complex, for Michael's sin involves multiple violations. On the most obvious level, Michael violates Ane by having intercourse with her out of wedlock. His bastard child, Maren Kirstine, testifies to this violation. It is also clear that this deed is a breach of religious duty and ethical obligation. Michael's turn to pietistic religion reflects his sensitivity to this aspect of his transgression. There are, however, less obvious dimensions of Michael's guilt. Ane, I have noted, had been the maid in the household of Michael and his first wife. The violation of Ane is at the same time a violation of Kirstine. As Thompson points out, "Long into the second marriage the old man continued to think of his first wife as the real one."[53]

The far-reaching implications of Michael's transgression are inseparably bound up with Ane's social status. It is too simple to regard the union of Michael and Ane as merely a matter of convenience. The economy of desire is always social as well as sexual. In their analysis of *The Politics and Poetics of Transgression*, Peter Stallybrass and Allon White argue:

> The opposition of working-class maid and upper-class male, then, depended upon a physical and social separation which was constitutive of desire but it was a desire which was traversed by contradictions. On the one hand, the "lowness" of the maid reinforced antithetically the status of the gentleman. . . . But on the other hand [the gentleman] worshipped [the maid's] physical strength and contrasted it to his own puniness and whiteness. . . . The maid, then, was not only a figure of "lowness;" she was also a figure of comfort and power.[54]

The power of the maid is often associated with sexuality. In the bourgeois household of the nineteenth century (and Michael and Kirstine's household was nothing if not bourgeois), "the upper middle-class parent rarely took 'any active part in the physical care of toddlers or infants.' "[55] As Freud's case histories make clear, part of this care involved direct and indirect initiation into sexual matters. It is, after all, the nurse and not the mother who explains "the meaning" of "The Sand-Man" to the children:

> On certain evenings his mother used to send the children to bed early, warning them that "the Sand-Man was coming;" and, sure enough, Nathaniel would not fail to hear the heavy tread of a visitor, with whom his father would then be occupied for the evening. When questioned about the Sand-Man, his mother, it is true, denied that such a person

existed except as a figure of speech; but his nurse could give him more definite information: "He's a wicked man who comes when children won't go to bed, and throws handfuls of sand into their eyes so that they jump out of their heads all bleeding. Then he puts the eyes in a sack and carries them off to the half-moon to feed his children. They sit up there in their nest, and their beaks are hooked like owls' beaks, and they use them to peck up naughty boys' and girls' eyes with."

The maid's bedtime stories are at least partly constitutive of the child's desire as well as its repression. In the absence of the mother, the maid becomes the mother.

It seems that Michael and Ane had no maid. Apparently Michael thought there was no need for a maid; Ane was already his domestic. But what role did Ane play in the economy of the Kierkegaard household? What secrets did she tell? Or not tell? Since none of the children left any direct testimony, it is impossible to be certain. However, since Ane was both mother and maid, it seems unlikely that she was as domesticated as Michael presumed. Never completely at home in the house of the father, Ane always remained *uhyggelig* . . . *unheimlich*. The fascination of the *uhyggelig/unheimlich* results from the simultaneity of attraction and repulsion. The strange "object" of desire, like the no-thing of anxiety, casts its spell by exercising *"a sympathetic antipathy* and *an antipathetic sympathy."*[56] To succumb to this dread is to become guilty–guilty with what Kierkegaard describes as "Hereditary Sin" (*Arvesynd*). If the sin of the father is visited upon the son, then the sin of the son might be the violation of the mother/maid. Perhaps this is the secret–the unspeakable secret that forever haunts the son and all he writes . . . that forever haunts every son and every text.

But the son's sin never actually took place, or the sin took place as not having taken place. That which never takes place or takes place as not taking (a) place is never present. Never present, the sin of the son is always already past and thus always yet to come. Having been exiled for a fantastic transgression, the son, following the traces of the Wandering Jew, searches for an inaccessible *heim* bordered by an uncrossable heimen. There is no end to this search.

Mor(e) crypts. *Mor* crypts. More crypts. The secret of secrets seems to be the mother who "is" not, or is not present, though she is not absent. Her impossible presence/unbearable absence could be the secret that secretes. This might be the secret Kierkegaard's texts betray . . . betray by *not* telling. In all of his published writings and throughout the twenty volumes of his Journals and Papers, Søren never once mentions the name Ane Sørensdatter Lund. There is, however, a fragment . . .a fragment dated 1836.

Children who remember their mother–[57]

Was Kierkegaard such a son? Do his texts, which express "love for an Other, for one missing or lacking," commemorate the m-other? Is the m-other who is never named the unnameable? A ventriloquist, I neglected to mention, speaks not only from the belly but also from the womb–*ventriloquism: tolku*, talk + *udero*, belly, womb. Kierkegaard . . . "a cemetery guard. The crypt is enclosed within the self, but as a strange, foreign place, prohibited, excluded. The self is not the proprietor of what he is guarding. He makes the rounds like a proprietor, but only the rounds. 'He stands there firmly, keeping an eye on the comings and goings of the nearest of kin who claim–under various titles–to have the right to approach the tomb. If he agrees to let in the curious, the injured parties, the detectives, it will only be to serve them with false traces and tombs."

If the secret of Kierkegaard's cryptic writings is the crypt that (impossibly) keeps alive the dead mother *as* dead, then every sentence he writes is, in effect, a "death sentence." Kierkegaard might well have summarized *The Point of View for My Work as an Author* by citing the concluding words of Blanchot's *L'Arrêt de Mor[-]t*:

As for me, I have not been the unfortunate messenger of a thought stronger than I, nor its plaything, nor its victim, because that *thought,* if it has conquered me, has only conquered through me, and in the end has always been equal to me. I have loved it and I have loved only it, and everything that happened I wanted to happen, and having had regard only for it, wherever it was or wherever I might have been, in absence, in unhappiness, in the inevitability of dead things, in the necessity of living things, in the fatigue of work in the faces born of my curiosity, in my false words, in my deceitful vows, in silence and in the night, I gave it all my strength and it gave me all its strength, so that this strength is too great, it is incapable of being ruined by anything, and condemns us, perhaps, to immeasurable unhappiness, but if that is so, I take this unhappiness on myself and I am immeasurably glad of it and to that thought I say eternally, "Come," and eternally it is there: *"Viens," et èternellement elle est là.*[58]

Elle . . . who . . . *El-le?* Is *El-le* the persona of *El?* Or is *El* the persona of *El-le?*[59]

12.

How to do Nothing with Words

Is there really nothing new to try? I mentioned
my hope, but it is not serious. If I could speak
and yet say nothing, really nothing.

Samuel Beckett

The ideal of literature might be this: to say
nothing, to speak and say nothing.

Maurice Blanchot

The face-to-face with the text has replaced the
face-to-face with God.

Edmond Jabès

Beyond the End

The end of theology is approaching . . . has always been approaching . . .
approaching from the beginning . . . even "before" the beginning . . . approaching without ever arriving . . . approaching "before" the beginning and
without end. The endless approach of the end of theology harbors an end that
is not merely an end *of* theology but is another end . . . a different end that is
not the end of difference. This alternative end, which eludes the closed
economy of ontotheology, implies the irreducible opening of the a/theological
imagination. The task of thinking at the end of theology is to think beyond
the end of theology by thinking the "beyond" of an end that is not theological.
This "beyond," which is neither simply immanent nor transcendent, has been
left unthought throughout the theological tradition. Indeed, theologies traditionally have been constructed in order *not to think* this strange end. But what
has theology not thought?

In an important essay entitled "The End of Philosophy and the Task of Thinking," Heidegger maintains that "Hegel, as little as Husserl, as little as all metaphysics, does not ask about Being as Being, that is, does not raise the question of how there can be presence as such."[1] From Heidegger's point of view, Western ontotheology attempts to comprehend everything by returning all things to their origin. Different philosophical and theological positions represent contrasting accounts of the original ground from which everything emerges and to which (the) all returns. This ground is always the ground of being—even when the notion of being is not explicitly invoked or appears in the guise of *a* being rather than being as such. Being, moreover, is that which is *present*. To be is to be present, though presence need not always be immediately present. If being is primal, everything else is secondary or derivative. To understand the originality of being is to grasp that which stands under all things.

In thinking the being of beings, ontotheology leaves nothing unthought. This claim must be understood in at least two ways. In the first place, originary or foundational thinking seeks to be comprehensive. To think the ground of all things is to comprehend everything. Belief in all-inclusive understanding need not necessarily claim that everything is actually grasped here and now but does imply the conviction that all things are *in principle* comprehensible. The assertion of total comprehension might require recourse to a point of view that transcends human awareness either as the actuality of divine self-consciousness or as the eschatological possibility of complete vision for human beings who now see through a glass darkly.

In the second place, ontotheology leaves nothing unthought by not thinking nothing. More precisely, ontotheology thinks nothing as reducible to or derivative from being. The most important formulation of the identity of being and nothing is presented in the introductory paragraph of the first chapter of Hegel's *Science of Logic*:

> *Being, pure being*, without any further determination. In its indeterminate immediacy it is equal only to itself. It is also not unequal relatively to an other; it has no diversity within itself nor any with a reference outwards. It would not be held fast in its purity if it contained any determination or content that could be distinguished in it or by which it could be distinguished from an other. It is pure indeterminateness and emptiness. There is *nothing* to be intuited in it, if one can speak here of intuiting; or, it is only this pure intuiting itself. Just as little is anything to be thought in it, or it is equally only this empty thinking. Being, the indeterminate immediate, is in fact *nothing*, and neither more nor less than *nothing*.[2]

Within the bounds of Hegel's dialectical logic, to insist that being is nothing is to claim that nothing is being. The nothing that is identical with being is no thing—no determinate thing or no thing in particular. If nothing is interpreted as no thing, it turns out to be nothing other than the fullness of being. When understood in this way, Hegel's dialectical logic expresses the truth glimpsed in various forms of negative theology. Since the ground of all things is no thing, it seems that we can speak of this ground, if at all, only negatively. Some negative theologians go so far as to argue that the primal ground of everything is even beyond being itself. This "beyond being," however, does not break with being but is, in the words of Meister Eckhart, "hyperessential being" (*überwesendes Wesen*). So understood, the beyond *of* being still belongs *to* being. Negative philosophers and theologians from Plotinus and Pseudo-Dionysus to Nicholas of Cusa and Jacob Boehme anticipate the conclusion that forms the foundation of Hegel's entire System: being and nothing are One. In the final analysis (and for Hegel and his precursors analysis is never interminable), difference gives way to identity—even when identity and difference are understood dialectically.

Throughout the ontotheological tradition, being is privileged in ways other than the reduction of nothing to being. Nothing can also be viewed as the absence *of* being. In this case, being defines nothing as the absence that constitutes its essence. The absence that defines nothing, however, remains bound to and by the presence of being. From this point of view, nothing is the presence of the absence of being. Tillich presents a variation of this account of the relationship between being and nothing when he argues that nothing is a negative and hence derivative concept. Interpreting nothing as nonbeing, which constitutes itself by the negation of being, Tillich argues:

> In a metaphorical statement (and every assertion about being-itself is either metaphorical or symbolic), one could say that being includes nonbeing but nonbeing does not prevail against it. "Including" is a spatial metaphor that indicates that being embraces itself and that which is opposed to it, nonbeing. Nonbeing belongs to being, it cannot be separated from it.[3]

Since nonbeing is the negation of being, it is dependent upon being, which transcends it as the creative ground of everything as well as of nothing. By grounding nonbeing in being, Tillich represses rather than thinks nothing.

Nothing lies "beyond" ontotheology. This nothing is the unthought that we are now called to think. The nothing that remains to be thought is not simply the opposite of being but "is" *neither* being *nor* nonbeing. As such, it does not exactly exist and yet is not nonexistent—it is not precisely present without being absent. As the difference between being and nonbeing as well as presence and absence, nothing might point toward something like a response to the unasked question of ontotheology: How can there be presence as such? The task of thinking at the end of theology is to think nothing otherwise than by not thinking. The nothing remaining after (the) all has been thought marks the end of theology by inscribing an end that does not belong to theology. This end implies the closure of theology, which at the same time is the opening of a previously unimaginable a/theology. To think this opening, it is necessary to think otherwise by learning to write differently. For the a/theologian, the question that repeatedly returns is: How to do nothing with words?

Linguistic Turnings

"The sign and the divinity," Derrida argues, "have the same place and time of birth. The age of the sign is essentially theological. Perhaps it will never *end*. Its historical *closure* is, however, outlined."[4] The age of the sign is theological because it is inscribed within the economy of re-presentation that presupposes a structure of reference grounded in the actual or possible presence of a transcendental signified. The sign is comprised of a signifier and a signified. The signifier points beyond itself to a signified that completes the sign by filling it with meaning. In different terms, the signifier signifies by re-presenting a signified. As the condition of the possibility of significant signs, the signified is transcendental. While not always explicitly theological, the transcendental signified is implicitly theological inasmuch as it is the ground of meaning. Like being itself, this ground assumes different forms at different moments in the Western tradition.

In what follows, I will examine four strategies of signification: constative, expressive, performative, and poetic. In the course of the analysis, it will become apparent that each of these interpretations of the linguistic sign falls within the economy of representation and thus is still ontotheological. To think beyond the end of theology, it is necessary to think beyond representation by thinking after the age of the sign.

The economy of representation is essentially mimetic. The signifier is intended to render present the signified through a process of reflective imitation. The goal of mimesis is the perfect transparency of the signified in the signifier. On the most basic level, signification is constative. Signs are words that describe by referring to things. Description and reference succeed when a word re-presents a thing or state of affairs that exists independent of and prior to the process of signification. A sign that does not or cannot refer is both insignificant and meaningless. The constative understanding of the sign involves an ambiguity that is rarely acknowledged. While intended to represent the signified in the signifier, the act of representation is actually the de-presentation of thing in word. Instead of representing something that is primordially present, the sign stands for an irreducible absence. Within the referential structure of the constative sign, the signifier inevitably remarks the presence of the absence that the sign is intended to erase.

The referential relation of signifier and signified is not limited to the interplay between word and thing or subject and object. Reference can also be intrasubjective.[5] When signifier and signified are both "within" the subject, the sign is expressive. The expressive sign can take at least three forms: ideational, emotional, and intentional. Accordingly, the meaning of a signifier can be understood in terms of a signified idea, feeling, or intention expressed by the signifying subject.

Signs can represent not only things but also ideas.[6] In this case, to understand the signifier is to grasp the idea standing behind it. Instead of translating thing into word, the ideationally expressive sign re-presents an idea through a linguistic signifier. The represented idea might be understood in terms of a self-conscious thought, the divine logos, idealistic logic, linguistic structures, or an archetypal or linguistic unconscious. What unites these otherwise contrasting readings of the sign is the agreement that signification involves a structure of reference in which the signifier points beyond itself to a signified that is in some sense ideational. The signified idea secures the foundation of meaning by establishing a clear referent for the expressive signifier. To read such a sign, one must reverse the process of expression by returning to the signified origin from which the signifier arises. If this origin is accessible, the sign is meaningful; if it is inaccessible, the sign is meaningless. While transparency is the goal of the constative sign, clarity is the ideal of the ideationally expressive sign.

Expressive signs extend beyond the sphere of ideas to the domain of feelings and emotions. Though statements involving expressive signs often appear to make assertions about objects or states of affairs, they frequently represent feelings or emotions of the asserting subject. Some analysts use the distinction between constative and emotively expressive signs to differentiate statements of fact from ethical and religious claims. A.J. Ayer, for example, argues:

> We begin by admitting that the fundamental ethical concepts are unanalysable, inasmuch as there is no criterion by which one can test the validity of the judgments in which they occur. . . .We say that the reason why they are unanalysable is that they are mere pseudo-concepts. The presence of an ethical symbol in a proposition adds nothing to its factual content. . . . It merely serves to show that the expression of it is attended by certain feelings in the speaker.[7]

For Ayer, a concept is, by definition, an ostensive sign that must be subjected to the criterion of verifiability. Signs that express emotions or feelings cannot be verified and thus yield no true knowledge. Though the emotively expressive sign is not empirically verifiable, it is nonetheless referential. Signifier and signified stand in a mimetic relationship that is isomorphic with the constative sign. Meaning remains referential and the sign representational.

By interpreting ethical statements in terms of emotional expression, Ayer points to a final modality of the expressive sign. Signs might re-present neither ideas nor feelings but the intention to perform certain actions. While the emotively expressive sign is grasped by returning it to the feeling from which it originates, the intentionally expressive sign is understood by referring to the end toward which it is directed. According to R. B. Braithwaite, "Just as the meaning of a moral assertion is given by its use in expressing the asserter's intention to act . . . in accordance with the moral principles involved, so the meaning of a religious assertion is given by its use in expressing the asserter's intention to follow a specified policy of behavior."[8] It is important to distinguish the expression of the intention to act from the act itself. While every expression is in some sense a deed, the statement of an intention is not its execution. When words not only express intentions but are themselves actions, language becomes performative.

Both constative and expressive signs presuppose the structure of reference in which the signifier finds its meaning beyond itself in an antecedent signified that it re-presents. But must language always be referential? In his well-known book *How to do Things with Words*, J. L. Austin claims: "It was for too long the assumption of philosophers that the business of a 'statement' can only be to 'describe' some state of affairs, or to 'state some fact,' which it must do either truly or falsely."[9] Responding to accounts of language deeply influenced by logical positivism, Austin insists that speech does not always refer to antecedent states of affairs, but can bring about states of affairs that previously did not exist. Words are not merely referential; they also perform certain actions. After listing several instances of speech acts, Austin avers: "In these examples it seems clear that to utter the sentence (in, of course, the appropriate circumstances) is not to *describe* my doing of what I should be said in so uttering to be doing or to state that I am doing it: it is to do it. . . . To name the ship *is* to say (in the appropriate circumstances) the words 'I name, etc.' When I say, before the registrar or altar, etc., 'I do,' I am not reporting on a marriage: I am indulging in it."[10]

Commenting on Austin's argument, Derrida explains:

> Differing from the classical assertion, from the constative utterance, the performative's referent (although the word is inappropriate here, no doubt, such is the interest of Austin's finding) is not outside it, or in any case preceding it or before it. It does not describe something that exists

outside and before language. It produces or transforms a situation, it operates; and if it can be said that a constative utterance also effectuates something and always transforms a situation, it cannot be said that this constitutes its internal structure, its manifest function or destination, as in the case of the performative.[11]

While it is not necessary to repeat the details of Derrida's analysis of Austin's account of performative utterance in this context, several points deserve emphasis. In contrast to constative utterances in which the referent is external, the performative's referent "is not outside it" but is internal to the statement. The "referent" is nothing other than the action performed by the statement. The performative is defined by what it does. A performative utterance always does something–always accomplishes some end. So interpreted, performative utterances cannot do nothing, or more precisely cannot do nothing with words. To understand exactly what the performative utterance can accomplish, it is necessary to stress that its referent is *internal* to the statement itself. In its performance, the utterance enacts *itself*. Since the performative utterance refers to itself, it is in a certain sense self-referential and autotelic. Its end, in other words, is nothing outside itself–nothing other than the successful completion or fulfillment of itself.

But can the performative's end be accomplished or is it an impossible dream that can never be realized? In the definition of the performative cited above, Austin insists that in order to be effective, the utterance must be made "in the appropriate circumstances." The question is whether the appropriate circumstances can ever be met. If the performative is to be successful (and it is important to note that an unsuccessful performative is no performative at all), the performing subjects must engage in their activity sincerely and self-consciously. Derrida points out:

> [One of the circumstances necessary for performative utterance] classically remains consciousness, the conscious presence of the intention of the speaking subject for the totality of his locutory act. Thereby, performative communication once more becomes the communication of an intentional meaning, even if this meaning has no referent in the form of a prior or exterior thing or state of things. The conscious presence of the speakers or receivers who participate in the effecting of a performative, their conscious and intentional presence in the totality of the operation, implies teleologically that no *remainder* escapes the present totalization. No remainder, whether in the definition of the requisite conventions, or the internal and linguistic context, or the grammatical form or semantic determination of the words used; no irreducible polysemia, that is no "dissemination" escaping the horizon of the unity of meaning.[12]

Leaving aside the not insignificant question of the possibility of sincere self-consciousness, one is left to wonder whether the remainder that would unsettle the conditions of performative utterance can ever be totally erased. From Derrida's perspective, the totalization of the semantic context requisite for performative utterance can never be realized. The linguistic structures necessary for performative utterance are constituted by an act of exclusion that renders them inevitably incomplete. Thus the condition of the possibility of performative utterance is at the same time the condition of its impossibility.

In addition to the difficulties raised by the inescapable incompletion of linguistic structures, it is possible to discern instabilities in Austin's own argument that pose problems for the successful completion of performative utterances. Austin's whole analysis rests on the distinction between performative and constative utterances. This distinction, however, is not as clear as Austin would have us believe. He begins his sixth lecture by admitting an obscurity he never really overcomes:

> Because we suggested that the performative is not altogether so obviously distinct from the constative—the former happy or unhappy, the latter true or false—we were considering how to define the performative more clearly. The first suggestion was a criterion or criteria of grammar or of vocabulary or of both. We pointed out that there was certainly no one absolute criterion of this kind: and that very probably it is not possible to lay down even a list of all possible criteria; moreover, they certainly would not distinguish performative from constative, as very commonly the *same* sentence is used on different occasions of utterance in *both* ways, performative constative.[13]

This is a remarkable admission. If the difference between constative and performative utterances *remains* obscure, and if clear self-consciousness is a necessary condition of the possibility of successful performative utterances, then can a performative ever be performed? If we can never be certain that a performative utterance is successful, then it seems we can never be sure that its referent is real or its end realized.

The end of the performative utterance, I have noted, is not external but is internal to the utterance itself. The uncertainty that is *necessarily* entailed in the performative utterance interrupts the completion of the autotelic circuit outlined in speech act theory. The question that remains in the wake of this ineradicable uncertainty is whether words sometimes are neither constative nor performative but function as an unthought third that allows words to do nothing.

Before attempting to respond to this question, it is necessary to consider the final strategy of signification identified above: poetic. The difference between constative and performative utterance points toward a shift from a mimetic to a poetic interpretation of language. While mimesis is imitative, poiesis is productive.[14] The productivity of poiesis is a function of the operation of the imagination. Words do not refer to preexisting objects but are products of the creative subject, which, in Ricoeur's terms, introduce a "semantic innovation." The imagination operative in such poetic production is generally understood to be both synthetic and constructive.[15]

In *The Theological Imagination: Constructing the Concept of God,* Gordon Kaufman argues:

> From Kant onward it has been understood that even the simplest experiences of objects are possible for us only because of the elaborate synthesizing powers of the mind: these enable us to bring together and hold together in enduring conceptual unities what is given to us only piecemeal and in separate moments of experience.[16]

The most comprehensive conceptual unity constructed by the imagination is, according to Kaufman, God. The word "God" does not refer to an extramental reality but designates a fabricated notion that functions like one of Kant's regulative ideas:

> God is the ultimate point of reference in terms of which all else is to be understood, and the ultimate focus of life and of human devotion. The technical theological vocabulary—including concepts like aseity, sin, creation, salvation, trinity, providence, miracle, revelation, incarnation, and the like—was developed over the centuries as an articulated schema for expressing and interpreting this claim, and it remains a principal resource and tool for theological work today. However, contemporary theological construction needs to recognize that these terms and concepts do not refer directly to "objects" or "realities" or their qualities and relations, but function rather as the building blocks or reference points which articulate the theistic world-picture or vision of life. For this reason it is a mistake to take over traditional vocabulary and methods uncritically, since these were worked out largely on the assumption that God-language was directly objectivist or referential, and thus they are usually cast in a reifying mode.[17]

What previously had been believed to be an objective reality existing independently of the mind, now is recognized as a construction of the mind itself:

> Since the terms and images which articulate these world-conceptions or world-pictures are never simply representations gained in direct perception, they should not be understood as directly descriptive of objects (of

experience). As products of and constitutive of a poetic or imaginative vision, they are properly understood as essentially elements within and functions of that overarching vision or conception.[18]

Contrasting images ground alternative frameworks of orientation for human life. Rather than being assessed by the accuracy of its re-presentation of objective reality, the validity of a concept is judged by its *usefulness* for the human subject. Kaufman makes this point explicitly when he argues:

> Theology also serves human purposes and needs, and should be judged in terms of the adequacy with which it is fulfilling the objectives we humans have set for it. "The sabbath was made for man," Jesus said, "not man for the sabbath" (Mark 2:27). That is, all religious institutions, practices, and ideas – including the idea of God – were made to serve human needs and to further our humanization (what has traditionally been called our "salvation"); humanity was not made for the sake of religious customs and ideas.[19]

It is important to appreciate the far-reaching implications of the poetic strategy of signification for our understanding of religious statements. Although rarely identified as such, poetic signification underlies many recent efforts to reclaim traditional religious ideas and symbols. While many people have difficulty believing that religious ideas and symbols refer to objective realities, it might be possible to entertain these notions as imaginative constructions that provide useful guidance for practical life. With the emergence of critical self-consciousness, religious ideas and symbols come to be understood as heuristic fictions. Insofar as we are active beings, we must, in Vaihinger's well-known phrase, act "as if" certain ideas are true. More recently, this line of analysis has returned under the guise of neopragmatism. For the pragmatist, the criterion of adjudication between and among competing ideas, symbols, and projects is their utility for individuals and communities. It is, however, neither a philosopher nor a theologian but a poet who best captures the gist of poetic signification. Wallace Stevens explains that in the modern world, "the final belief is to believe in a fiction, which you know to be a fiction, there being nothing other. The exquisite truth is to know that it is a fiction and that you believe it willingly."[20] When no longer a victim of naive faith, one is free to recognize that the objects of belief are unavoidably fictive.

This realization need not lead to nonbelief. Indeed, critical self-consciousness suggests that all awareness is in some sense fictive. In this situation, belief seems both impossible (since its object has "disappeared") and inevitable (since we must believe in order to understand anything). It is not, however, clear that this analysis significantly alters either belief or conduct. All too often, the movement toward what is supposed to be postcritical faith, which, according to Ricoeur, involves a "second naiveté," really amounts to a difference that makes no difference. Old ideas and symbols do not change significantly but return only to be suspended between quotation marks. Though everything seems different, nothing really changes. But does nothing change? And if so, how?

Poetic, like constative, expressive, and performative, signification remains within the economy of representation that is characteristic of ontotheology. To see how and why this is so, it is necessary to realize that the difference between mimesis and poiesis is as unstable as the difference between constative and performative utterance. The mimetic dimension of poiesis becomes apparent when one analyzes the notion of the subject presupposed by poetic signification. Within the framework of poetic signification, signs are nonreferential – that is, they do not refer to independent and antecedent objects or states of affairs. To the contrary, signs represent objects produced by the imagination of the creative subject. What appears to be an independent object is really a construction of the subject. In other words, the signifier represents a signified that is actually an imaginary production of creative subjectivity. The object is, in effect, the objectification of the subject. Through the process of poetic signification, the subject re-presents itself to itself. This structure of signification perfectly mirrors the structure of the modern subject that begins with Descartes and comes to completion in Hegel's speculative or specular System. Sign and subject are thoroughly reflexive, totally self-referential, and, to use a term previously invoked, perfectly autotelic. In representing the sign, the poetic subject produces nothing other than itself; production is autoproduction.

One can discern the mimetic dimension of poiesis by returning to the point at which the notion of poetic production, which still informs most interpretations of reflection, first emerges – nineteenth-century romanticism and idealism. In their important book, *The Literary Absolute: The Theories of Literature in German Romanticism,* Philippe Lacoue-Labarthe and Jean-Luc Nancy chart the genesis of the relationship between the idea of poiesis and the modern conception of the creative subject. The central figures in Lacoue-Labarthe and Nancy's account are the members of the romantic circle that formed in Jena around the Schlegel brothers. Lacoue-Labarthe and Nancy note:

> [Friedrich Schlegel] spoke of the *symbol*[21] – or of the "symbolic forms," whose symbolism consisted, he said, in "that by which, everywhere, the appearance of the finite is placed in relation with the truth of the eternal and, in this manner, precisely dissolved therein." But he also speaks in analogous terms of man himself. Thus, in the *Ideas*: "Think of the finite formed *(gebildet)* into the infinite, and you will think of a man."

Therefore, what was at stake in the question of the formation of form—
in the "religious" question *par excellence*—was indeed the possibility
of thinking the "subject-work," in other words, the becoming-artist of
the work or the absolute auto-production itself: man as the work of art
creating itself, art henceforth identified with the being-artist. It thus
becomes understandable that the "religious" motif of the mediator plays
such an important role in the *Ideas*. In the order of *Bildung* in general, it
is the motif of the subject-work, of the possibility of a presentation of
the infinite as the auto-production of the subject. This is why "idea" 44
makes the mediator "the one who perceives the divine within himself"
and who, in a gesture comparable to (although the inverse of) the movement that animates the Hegelian Absolute, sacrifices himself in order to
present (*darzustellen*) this divinity to all mankind."[22]

The work of art—and it is important to stress that "work" in this context
must be understood as both a noun and a verb—is the autoproduction of the
poetic subject in which it discloses its own divinity. Tzevetan Todorov extends Lacoue-Labarthe and Nancy's analysis when he argues that "rather than
being content to juxtapose forms, the artist has to rival the spirit of nature that
is expressed through these forms. Nature herself is imbued with an artistic impulse; and, conversely, artistic creation extends divine creation. As Novalis
says, 'nature possesses an artistic instinct.' And Friedrich Ast writes: 'Artistic
production (*Bildung*) is consequently as much a goal in itself as the divine production of the universe; and the one is as original and based on itself as the
other: for the two are one and God is revealed in the poet as he produces
(*gebildet*) corporally in the visible universe.' "[23]
Poiesis becomes mimesis when the creative production of the artist im-
itates the creative production of God. Instead of escaping the economy of
representation, such poetic signification re-presents the autoproduction of the
divine subject in the autoproduction of the human subject. As Derrida, commenting on Kant, points out:

> Mimesis here is not the representation of one thing by another, the rela-
> tion of resemblance or of identification between two beings, the
> reproduction of a product of nature by a product of art. It is not the rela-
> tion of two products but of two productions. And of two freedoms. The
> artist does not imitate things in nature, or, if you will, in *natura naturata*,
> but the acts of *natura naturans*, the operations of the *physis*. But since an
> analogy has already been made, *natura naturans*, the art of the creative
> subject, and one could even say, of an artist-god, mimesis displays the
> identification of human action with divine action—of one freedom with
> another freedom.[24]

The identification of human action with divine action marks the end of theology beyond which – or the "beyond" of which – we are now called to think. This beyond is, strictly speaking, unrepresentable. It cannot, therefore, be inscribed within the economy of representation. Insofar as constative, expressive, performative, and poetic strategies of signification remain bound to and by the structure of representation, they cannot think the strange nothing that remains to be thought after the end of theology. Though nonsignifiable, nothing is not insignificant. To think that which is unrepresentable, it is necessary to rethink the binary oppositions that found and ground the economy of representation. As I have suggested, foundational couples like constative/performative and mimesis/poiesis are unstable or "undecidable." Each passes into the other, thereby creating an irreducible obscurity that both beckons and frustrates thought. Derrida contends:

> Such an undecidability is the *condition* of all deconstruction: in the sense of condition of possibility, indeed, efficacy, and at the same time in the sense of situation and destiny. Deconstruction is, *on this condition* and *in this condition*. There is in this a power (a possibility) and a limit. But this limit, this finitude, empowers and makes one write; in a way that it obliges deconstruction to write, to trace its path by linking its "act," always an act of memory, to the promised future of a text to be signed. The very oscillation of undecidability goes back and forth and weaves a text; it makes, if this is possible, a path of writing through the aporia. This is impossible, but no one has ever said that deconstruction, as a technique or a method, was possible; it thinks only on the level of the impossible and of what is still evoked as unthinkable.[25]

The very oscillation of undecidability stages the eternal return of an altarity that can be thought – if at all – only by re-imagining the imagination. The imagination settles nothing . . . settles nothing by unsettling everything . . . unsettles everything by forever oscillating, alternating, vibrating, shaking, trembling. Imagine trembling: the fear of it . . . the fear of it.

Imagine Nothing

The most influential treatment of the imagination in the modern period is presented in Kant's *Critique of Judgment*. Within the Kantian critical philosophy, the imagination functions as a synthetic third that attempts to unite opposites. Kant stresses the importance of the synthetic role of the imagination by the strategic placement of the *Critique of Judgment*. The Third Critique is supposed to resolve the tensions within each of the first two Critiques as well as to unite the analyses of theoretical and practical reason.

The groundwork for this interpretation of the imagination is laid in the First Critique. In a certain sense, Kant's account of the imagination implies a possible answer to the question that Heidegger claims Western metaphysics has never asked: How can there be presence as such? Within the Kantian archetectonic, the imagination is the mental capacity through which objects become *present* to the knowing subject. In the First Critique Kant describes the transcendental imagination as "a fundamental faculty" of the mind, which by uniting intuition and concepts through the schematism, is the condition of the possibility of the presentation of objects to consciousness:

> If each representation were completely foreign to every other, standing apart in isolation, no such thing as knowledge would ever arise. For knowledge is a whole in which representations stand compared and connected. As sense contains a manifold in its intuition, I ascribe to it a synopsis. But to such synopsis a synthesis must always correspond; receptivity can make knowledge possible only when combined with spontaneity. Now this spontaneity is the ground of a threefold synthesis which must necessarily be found in all knowledge; namely, the *apprehension* of representations as modifications of the mind in intuition, their *reproduction* in imagination, and their *recognition* in a concept. These point to three subjective sources of knowledge which make possible the understanding—and consequently all experience as its empirical product.[26]

In anticipation of points developed below, it is important to note that inasmuch as the imagination is the condition of the possibility of all presentation, it cannot itself be properly presented, actually present, or truly re-presented.

In his important study of Kant, Heidegger points out that Kant's argument changes subtly but significantly between the first and second editions of the *Critique of Pure Reason*. From the outset, Kant regards his investigation of the foundation of reason as a daring venture. "The reader," he warns, "must not . . . be deterred by obscurities in these early sections. They are unavoidable in an enterprise never before attempted."[27] As Kant probes deeper and deeper, he is unable to heed his own advice. His *is* finally deterred and turns away from the obscurity surrounding the imagination. As I have indicated, in the first edition of the *Critique of Pure Reason*, Kant describes the imagination as the synthetic third that cannot be reduced to either understanding or intuition. By the time of the second edition, the task of synthesizing intuitions and concepts is taken over by understanding. In other words, Kant erases the synthetic third and replaces it with a binary opposition in which one term (understanding) is privileged over the other (intuition). The imagination "is no longer a 'function' in the sense of an autonomous faculty, but is now a 'function' only in the sense of an operation of the faculty of understanding. While in the first edition, all synthesis, i.e., synthesis as such, arises from the imagination as a faculty not reducible either to sensibility or understanding, in the second edition the understanding alone assumes the role of origin for all synthesis."[28]

As the agency that effects the union of intuition and concepts, the imagination is, in effect, the origin or foundation of knowledge. At some point between 1781 and 1787, this ground turns into an abyss that Kant feels compelled to cover or remove. "By his radical interrogation," Heidegger concludes, "Kant brought the 'possibility' of metaphysics before this abyss. He saw the unknown; he had to draw back. Not only did the imagination fill him with alarm, but in the meantime [between the first and second editions] he had also come more and more under the influence of pure reason as such."[29] Why did the imagination fill Kant with alarm? What was the abyss before which he trembled and from which he fled into the waiting arms of pure reason? The answers to these questions begin to emerge three years later with the publication of the *Critique of Judgment.*

The Third Critique, we have seen, is intended to resolve the tensions within and between the first two Critiques. In keeping with the position developed in the first edition of the First Critique, the agency of synthesis in the Third Critique is the imagination. By setting limits on the role of the imagination in the *Critique of Judgment,* Kant is able to return to the question of the function of the imagination in mental life. Kant insists that esthetic judgment *is not* a matter of knowledge. Instead of stating a relation between subject and object, as must every cognitive assertion, esthetic judgments articulate contrasting relations of the subject to itself. More precisely, different forms of esthetic judgment reflect different relations among the mental faculties of intuition or sensibility, imagination, understanding, and reason. Kant identifies two types of esthetic judgment: beauty and sublimity.

Beauty, Kant maintains, "conveys a finality in its form, making the object appear, as it were, preadapted to our power of judgment, and thus constitutes in itself an object of satisfaction."[30] Form is apprehended by the imagination and *presented* to understanding. A judgment of beauty reflects a harmonious accord between imagination and understanding in which the form of the object appears to be "preadapted" (*vorherbestimmt*) to the judging subject. It is essential to recognize that the harmony discerned in the judgment of beauty is not between subject and object but is intrasubjective. As John Sallis explains:

> The object enters, as it were, into the judgment only as form, through
> the apprehension of its form in imagination, that is, in and through the
> operation of the imagination. Hence, the relation between the object

and the faculties is not a simple external relation of the object to the subject but rather is a relation in which one faculty, namely, imagination, is already involved. Thus, to say that the object is in harmony with the faculties is already to refer to the harmony between those faculties, that is, to the preeminent sense of harmony.[31]

The "preeminent sense of harmony" that constitutes the beautiful grows out of "the free play of cognitive powers." In the first book of the "Analytic of the Beautiful," Kant discloses the significance of this play:

> The cognitive powers brought into play by this representation are here engaged in a free play, since no definite concept restricts them to a particular rule of cognition. Here the mental state in this representation must be one of a feeling of the free play (*freien Spiels*) of the powers of representation in a given representation for a cognition in general. Now a representation, whereby an object is given, involves, in order that it may become a source of cognition at all, *imagination* for gathering together the manifold of intuition, and *understanding* for the unity of the concept uniting the representations. This state of *free play* of the cognitive faculties attending a represenation by which an object is given must admit of universal communication: because cognition, as a definition of the object with which given representations (in any subject whatever) are to accord, is the one and only representation which is valid for everyone.[32]

It is important to understand the precise nature of this free play. Play is free when players are unaffected by anything other than themselves. In esthetic judgment, the subject plays with itself by representing itself (as imagination) to itself (as understanding). The harmony of such autoaffection is expressed in the judgment of beauty, which is the occasion for the judging subject's experience of pleasure:

> The consciousness of mere formal finality in the play of the cognitive faculties of the subject attending a representation whereby an object is given, is the pleasure itself, because it involves a determining ground of the subject's activity in respect of the quickening of its cognitive powers, and thus an internal causality (which is final) in respect of cognition generally, but without being limited to a definite cognition, and consequently a mere form of the subjective finality of a representation in an aesthetic judgment.[33]

Since the object of esthetic judgment is not external to the judging subject but is a representation of the subject, the subject relates to itself in the object that appears to be other than itself. In the course of summarizing Kant's account of beauty, Jean-Luc Nancy underscores the self-reflexivity involved in the judgment of beauty and the autoaffective character of the feeling of pleasure:

> What is the only beauty? The only beauty, or beauty alone, isolated for itself, is the form in its pure accord with itself or, to say the same thing, in its pure accord with imagination, with the faculty of presentation (or formation). Beauty alone, without interest, without concept, or without Idea is the simple accord, which by itself is a pleasure of the thing presented with its presentation. At least modern beauty has tried to be such; a successful presentation without remainder, in tune with itself. . . . The beautiful is the figure that figures itself in accord with itself, the strict accord of the contour with its outline (*tracé*).[34]

Kant's notion of the beautiful implies the romantic idea and symbol as well as the idealistic idea and reason. As proleptic of reason, beauty is not abyssal. That is why it can be enjoyed without fear and trembling. If, as Heidegger suggests, Kant's quest for the foundation of reason leads to an abyss from which he withdraws, the imagination must approach something other than beauty. The other that is beyond beauty is sublime.

While the beautiful presupposes inner harmony that is experienced as pleasure, the sublime interrupts harmonious autoaffection and issues in what Kant describes alternatively as "a negative pleasure" or "a feeling of displeasure, arising from the inadequacy of the imagination":

> For the beautiful is directly attended with a feeling of the furtherance of life, and is thus compatible with charms of a playful imagination. On the other hand, the feeling of the sublime is a pleasure that arises only indirectly, being brought about by the feeling of a momentary check (*einer augenblicklichen Hemmung*) to the vital forces, followed at once by a discharge all the more powerful, and so it is an emotion (*Rührung*) that does not seem to be play, but deadly earnest in the affairs of the imagination. Hence charms are repugnant to it; and, since the mind is not simply attracted by the object, but is also alternately repelled thereby, the satisfaction in the sublime does not so much involve positive pleasure as admiration or respect, which rather deserves to be called negative pleasure (*negative Lust*).[35]

The pleasure of beauty, we have observed, derives from the harmony between the form of an object apprehended by the imagination and the understanding. The sublime, by contrast, *exceeds* every form and *escapes* all formation. Kant argues:

The beautiful in nature is a question of the form of the object, and this consists in limitation (*Begrenzung*), whereas the sublime is to be found in an object even devoid of form, so far as it immediately involves, or else by its presence provokes a representation of unlimitedness (*Unbegrenztheit*), and yet its totality is also present to thought. Thus the beautiful seems to be regarded as a presentation of an indeterminate concept of understanding, the sublime as a presentation of an indeterminate concept of reason.[36]

Whereas the presentation of form to understanding in the judgment of beauty reveals the unity of intuition, imagination, and understanding, the presentation of unlimitedness to reason in the judgment of sublimity discloses differences among intuition, imagination, and reason. Kant explores these differences through a consideration of two modalities of the sublime: mathematical and dynamic.

The sublime erupts at the *limits* of human consciousness. Indeed, the sublime might be understood as the experience of limit as such – if, that is, limit as such could be experienced. Paradoxically, limit is encountered in and through the irreducible excess of the unlimited. In the "Analytic of the Sublime," Kant identifies two orders of excess: magnitude, described as the mathematical sublime, and power, defined as the dynamic sublime.

The mathematical sublime marks the boundary between reason's demand for totality and the imagination's inability to deliver it. In seeking to satisfy reason's desire for "absolute totality," the mind is "pushed to the point at which our faculty of imagination breaks down in presenting the concept of a magnitude, and proves unequal to the task."[37] The tear of the imagination is the opening of the sublime. Kant cites two examples of the mathematical sublime – the Egyptian pyramids and St. Peter's in Rome. In both cases, one is forced to admit that "comprehension is never complete, the totality of reason is repeatedly deferred. At this point, one suffers the feeling "of the inadequacy of his imagination for presenting the idea of a whole within which the imagination attains its maximum."[38]

Something can be *de trop* not only because of its excessive magnitude but because of its excessive power. Anticipating the romantic preoccupation with nature, Kant argues that the dynamic sublime is encountered in the overwhelming power of nature. "In the immeasurableness of nature and the insufficiency of our faculties for adopting a standard proportionate to the aesthetic estimation of the magnitude of its realm," he maintains, "we find our own limitation."[39] The dynamic sublime traces the *difference* between natural power and the human capacity to grasp or master it. As in the case of the mathematical sublime, reason demands a totality the imagination cannot deliver. Rather than an endless series of forms, the dynamic sublime exceeds all form. Kant argues that "in what we are accustomed to call sublime in nature there is such an absence of anything leading to particular objective principles and forms of nature corresponding to them that it is rather in its chaos or its wildest and most irregular desolation, provided size and might are perceived, that nature chiefly excites in us the ideas of the sublime."[40] "In both types of judgments of the sublime [i.e., mathematical and dynamic] the apprehensive moment is thus found to issue in the disclosure of a certain difference. This disclosure is the site of the sublime, its site within experience, within the subject. The authentically sublime—in distinction from those objects commonly but improperly called sublime—is precisely the difference that comes to be disclosed at this site, the difference between nature and the sensible powers of man, imagination constituting the central yet complex element of the latter."[41]

The site of the sublime is a site of difference—irreducible difference that can be reduced to neither identity nor unity. In this uncanny space, which we shall see is also a strange time, understanding and reason are checked and held in suspense. In relation to the sublime, the imagination *is not* synthetic. Instead of reconciling or uniting opposites, the imagination constantly alternates, oscillates, or hovers between differences it simultaneously brings together and holds apart. This ceaseless alternation keeps the imagination in motion and allows it no rest. In one of his most important comments on the imagination, Kant writes:

> The mind feels itself *moved* in the representation of the sublime in nature, while the aesthetic judgments about the beautiful it is in *restful* contemplation (*ruhiger Kontemplation*).[42] This movement, especially in its inception, may be compared to a vibration or tremor (*Erschütterung*), i.e., to a rapidly alternating attraction toward, and repulsion from, the same object. That which is excessive (*das Überschwengliche*) for the imagination (toward which it is impelled in the apprehension of intuition) is, as it were, an abyss (*Abgrund*), in which it fears to lose itself; but for the rational idea of the supersensible it is not excessive but lawful to bring forth such a striving of imagination, and consequently here there is the same amount of attraction as there was of repulsion for the mere sensibility.[43]

This is the abyss from which Kant had turned in the First Critique. The tremor (*Erschütterung*) of the imagination leaves one shaking, shuttering, trembling (*erschütternd*). Far from synthesizing opposites in a comprehensive whole or absolute totality, the imagination disturbs, upsets, unsettles (*erschüttert*). Neither exactly pleasurable nor displeasurable, the sublime is, as I have noted, "a negative pleasure."[44] Rapidly alternating between opposites it cannot unite, the imagination creates a sense of vertigo—as if the foundation were shaking, cracking, tearing . . . as if the ground were falling from beneath one's feet. And yet when one attempts to define the sublime that sets the mind spinning, words fail. The sublime is unpresentable and thus eludes or overflows the economy of representation. Forever unrepresentable, the sublime is never present; never present, the sublime is unrepresentable. If the sublime approaches, which is not to say arrives, it is at the limit, edge, margin, border of form – "in" the gaps, fissures, faults, tears of structure. The sublime, Jean-Luc Nancy explains, "is the unlimited beginning of the delimitation of a form and thus of the state of a form and the form of a state. The unlimited removes itself by delimiting. It does not consist by itself in a delimitation, even if it were negative, for so understood, it still would be precisely a delimitation and the unlimited would end up by having its own form, let us say the form of the infinite."[45]

The unlimited beginning of the de-limitation of form is a strange beginning. It is a beginning that forever withdraws. The space that remains in the wake of this withdrawal allows the presencing that creates the clearing where everything present emerges. The space in which the imagination operates and presencing occurs is in a sense unimaginable:

> The imagination is thus destined to the beyond of the image, which is not a primordial or ultimate presence (or an absense), which the image would present, or which the images would present as non-representable. But the beyond of the image, which is not a "beyond" that is on the limit, is in the *Bildung* of the *Bild* itself and thus is at one with the *Bild*, at one with the outline of the figure, the tracing, the separating-uniting incision, the fluttering scheme: the syncope, which is, in effect, the other name of the scheme, its sublime name, if there are sublime names.[46]

This beyond, which is neither a presence nor an absence, implies a spacing "beyond" yet "within" time. Since the spacing that is the condition of the possibility of presence can never itself be present, it is always already past. By suffering the restraint (*Hemmung*) of the sublime, the imagination draws near what Emmanuel Levinas describes as "the unrepresentable before," which both escapes and releases all represenation. This "before" is not a past present but is a radical past – the "terrifyingly ancient" – that is "before" every present and "antecedent" to all presense. It is, in the words of Maurice Blanchot, *le pas au-delà*:

> Time, time: the step/not beyond (*le pas au-delà*), which is not accomplished in time, would lead outside of time, without this outside being timeless, but there where time would fall, fragile fall, according to

this "outside of time in time" toward which writing would draw us, if it were permitted of us, vanished from us, from writing the secret of the ancient fear.[47]

Le pas au-delà takes us one step closer to nothing. In a certain sense, *nothing is sublime.* The nothing that is sublime is neither the presence of no thing that is everything nor the absence of all things. Neither present nor absent, nothing is, but of course it is not, the margin of difference inscribed in and through the endless alternation of the imagination. This nothing is other—wholly other. Its name, if it had a name, would be altarity. Altarity "is" that "toward which writing would draw us." To think the unthinkable *pas au-delà* is to think the "beyond" that is not the end *of* theology. This beyond can be thought only "within" the unsettling spacing-timing of the nonsynthetic imagination. To think "in" this tear—to think with this tear, is to write "the secret of the ancient fear" with trembling.

Parapraxis

The problem . . . is that the inadequacy of language . . . runs the risk of never being sufficiently inadequate. Lack of language: what this means (to begin with) is two things—a lack with respect to what has to be signified, but at the same time a lack that is the center and the life of meaning, the reality of speech (and the relationship between these two lacks is itself incommensurable). To speak—as we know today—is to bring this kind of lack into play, maintain it and deepen it in order to make it *be* more and more, and in the end what it puts in our mouths and under our hands is no longer the pure absence of signs but the prolixity of an indefinitely and indifferently signifying absence: a designation that remains impossible to annul, even if it carries nullity within it. If it were not this way, we would all have been satisfied with silence long ago.[48]

To write beyond the end of theology is to write the lack of language that is (a) nothing other than the nothing of silence. Neither speech nor silence, this lack of language is inscribed in and as the failure of words. Language fails in what Edmond Jabès describes as "wounded words." The wound of words is a tear that cannot be mended—a tear that can never be wiped away. This tear, which interrupts the system of exchange—linguistic and otherwise, is neither exactly inside nor outside the text. As such, it eludes the economy of representation. That which is neither outside nor inside cannot be represented either referentially or self-reflexively. To write the "beyond" that is not the end of theology, it is necessary to write in a way that is nonreferential without being self-reflexive.

In an effort to describe the distinguishing features of this alternative a/theological writing, I have borrowed a term from Freud: parapraxis. While Freud first uses the term "parapraxis" in a letter to Fliess dated August 26, 1898, he does not define it until he publishes *The Psychopathology of Everyday Life*. In chapter 12, entitled "Determinism, Belief in Chance and Superstition–Some Points of View," Freud explains that a psychical parapraxis "must be in the nature of a momentary and temporary disturbance. The same function must have been performed by us more correctly before, or we must at all times believe ourselves capable of carrying it our more correctly. If we are corrected by someone else, we must at once recognize the rightness of the correction and the wrongness of our own physical process."[49] A parapraxis, then, involves a failure, slip, error, or mistake. This feature of actions categorized as parapraxes, Freud points out, is suggested by the German prefix *ver-*, which is the equivalent of the English mis-:

> There thus remain in this group the cases of forgetting (*Vergessen*), the errors in spite of better knowledge, the slips of the tongue (*Versprechen*), misreadings (*Verlesen*), slips of the pen (*Verschreiben*), bungled actions (*Vergreifen*) and the so-called "chance actions." Language points to the internal similarity between most of these phenomena: they are compounded alike [in German] with the prefix *ver-*.[50]

The slip of the tongue or pen underscores the irreducible errancy of parapraxis. In this case, error *betrays*. Such betrayal always takes place along a border–at the limits of language. J. Hillis Miller points out:

> "Para" is a double antithetical prefix signifying at once proximity and distance, similarity and difference, interiority and exteriority, something inside a domestic economy and at the same time outside it, something simultaneously this side of a boundary line, threshold, or margin, and also beyond it, equivalent in status and also secondary or subsidiary, submissive, as of guest to host, slave to master. A thing in "para," moreover, is not only simultaneously on both sides of the boundary line between inside and out. It is also the boundary itself, the screen which is a permeable membrane connecting inside and outside. It confuses them with one another, allowing the outside in, making the inside out, dividing them and joining them. It also forms an ambiguous transition between one and the other.[51]

Parapraxical writing is the praxis of the "para." This praxis involves the inscription of the boundary, threshold, margin, or limit. To write paraprax- ically is to write the limit as such rather than to write *about* the limit. The "para" inscribed in parapraxis is "inside" the written text as a certain "outside" that cannot be internalized. Thus parapraxical writing falls *between* referential and self-referential discourse. There is an inescapably performative dimension to parapraxis. However, in contrast to performative utterance, which always does *something* with words, parapraxis struggles to do *nothing* with words. It succeeds by failing. By doing nothing with words, parapraxical writing *stages* the withdrawal of that which no text can contain, express, or represent. In *The Writing of the Disaster*, Blanchot explains:

> It is upon losing what we have to say that we speak—upon an imminent and immemorial disaster—just as we say nothing except insofar as we can convey in advance that we take it back, by a sort of prolepsis, not so as finally to say nothing, but so that speaking might not stop at the word—the word that is, or is to be, spoken, or taken back. We speak by suggesting that something not being said is speaking: the loss of what we were to say; weeping when tears have long since gone dry.[52]

It is important to stress that parapraxis is not simply a latter-day version of negative theology. The nothing toward which parapraxis is drawn *is not* the nothing of negative theology. While negative theologians tend to regard nothing as the binary or dialectical opposite of being, the a/theologian interprets nothing as neither being nor nonbeing. Parapraxis, therefore, is no more positive than negative, no more assertion than negation. Instead of employing a strategy of simple negation, parapraxis engages in what Kierkegaard labels "indirect communication." The wound of words renders all discourse indirect. That which is unrepresentable cannot be approached directly but must be approached indirectly through linguistic twistings and turnings that can never be straightened out.

To claim that the discourse of the writer is always indirect is to insist that parapraxis is unavoidably tropological. Words are tropes (*tropos*, a turn), which, as Blanchot explains, are "turned toward that which turns away" (*tourné vers cela qui détourne*).[53] The turnings of parapraxical writing create what Michel de Certeau identifies as "a rhetoric of withdrawal."[54] Describing the operation of mystic speech, de Certeau writes:

> It is by taking words seriously, a life and death game in the body of language, that the secret of what they give is torn from them—and, as St. John of the Cross says in relation to the "holy *doctors*," to do that is to make them confess the secret of their "impotence," of what they cannot "give." One more thing, perhaps, is mystical: the establishment of a space where change serves as a foundation and saying loss is another beginning. Because it is always *less* than what comes through it and

allows a genesis, the mystic poem is connected to the *nothing* that opens the future, the time *to come*, and more precisely, to that single work, "Yahweh," which forever makes possible the self-naming of that which induces departure.[55]

Through an unexpected metalepsis, the past that was never present and hence cannot be re-presented returns as the "*nothing* that opens the future, the time *to come*." The approach of this ever-outstanding future induces an endless departure that is deeply unsettling.

Paradoxically, the "less," which de Certeau suggests, is associated with the "lack" of nothing is at the same time a certain more. Every trop-e, in other words, is always *de trop*–too much . . . excessive. The excess of language is not a result of its inexhaustible plenitude but is a function of its inescapable poverty. To say less, one must always write more. Forever more or less, parapraxical words mean, if they mean anything, only more or less what they seem to say. In this case, the lack of univocity does not point to polysemy but entails a strange "anasemia," which both escapes and engenders discourse.[56] The absence of univocality leaves parapraxical writing irreducibly duplicitous; its meaning is indeterminate, its sense undecidable. Such indeterminacy and undecidability harbor an obscurity that cannot be dispelled.

The obscurity generated by the excessive oscillation or alternation of parapraxical writing recalls the obscurity of the Kantian imagination. This obscurity, we have seen, results from the endless *Erschütterung* of the mind as it struggles vainly to synthesize the opposites between which it is suspended. Parapraxis is a function of the *nonsynthetic* imagination. Instead of uniting or reconciling contraries, the praxis of the para involves disjunctive conjunction and conjunctive disjunction. Every bringing together is at the same time a holding apart and vice versa. The parapraxical imagination, therefore, does not seek to heal the wound of words but keeps the mind open by refusing to mend its tear.

There is, to be sure, a certain violence involved in the nonsynthetic imagination. Again drawing on de Certeau's analysis of mystic speech, parapraxis "denatures language: it removes it from the function that intends an imitation of things. It also undoes the coherence of signification so as to insinuate in every semantic unity the sly and 'meaningless' games of relations that the subject plays with others and itself: it torments words in order to make them say that which literally they do not say."[57]

To undo the coherence of signification, it is necessary to think beyond representation by thinking after the "theological" age of the sign. Words are wounded when language goes astray. The nonsynthetic imagination employs aberrant syntax to create a text that lacks semantic plenitude. This lack is the tear in the text that implies the "unrepresentable before," which is the condition of the possibility of all presentation and thus all re-presentation. The trope that most clearly suggests the strategy of the parapraxical imagination is catachresis (*katakrēsis*, excessive use, misuse, from *katachrēsthai*, to misuse). In *The Ethics of Reading*, J. Hillis Miller points to an important relation between catachresis and Kant's analysis of the imagination:

> The name for this procedure of naming by figures of speech what cannot be named literally because it cannot be faced directly is catachresis or, as Kant calls it in paragraph fifty-nine of the *Critique of Judgment*, "hypotyposis" (hypotypose). Kant's linguistic procedure in this footnote is an example of the forced or abusive transfer of terms from an alien realm to name something which has no proper name in itself since it is not an object which can be directly confronted by the senses. That is what the word *catachresis* means; etymologically: "against usage."[58]

To use language "against usage" is to use language against itself. Aberrant use entails linguistic abuse through which the writer attempts to say the unsayable by allowing language to do violence to itself. The unsaying of language is not the same as mere silence. By simultaneously inscribing and erasing, parapraxis allows the withdrawal of language to approach in and through the tangled lines of the text. These lines weave the disjunctive conjunction and conjunctive disjunction glimpsed when the imagination succeeds by failing to synthesize opposites:

> The combination of two terms substitutes itself for the existence of a third term and positions it as absent. This combination creates a hole in language. It cuts out a pointed space that directs nonlanguage. In this respect also it "deranges the lexic." In a world that is supposed to be entirely written and spoken, thus lexicalizable (*lexicalisable*), it opens the void of an unnameable, it points to an absence of correspondence between things and words.[59]

The absence of correspondence breaks the circuit of communication that it nonetheless leaves open. Writers who do nothing with words are always ex-communicated, for their nonmessage is forever ex-communication. This *ex-* erases without completely removing the economy of re-presentation characteristic of all ontotheological discourse:

> An initial cleavage renders impossible the "ontological" statement that would be the *said* (*le dit*) of the intended thing. The mystical sentence escapes this logic and puts in its place the necessity of only producing in language effects relative to that which is not in language. That which

must be said can only be said in the fissure of the word. An internal cleavage makes words avow or confess the mourning that separates them from what they show.[60]

From this point of view, to write is to mourn. But for whom or for what? Jabès sketches a graphic answer to this question. (See Figure 20.)

The X of the text is the ex- that is forever barred from proper discourse or discourse proper. Within and without the parapraxical text, this X is the trace of what once was named God. The death of God is God's betrayal. This death is the death the writer mourns . . . mourns in a writing that becomes ever-more literary. To appreciate the significance or insignificance of the literary, it is necessary to return to Sartre's question, "What is literature?"

Literature is, above all else, a work of art. The work of art—as both noun and verb—lies along a margin that marks and remarks a limit that brings together what it holds apart and holds apart what it brings together. "Art," after all, derives from *ar,* which means, among other things, joint. A joint, where the excommunicated often hang out, is "a point of connection or articulation." Articulation presupposes the endless alternation of connection and disjunction. The work of art inscribes, without representing, the altarity of this alternation. As Kant's analysis of the sublime suggests, art does not always bring pleasure but often occasions "displeasure" or "negative pleasure." Heidegger effectively de-scribes the pain of the work of art:

> But what is pain? Pain tears or rends (*reisst*). It is the tear or rift (*Riss*). But it does not tear apart into dispersive fragments. Pain indeed tears asunder, it separates, yet in such a way that it at the same time draws everything together to itself. Its rending, as a separating that gathers, is at the same time that drawing, which, like the pre-drawing (*Vorriss*) and sketch (*Aufriss*), draws and joins together what is held apart in separation. Pain is the jointing (*Fügende*) in the tearing/rending that divides and gathers. Pain is the joining or articulation of the rift. The joining is the threshold. It delivers the between, the mean of the two that are separated in it. Pain articulates the rift of the difference. Pain is dif-ference (*Unter-schied*) itself.[62]

The tear of dif-ference is the para inscribed in the praxis of the writer. This dif-ference is written "in" the literary text. In the course of our consideration of Kant's interpretation of beauty, we discovered that for the romantics, the self-reflexive totality that is constitutive of beauty is supposed to be embodied in the literary *oeuvre.* This work, however, is never complete or is

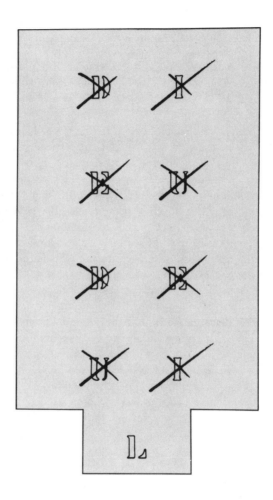

DIEU: God
DEUIL: mourning[61]

Figure 20. Edmond Jabès, *El, or The Last Book.*

forever deferred. Thus literature inadvertently becomes the writing of the failure of the work of art:

> Literature, as we discern it, is held apart from every excessively strong determination, hence it is repugnant to masterpieces and even withdraws

from the idea of a work (*oeuvre*) to the extent that it makes of it a form
of nonwork or unemployment (*désoeuvrement*). Creative, perhaps, but
that which it creates is always hollow with respect to what it is and this
hollowing produces not only what is more slippery, less sure of being,
and because of that, as though attracted to another measure, that of its
unreality where, in the play of infinite difference, that which nonetheless affirms itself by withdrawing under the veil of the not.[63]

The veil of the not is the infinite play of difference. This is not the satisfying play that Kant describes as the beautiful, but is the unsettling play of the
sublime that interrupts all satisfaction. Rather than re-presenting the self to
itself in the play of autoaffection, the play of literature is a heterological performance in which nothing is said by not speaking through writing. In a provocative essay entitled "The Absence of the Book," Blanchot maintains that
"to write is to produce the absence of the work (the out-of-work [*le désoeuvrement*]). Or again, writing is the absence of the work as it *produces itself* through
the work, throughout the work. Writing as unemployment (in the active sense
of the word) is the chance between reason and unreason."[64]

The space *between* reason and unreason is the place or nonplace of
literature. Literature is less a type of writing than a way of writing. "All important literary work," Blanchot argues, "is all the more important when it puts
into work more directly and more purely the meaning of this turning, which at
the moment it emerges, makes the work vacillate or alternate strangely, work
where there is withheld as its always decentered center, the nonwork (*le
désoeuvrement*) : the absence of work. The absence of work whose other name
is madness (*la folie*). The absence of work where discourse ceases so as outside speech, outside language, the movement of writing, under the attraction
of the outside, can come into being."[65]

The absence of the work is not its simple negation. As the duplicitous
word "of" implies, this absence in some sense belongs to the work. It is,
therefore, what Blanchot describes as a "nonabsent absence," which
nonetheless *is not* a presence. More profound than the absence that is the
absence of presence, this nonabsent absence is an other that is wholly other.
Eluding every binary and dialectical economy, this haunting other is nearer
than presence and more distant than absence. When we try to name it, we
can, indeed we must, say nothing. To *say* nothing, however, is to do nothing
with words.

When we do nothing with words, nothing happens. The nothing that
happens when words fail cannot, of course, be experienced. This nothing,
which is neither the presence of the no thing that is the ground of everything nor
the absence of all things, can never be experienced as such. To approach this
limit of experience is to undergo the experience of limit. The limit-experience,
according to Blanchot, is "the experience of nonexperience":

We speak of it as though it were an experience and nevertheless we are never able to say that we have undergone it. Experience that is not a lived event . . . : at most the limit-experience, where perhaps the limits fall and which only reaches us at the limit, when all the future that has become present, by the resolution of the decisive Yes, affirms the grasp upon which there is no more grip (*l'emprise sur laquelle il n'y a plus de prise*). Experience of the non-experience. Detour of all visible and all invisible.[66]

As I approach an end, which I hope is "beyond" the end of theology, I would like to suggest that the liminal experience of nonexperience might be the way in which the sacred is "experienced" today. The sacred *is not* God but is that which remains and approaches when gods fail . . . fail to arrive, to be present, or to be present again in our re-presentations. The failure of God betrays the sacred. The site of this betrayal is the (literary) text inscribed in parapraxis. Through parapraxis, the a/theological writer struggles to restage the sacrifice of the Word. This sacrifice is radical – it is an expenditure without return. The sacrifice of the Word in writing is the betrayal of language that mourns the death *of* God. In the wake of this mourning, nothing is left . . . nothing remains . . . always remains. To write after the death of God . . . to write beyond the end of theology is to betray nothing. To betray nothing by writing . . . to write by doing nothing with words. An impossible dream or the dream of the impossible – the impossible that might impossibly be the "real"?

Write in order not simply to destroy, in order not simply to conserve, in order to transmit; write under the attraction of the impossible real, that share of disaster where every reality, safe and sound, founders.[67]

How to do nothing with words? Write to betray nothing. An end "beyond" the end of theology. An end that never arrives but always betrays.

God: language speaks only as
the sickness of language inasmuch as fissured, split open,
broken, failure that language
recuperates immediately as its
validity, its power, and its
health, recuperation that is
most intimate sickness, of
which God, name always irre-
cuperable, which is always to
be named and never names anything, seeks to cure us, a cure
in itself incurable.

Maurice Blanchot

Notes

Chapter 1

1. Mircea Eliade, *The Sacred and the Profane: The Nature of Religion*, trans. W. R. Trask (New York: Harper and Row, 1961), p. 20.

2. Ibid., p. 68.

3. See *Natural Supernaturalism: Tradition and Revolution in Romantic Literature* (New York: Norton and Norton, 1973).

4. Thomas J. J. Altizer, *Total Presence: The Language of Jesus and the Language of Today* (New York: Seabury, 1980), pp. 31–32.

5. Ibid., p. 33.

6. Altizer devotes one of his early books to an examination of Eliade's works: *Mircea Eliade and the Dialectic of the Sacred* (Philadelphia: Westminster, 1963).

7. Maurice Blanchot, *The Space of Literature*, trans. A. Smock (Lincoln: University of Nebraska Press, 1982), p. 244.

8. Ibid., p. 229.

9. Maurice Blanchot, *Le pas au-delà* (Paris: Gallimard, 1973), p. 8.

10. Blanchot, *Space of Literature*, p. 30.

11. Ibid., p. 238.

12. Heinrich Klotz, *Postmodern Visions: Drawings, Paintings and Models by Contemporary Architects* (New York: Abbeville), p. 9.

13. Anne et Patrick Poirier, *Voyages . . . et caetera, 1969–1983* (Milan: Electra, 1983). This catalogue is for an exhibit in Paris at Chapelle de la Salpêtrière from October 30 to December 5, 1983, and in Milan at the church of San Carpoforo in 1984. Translations from this text are my own.

14. Ibid., p. 72.

15. Ibid., p. 118.

16. Quoted by Claude Gintz in "Ruins and Rebellion," *Art in America* (April 1984), pp. 149–50.

17. Poiriers, *Voyages*, p. 118.

18. Ibid.

19. See "Différance," in *Margins of Philosophy*, trans. A. Bass (Chicago: University of Chicago Press, 1982).

20. See, inter alia, *Visions of Excess, Selected Writings, 1927–1939*, trans. A. Stoekl, C. R. Lovitt, and D. M. Leslie (Minneapolis: University of Minnesota Press, 1985).

21. See, inter alia, "The Origin of the Work of Art," in *Poetry, Language, Thought*, trans. A. Hofstadter (New York: Harper and Row, 1971).

22. Maurice Blanchot, *The Writing of the Disaster*, trans. A. Smock (Lincoln: University of Nebraska Press, 1986), p. 1.

23. Maurice Blanchot, *Thomas the Obscure*, trans. R. Lamberton (New York: David Lewis, 1973), p. 7.

Chapter 2

1. Jacques Derrida, "Living On/Border Lines," in *Deconstruction and Criticism*, Harold Bloom et al. (New York: Seabury, 1984), pp. 172–73.

2. G. W. F. Hegel, *Phenomenology of Spirit*, trans. J. N. Findlay (New York: Oxford University Press, 1977), chapter 6.

3. *Bespangled, Painted and Embroidered: Decorated Masonic Aprons in America, 1790–1850* (Lexington, Mass.: Museum of Our National Heritage), p. 25.

4. Jacques Derrida, *Dissemination*, trans. B. Johnson (Chicago: University of Chicago Press, 1981), pp. 92–93.

5. Hegel, *Phenomenology*, p. 14.

6. Throughout his writings, Derrida relentlessly criticizes Hegel's realized eschatology. In the following text from *Of Grammatology*, Derrida underscores the importance of this issue:

> The horizon of absolute knowledge is the effacement of writing in the logos, the retrieval of the trace in parousia, the reappropriation of difference, the accomplishment of what I have elsewhere called the *metaphysics of the proper* [*le propre*–self-possession, propriety, property, cleanliness, literal]. Yet, all that Hegel thought within this horizon, all, that is except eschatology, may be reread as a meditation on writing. Hegel is *also* the first thinker of irreducible difference. He rehabilitated thought as the *memory productive* of signs. And he reintroduced, as I shall try to show elsewhere, the essential necessity of the written trace in a

philosophical–that is to say Socratic discourse–that had always believed it possible to do without it; the last philosopher of the book and the first thinker of writing. [*Of Grammatology*, trans. G. Spivak (Baltimore: Johns Hopkins University Press, 1976), p. 26.]

See also Jacques Derrida, "Of an Apocalyptic Tone Recently Adopted in Philosophy," *Semeia*, vol. 23 (1982), pp. 63–97.

7. Maurice Merleau-Ponty, *Phenomenology of Perception*, trans. C. Smith (London: Routledge and Kegan Paul, 1978), p. 372.

8. Ibid., p. 415.

9. Maurice Merleau-Ponty, *The Visible and the Invisible*, trans. A. Lingis (Evanston: Northwestern University Press, 1968), pp. 32–33.

10. Bataille, *Visions of Excess*, pp. 57–58.

11. Ibid., p. 215.

12. Ibid., p. 220.

13. See "The Absence of the Book," in *The Gaze of Orpheus*, trans. L. Davis (Barrytown, N.Y.: Station Hill Press, 1981), pp. 145–60.

14. Jacques Derrida, "Différance," in *Margins of Philosophy*, p. 13.

15. Ibid., p. 26.

16. Ibid., pp. 3–4.

17. Jacques Derrida, *Glas* (Paris: Editions Galilée, 1974), pp. 258–59.

18. Ibid., p. 244.

19. Ibid., p. 255.

20. Ibid., pp. 255–56.

21. See above, note 6.

22. Derrida, *Glas*, p. 245.

23. Ibid., p. 252.

Chapter 3

1. Michel Foucault, *Discipline and Punish: The Birth of the Prison*, trans. A. Sheridan (New York: Random House, 1979), p. 200.

2. Somewhere Lacan suggests that the significance of the Freudian revolution might best be understood in terms of the shift from talking in circles to thinking in ellipses.

3. "The return of the book is of an *elliptical* essence. Something invisible is missing in the grammar of this repetition. As this lack is invisible and undeterminable, as it completely redoubles and consecrates the book, once more passing through each point along its circuit, nothing has budged. And yet all meaning is altered by this lack. Repeated, the same line is no longer exactly the same, the ring no longer has exactly the same center, *the origin has played*. Something is missing that would make the circle perfect" (Jacques Derrida, "Ellipsis," in *Writing and Difference,* trans. A. Bass [Chicago: University of Chicago Press, 1978], p. 296).

4. Martin Heidegger, "The End of Philosophy and the Task of Thinking," in *On Time and Being,* trans. J. Stambaugh (New York: Harper and Row, 1972), p. 56. In order to stress the intersection of theology and philosophy, Heidegger describes the Western tradition as "ontotheological."

5. Charles Jencks, *What is Postmodernism?* (New York: St. Martin's Press, 1986), p. 14.

6. Ibid.

7. Heinrich Klotz, "Das Pathos des Functionalismus," *Werk/Architheses,* March 1977 (with reference to a symposium held in Berlin in 1975). See also *Moderne und Postmoderne: Architektur der Gegenwart, 1960–1980* (Braunschweig: Friedr. Vieweg & Sohn, 1985).

8. Friedrich Nietzsche, *The Will to Power,* trans. W. Kaufmann (New York: Random House, 1968), p. 267.

9. Wallace Stevens, *Collected Poems* (New York: Knopf, 1981), pp. 250–51.

10. Wallace Stevens, *Opus Posthumous* (New York: Knopf, 1957), p. 163.

11. Søren Kierkegaard, *The Concept of Irony,* trans. L. Capel (Bloomington: University of Indiana Press, 1969), p. 349.

12. Stevens, *Collected Poems,* p. 251.

13. Heidegger, "Language," in *Poetry, Language, Thought,* p. 204.

14. Blanchot, *Writing of the Disaster,* p. 5.

15. Emmanuel Levinas, *Otherwise than Being or Beyond Essence,* trans. A. Lingis (Boston: Martinius Nijhoff, 1981), p. 9.

16. Ibid., p. 100.

17. Ibid., p. 9. For an elaboration of Levinas's notion of the trace, see "The Trace of the Other," in *Deconstruction in Context: Literature and Philosophy,* ed. Mark C. Taylor (Chicago: University of Chicago Press, 1986), pp. 345–59.

18. Emmanuel Levinas, *Dieu qui vient à l'idée* (Paris: Librairie Philosophique, J. Vrin, 1986), p. 16.

19. Ibid., p. 110.

20. See Maurice Blanchot, *Death Sentence*, trans. L. Davis (Barrytown, N.Y.: Station Hill Press, 1978).

21. Søren Kierkegaard, *Journals and Papers*, trans. Howard and Edna Hong (Bloomington: Indiana University Press, 1967), no. 253.

Chapter 4

1. This letter was written in response to Peter Eisenman's remarkable book PETEREISENMANHOUSEOFCARDS (New York: Oxford University Press, 1987). In addition to reproductions of Eisenman's drawings, plans, models, and photographs of several of his houses, the book contains an essay by Eisenman entitled "*Misreading* Peter Eisenman," as well as critical essays by Rosalind Krauss ("Death of a Hermeneutic Phantom: Materialization of the Sign in the Work of Peter Eisenman") and Manfredo Tafuri ("The Meditations of Icarus").

Chapter 5

1. Thomas J. J. Altizer, *History as Apocalypse* (Albany: State University of New York Press, 1985), p. 254. Hereafter references to this book are given in the text.

2. This essay is a postscript to my earlier assessment of Altizer's work: "Altizer's Originality," *Journal of the American Academy of Religion,* vol. 52, no. 3, pp. 570–84.

3. Jean-Michel Rabaté, "Lapsus ex machina," in *Post-Structuralist Joyce: Essays from the French,* ed. D. Attridge and D. Ferrer (New York: Cambridge University Press, 1984), p. 97.

4. Thomas J. J. Altizer, *The New Apocalypse: The Radical Christian Vision of William Blake* (Ann Arbor: Michigan State University Press, 1967).

5. Jacques Derrida, "Of an Apocalyptic Tone Recently Adopted in Philosophy," p. 81.

6. Freidrich Nietzsche, *Nietzsche Werke: Kritische Gesamtausgabe,* ed. G. Colli and M. Montinari, vol. 4 (New York: Walter de Gruyter, 1978), pp. 48–49. Quoted in Derrida, "Of an Apocalyptic Tone," p. 81.

7. Maurice Blanchot, *Le Dernier Homme* (Paris: Gallimard, 1957). See also *Le denier à parler* (Paris: Editions fata morgana, 1984).

8. I borrow this term from Maurice Blanchot who distinguishes *la voix nar-ratrice* from *la voix narrative* (narrative voice). See, inter alia, "The Narrative Voice (the

'he,' the neuter)," *The Gaze of Orpheus*, pp. 133–42. I will return to the question of the narrative voice in the final section of this essay.

9. For an examination of the role of the "we" in the *Phenomenology*, see Mark C. Taylor, *Journeys to Selfhood: Hegel and Kierkegaard* (Berkeley: University of California Press, 1980), pp. 71–90.

10. Thomas J. J. Altizer, *Total Presence: The Language of Jesus and the Language of Today* (New York: Seabury, 1980), p. 3.

11. Ibid., p. 6. It is important to underscore Altizer's repeated use of terms characteristic of what Heidegger labels "the ontotheological tradition" or what Derrida describes as "onto-eschato-tele-ological" reflection: "purity," "origin," "immediacy," "speech," and "presence."

12. Ibid., p. 7–8.

13. Ibid., pp. 16, 4. For a discussion of the notions of metaphor and allegory that Altizer resists, see Paul De Man, *Allegories of Reading: Figural Language in Rousseau, Nietzsche, Rilke, and Proust* (New Haven: Yale University Press, 1979), especially chapters 7, 9, 10. De Man's analysis is especially helpful, for he presents an alternative reading of some of the writers who play a crucial role in Altizer's argument.

14. Ibid., pp. 15–16.

15. Ibid., p. 18. It is clear that Altizer does not use the term "text" in the way it is currently employed by literary critics. Nonetheless, his insistence on the "speechly" character of *Finnegans Wake* transforms what many regard as a "writerly" text into an "antitext" that is the fulfillment of the book. I will return to the textuality of the *Wake* in my reexamination of the relationship between speech and writing.

16. Ibid., p. 81.

17. Ibid., pp. 86–87. Altizer argues that the true voice of the Gospels is "an anonymous voice" that "is a total presence of voice which can realize itself only by dissolving every other form of presence" (p. 42).

18. For an account of Altizer's interpretation of the bad infinite, see *The New Apocalypse*, pp. 7–9. Altizer identifies Hegel's bad infinite and Blake's Urizen.

19. See "The Anonymity of God," in *Total Presence*, pp. 19–36.

20. Thomas J. J. Altizer, *The Self-Embodiment of God* (New York: Harper and Row, 1977), p. 82. Altizer repeats in a theological register Hegel's interpretation of the dialectical relationship of identity and difference. See "The Doctrine of Essence," in *Hegel's Science of Logic*, trans. A.V. Miller (New York: Humanities Press, 1969). Altizer, like Hegel, privileges identity by insisting upon the *identity* of identity and difference, and the *union* of union and nonunion.

21. In view of Altizer's admission that the original language of Jesus is lost as soon as it is inscribed in writing, it would be more accurate to say that for those other

than his contemporaries, Jesus's parabolic language becomes present *for the first time* in the words of Joyce and, by extension, of Altizer.

22. In this passage Altizer seems to be using "text" to refer to what he elsewhere designates "antitext."

23. *The Self-Embodiment of God*, p. 92.

24. This is, of course, the famous phrase Hegel uses to describe the *Phenomenology*. From beginning to end, the prototype for *History as Apocalypse* is the *Phenomenology of Spirit*. But whereas Hegel intends the *Phenomenology* as a preface to his System as a whole, *History as Apocalypse* is supposed to be the conclusion of a line of thought that has been unfolding for "some thirty-five years." As we will see in the next section, the similarities between the *Phenomenology* and *History as Apocalypse* suggest that, claims to the contrary notwithstanding, Altizer's book (like all books) remains a preface—a preface to something other, which the Book itself can never contain.

25. The "sheer immediacy" (p. 226) of this "Now" marks the return of the immediacy with which Hegel begins the *Phenomenology*. For Hegel, as for Altizer, this immediacy disappears when the *hic et nunc* passes into writing. The recovery of immediacy presupposes the return of the Word that had been scattered in space (i.e., nature) and time (i.e., history) through a process that Hegel describes in terms of sexuality and digestion, two activities that are closer to each other than Hegel realized. "This Becoming [i.e., the Becoming that is the truth of Being itself] presents a slow-moving succession of Spirits, a gallery of images, each of which, endowed with all the riches of Spirit, moves thus slowly just because the Self has to penetrate and digest this entire wealth of its substance" (*Phenomenology*, p. 492).

26. Friedrich Nietzsche, *Thus Spoke Zarathustra*, trans. M. Cowan (Chicago: Henry Regnery Co., 1957), pp. 334–35.

27. Blanchot, *Space of Literature*, p. 116.

28. Kierkegaard, *Journals and Papers*, no. 1604.

29. Ibid., no. 1605.

30. Hegel, *Phenomenology*, p. 19.

31. Jacques Derrida, "From Restricted to General Economy: A Hegelianism without Reserve," in *Writing and Difference*, p. 259.

32. Georges Bataille, *L'expérience intérieure* (Paris: Gallimard, 1954), p. 127.

33. Georges Bataille, "The Use Value of D.A.F. Sade," in *Visions of Excess*, p. 94.

34. I borrow this phrase from Blanchot's important essay "The Absence of the Book," in *The Gaze of Orpheus*, p. 146.

35. Nowhere is this more evident than in Altizer's misreading of Derrida. The terms Derrida deploys to solicit altarity (e.g., *différance*, margin, limen, hymen, tym-

pan, etc.) can be understood as variations of Bataille's *ganz Andere* and Blanchot's "nonabsent absence." When faced with such "nonconcepts," Altizer transforms non-dialectical difference into a dialectical other that can be reversed:

> At bottom God or logos is the source and ground of the exclusion or negation of all alien sources of self-presence, and it is so precisely because God is total presence, a presence which negates and excludes everything which cannot become present, and which cannot become present in consciousness and history. Derrida is dedicated to resurrecting that excluded or negated absence, even if such a resurrection can never be effected in history, consciousness, or language, and cannot be so effected if only because the irreversible event of God's total self-presence has already occurred." ["History as Apocalypse," *Deconstruction and Theology* (New York: Crossroad, 1982), p. 153.]

Altizer's response to Derrida is, in effect, the response Kierkegaard expected from Hegel. Kierkegaard predicted that Hegel would have reacted to his writings by transforming his philosophical fragments into a paragraph in the System. Altizer writes: "Upon reflection, one wonders if it would be possible to be more Hegelian than Derrida; or, more Hegelian in a post-Hegelian or posthistorical age" (ibid., p. 154).

Altizer's unwillingness to acknowledge the *differences* between Hegel and writers like Bataille, Blanchot, and Derrida helps to explain his tendency to collapse postmodernism into modernism. Within Altizer's Hegelian dialectic, there is no place for the postmodern. The identification of modernism and postmodernism obscures much of what is distinctive in contemporary thought.

36. The inversion of the western theological tradition is not its subversion. The subversive thinker must think what the tradition has left unthought by writing (on) the margin of neither/nor.

37. Hélène Cixous, "Joyce: The (r)use of writing," in *Post-Structuralist Joyce*, p. 21.

38. Derrida, "Two words for Joyce," in *Post-Structuralist Joyce*, p. 155. As the translator points out, the last sentence—*Là ou c'était, Il fut*—is a play on Freud's famous *Wo es war, soll Ich werden.*

39. Derrida, *Of Grammatology*, p. 98.

40. Blanchot, "The Narrative Voice (the 'he,' the neuter)," pp. 141–42.

41. Blanchot, *Thomas the Obscure*, pp. 107–8.

42. This is the title of one of Blanchot's most provocative works. *Pas* can be translated as either "step" or "not." *"Au-delà"* means "beyond." Accordingly, the title might be translated *(The) Step/Not Beyond.*

43. These are the words with which a "book" entitled *Erring: A Postmodern A/theology* "ends." Compare the way in which Altizer *ends The Self-Embodiment of God:* "The real ending of speech is the dawning of resurrection, and the final ending of speech is the dawning of a totally present actuality. That actuality is immediately at

hand when it is heard, and it is heard when it is enacted. And it is enacted in the dawning of the actuality of silence, an actuality ending all disembodied and unspoken presence. Then speech is truly impossible, and as we hear and enact that impossibility, then even can we say: 'It is finished' " (p. 96).

44. These are the words with which Joyce almost ends *Finnegans Wake*. An unconcluding p.s.: Altizer stresses the importance of presence in and as woman at the end of *Finnegans Wake*. One with an ear for Danish can hear something other in these penultimate words. The Danish word for father is *far*, which is pronounced like the English word "far." After the End, how are we to read: "Far calls. Coming, far!"?

Chapter 6

1. Derrida, *Glas*, p. 259.

2. Joseph Shipley, *The Origins of English Words: A Discursive Dictionary of Indo-European Roots* (Baltimore: Johns Hopkins University Press, 1984), p. 264.

3. *The American Heritage Dictionary of the English Language* (New York: Houghton Mifflin, 1970), p. 46.

4. Karl Barth, *The Epistle to the Romans*, trans. E. C. Hoskyns (London: Oxford University Press, 1968), p. 242.

5. Altizer, *The Self-Embodiment of God*, p. 81.

6. Derrida, "Différance."

7. Martin Heidegger, "The End of Philosophy and the Task of Thinking," p. 56.

8. Ibid., p. 70.

9. Derrida, "Différance," pp. 7–8.

10. Thomas J.J. Altizer, "Eternal Recurrence and the Kingdom of God," *The New Nietzsche: Contemporary Styles of Interpretation*, ed. D.B. Allison (New York: Dell, 1977), p. 240.

11. Ibid., p. 240.

12. Blanchot, *Le pas au-delà*, pp. 34–35.

13. Ibid., p. 49.

14. Paul Tillich, "The Two Types of the Philosophy of Religion," *Theology and Culture* (New York: Oxford University Press, 1959), p. 10. All the quotations from Tillich in the following pages can be found in this essay.

15. Blanchot, *Writing of the Disaster*.

16. Samuel Beckett, *The Unnameable* (New York: Grove Press, 1958), p. 20.

1. Jean Hyppolite, *Logique et existence: essai sur la logique de Hegel* (Presses Universitaires de France, 1953), p. 131.

2. Rodolphe Gasché, *The Tain of the Mirror: Derrida and the Philosophy of Reflection* (Cambridge: Harvard University Press, 1986), p. 2, emphasis added. Hereafter references to this book are given in the text.

3. Richard Rorty, *The Consequences of Pragmatism* (Minneapolis: University of Minnesota Press, 1982), pp. 103–4. For a fuller account of Rorty's position, see below, chapter 9.

4. G. W. F. Hegel, *Lectures on the Philosophy of Religion*, trans. E. B. Speirs and J. B. Sanderson (New York: Humanities Press, 1968), vol. 1, p. 191.

5. Ibid., pp. 18–19.

6. G. W. F. Hegel, *The Difference between Fichte's and Schelling's System of Philosophy*, trans. H. S. Harris and W. Cerf (Albany: State University of New York Press, 1977), pp. 89, 91.

7. Ibid., p. 156.

8. Gasché effectively contrasts the philosophy of reflection with speculative philosophy, but his terminology sometimes confuses these two positions. In an effort to avoid unnecessary difficulties, I use *reflection* when considering the philosophy of reflection and *reflexion* to refer to Hegel's speculative philosophy. When it has been impossible to avoid citing Gasché's use of the word "reflection" to designate Hegelianism, I have suspended the term between quotation marks.

9. Derrida, *Glas*, p. 83.

10. The text Gasché cites in this passage is from Derrida's *La vérité en peinture* (Paris: Flammarion, 1978), p. 56.

11. Jacques Derrida, *Spurs: Nietzsche's Styles*, trans. B. Harlow (Chicago: University of Chicago Press, 1978), p. 117.

12. Blanchot, *Writing of the Disaster*, p. 40.

13. Ibid., p. 35.

14. Sylviane Agacinski, *Aparté: Conceptions and Deaths of Søren Kierkegaard*, trans. K. Newmark (Tallahassee: Florida State University Press, 1988).

15. Blanchot, *Writing of the Disaster*, p. 2.

16. Kierkegaard, *Journals and Papers*, no. 3034.

18. Jacques Derrida, "Des Tours de Babel," in *Difference in Translation*, ed. J. F. Graham (Ithaca: Cornell University Press, 1985), p. 203.

Chapter 8

1. Rudolf Otto, *The Idea of the Holy: An Inquiry into the Non-rational Factor in the Idea of the Divine and its Relation to the Rational*, trans. by J. W. Harvey (New York: Oxford University Press, 1965). *Das Heilige: Über das Irrationale in der Idee des Göttlichen und sein Verhältnis zum Rationalen* (Gotha: Leopold Klotz, 1929).

2. Ibid., p. 5 (German, pp. 5–6).

3. Ibid., p. 40 (German, pp. 55–56).

4. Martin Heidegger, "What are Poets For?" in *Poetry, Language, Thought*, p. 91.

5. Martin Heidegger, *The Question Concerning Technology and Other Essays*, trans. W. Lovitt (New York: Harper and Row, 1977), p. 154.

6. Martin Heidegger, *Identity and Difference*, trans. J. Stambaugh (New York: Harper and Row, 1969), p. 50.

7. Martin Heidegger, "Letter on Humanism," in *Basic Writings*, trans. and ed. D. Krell (New York: Harper and Row, 1977), p. 235.

8. Ibid., p. 236.

9. Heidegger, *Identity and Difference*, p. 71.

10. Ibid., p. 235. In what follows, I will examine the way in which Heidegger shifts from philosophical to artistic language to express that which remains conceptually inexpressible.

11. Ibid., p. 47.

12. Ibid., p. 64.

13. Ibid., pp. 63, 65.

14. Ibid., p. 68.

15. Heidegger, *Poetry, Language, Thought*, p. 202.

16. Ibid., p. 218.

17. Heidegger, *Identity and Difference*, p. 28.

18. Heidegger, *Discourse on Thinking*, trans. by J. M. Anderson and E. H. Freund (New York: Harper and Row, 1966), p. 83.

19. Heidegger, *On Time and Being*, pp. 24, 43.

20. Ibid., p. 6.

21. *Verstellung,* which recalls *Vorstellung,* carries a rich range of associations. *Verstellen* is to put one thing in the place of another, transpose, shift, adjust, remove, change the position or order of, put in the wrong place, misplace, disarrange, bar, block, obstruct; feign, sham, disguise, conterfeit. Accordingly, *Verstellung* can also mean presence, make-believe, disguise, dissimulation, hypocrisy. *Verstellen* and *Verstellung* are central aspects of Freud's analysis of dreamwork. As will become apparent in what follows, there is an important relationship between Heidegger's *Verstellung* and the inevitable oblivion that renders consciousness forever incomplete.

22. Heidegger, *Poetry, Language, Thought,* p. 60.

23. Heidegger, *Identity and Difference,* pp. 50–51.

24. Ibid., pp. 48–49.

25. Martin Heidegger, *Early Greek Thinking,* trans. D. F. Krell and F. A. Capuzzi (New York: Harper and Row, 1975), p. 121.

26. Heidegger, "Letter on Humanism," p. 199.

27. Heidegger, *On Time and Being,* p. 18.

28. In a similar way, *tempus* means a division, section. In relation to time, *tempus* is a portion of time or a period of time.

29. *Cassell's Latin Dictionary* (New York: Macmillan, 1968).

30. Heidegger, *Poetry, Language, Thought,* pp. 41, 42.

31. Ibid., pp. 17, 72, 47–48.

32. Ibid., p. 63.

33. Ibid., p. 204.

34. Ibid., p. 55.

35. Heidegger, *Early Greek Thinking,* p. 26.

36. Heidegger, *Poetry, Language, Thought,* p. 53.

37. Ibid., p. 68.

38. Heidegger, *On Time and Being,* p. 70.

39. Heidegger, *Poetry, Language, Thought,* p. 72.

40. By translating this phrase "saying sketchily," I have attempted to stress the way in which saying implies that which withdraws or conceals itself. "Sketchily" also has the virtue of suggesting an association with the various forms of *Riss* (e.g., *Aufriss, Vorriss, Umriss*) that we have already explored.

41. Heidegger, *Poetry, Language, Thought*, p. 74.

42. Ibid.

43. Ibid., p. 132.

44. Heidegger, *Early Greek Thinking*, p. 71.

45. Heidegger, *Identity and Difference*, p. 69.

46. Throughout this essay, Heidegger probes the interplay of differences, in and through which everything arises and passes away, in terms of the fourfold relationship of "sky, earth, mortals, and divinities."

47. Heidegger, *Poetry, Language, Thought*, p. 206.

48. Ibid., p. 207.

49. Heidegger, *Discourse on Thinking*, p. 61.

50. Heidegger, *Poetry, Language, Thought*, p. 130.

51. This association of terms is underscored by Heidegger's repetition of Hegel's hyphenation of *Er-innerung*. In both cases, the division of the word calls attention to the notion of inwardness or interiority. The difference between Hegel and Heidegger concerns the way in which this *Innerung* is understood.

52. Heidegger, *Poetry, Language, Thought*, p. 120.

53. Ibid., p. 94.

54. Ibid., p. 125. Heidegger borrows this line from Rilke.

55. Blanchot, *Writing of the Disaster*, pp. 48–49.

56. Blanchot, *Thomas the Obscure*, pp. 108–9.

57. Wallace Stevens, "Snow Man," *Collected Poems*, p. 10.

Chapter 9

1. Peter Stallybrass and Allon White, *The Politics and Poetics of Transgression* (Ithaca: Cornell University Press, 1986), p. 143.

2. Michel Serres, *The Parasite*, trans. L. Schehr (Baltimore: Johns Hopkins University Press, 1982), pp. 3, 12.

3. Joseph Shipley, *The Origins of English Words*, p. 9.

4. *The Oxford English Dictionary*.

5. Richard Rorty, *Consequences of Pragmatism*, pp. 103–4.

6. Ibid., p. 92.

7. See, inter alia, M. H. Abrams, *Natural Supernaturalism: Tradition and Revolution in Romantic Literature*, and Jean Hyppolite, *Genesis and Structure of Hegel's Phenomenology*, trans. S. Cherniak and J. Heckman (Evanston: Northwestern University Press, 1974).

8. Richard Rorty, *Philosophy and the Mirror of Nature* (Princeton: Princeton University Press, 1979), p. 318.

9. It is precisely Hegel's rejection of the notion of "edification" that leads Kierkegaard to describe some of his own writings as "Edifying Discourses." See *Edifying Discourses*, trans. David F. and Lillian M. Swenson (New York: Harper and Row, 1958).

10. The etymology of the word "edify" underscores the close relationship between edification and building or construction. "Edify" derives from the Latin *æficiare, ædes, ædis*, dwelling + *ficare*, to make. The Danish word for "edify" is *opbygge, op*, up + *bygge*, to build. Compare the German *erbauen*, build, raise, erect, construct; edify. Apparently opting for "accuracy" rather than elegance, the most recent translators of Kierkegaard's writings insist on rendering *Opbyggelige Taler* as "Upbuilding Discourses."

11. Rorty, *Philosophy and the Mirror of Nature*, pp. 358–59.

12. Ibid., p. 359.

13. Hans-Georg Gadamer, *Truth and Method* (New York: Seabury, 1975), p. 12. Quoted by Rorty, *Philosophy and the Mirror of Nature*, p. 362.

14. Rorty, *Philosophy and the Mirror of Nature*, p. 377. Rorty misleadingly cites Kierkegaard's *Concluding Unscientific Postscript* at this point. When read in the context of his overall argument, Kierkegaard's claim that "truth is subjectivity" calls into question the kind of humanism that Gadamer and Rorty support.

15. Rorty, *Philosophy and the Mirror of Nature*, p. 360.

16. Hegel, *Phenomenology*, p. 10. This passage calls for two additional comments. First, Hegel clearly indicates his low esteem for edification by his use of the verb *sinken*. Second, a phrase like *ein Spielen der Liebe mit sich selbst* makes Derrida's discussion of the significance of Rousseau's preoccupation with masturbation much more telling than many commentators are willing to admit. See *Of Grammatology*, especially pp. 141–64.

17. The recognition of the role played by Schiller and Kant in the genesis of hermeneutics is important for several reasons. In the first place, Schiller's *Letters* present a notion of *Bildung* that dominates later thinking. Second, Kant's use of the notion of play in his account of the work of art exercises considerable influence on nineteenth- and twentieth-century esthetic theory. As we shall see, Gadamer develops his views of play in the context of his discussion of the work of art. For a more complete account of the importance of Schiller's notion of play for Hegel's philosophy, see Mark C. Taylor, *Journeys to Selfhood*, pp. 71–90.

18. Hegel, *Phenomenology,* p. 10.

19. Gadamer, *Truth and Method,* p. 97, emphasis added.

20. Ibid.

21. Ibid., p. 111.

22. Ibid.

23. Ibid., pp. 113–14.

24. Ibid., p. 341. In this passage, Gadamer is concerned with dialogue partners who are contemporaries. As the following text makes clear, the implications of conversation are the same when the discussion partner is in the "past":

> Every encounter with tradition that takes place within historical consciousness involves the experience of the tension between text and the present. The hermeneutic task consists in not covering up this tension by attempting a naive assimilation but consciously bringing it out. This is why it is part of the hermeneutic approach to project an historical horizon that is different from the horizon of the present. Historical consciousness is aware of its own otherness and hence distinguishes the horizon of tradition from its own. On the other hand, it is itself, as we are trying to show, only something laid over a continuing tradition, and hence it immediately recombines what it has distinguished in order, in the unity of the historical horizon that it thus acquires, to become again one with itself. [p. 273]

25. This is not, of course, to imply that Gadamer and Rorty agree about everything. It is obvious that they differ on a variety of relevant details. I would insist, however, that they concur on most of the basic points in their theories of interpretation.

26. Derrida, *Writing and Difference,* p. 292.

27. Rorty, *Consequences of Pragmatism,* p. 92.

28. Ibid., p. 140.

29. Ibid., pp. 94–95.

30. Derrida, *Writing and Difference,* p. 292. Another way to approach Rorty's misprision of Derrida is to examine his understanding of presence and absence. Having failed to recognize the difference between Gadamer's and Derrida's views of play, Rorty tends to regard absence as the absence of presence, which is the *presence* of absence. What Rorty has not thought is that which "must be conceived before the alternative of presence and absence." In hermeneutical terms, the presence of the absence of the represented object creates the possibility of the self-presence of the representing subject. To think that which is neither present nor absent is to think the impossibility of presence as such.

31. Ibid., p. 293.

32. Blanchot, *Le pas au-delà*, p. 158.

33. Ibid., p. 158.

34. Jean-Luc Nancy, *Le partage des voix* (Paris: Galilée, 1982), p. 86.

35. Heidegger, "Language," in *Poetry, Language, Thought*, pp. 206–7. Those who espouse hermeneutics frequently cite the first sentence in this quotation. They usually do not recognize the difficulties that the notion of difference suggested in the rest of the text pose for the hermeneutical reading of language. For a more extensive consideration of Heidegger's position, see above, chapter 10.

36. One of Nancy's chief concerns in *Le partage des voix* is to show how the notion of the *Riss* necessitates a reinterpretation of Heidegger's hermeneutical circle.

37. Nancy, *Le partage des voix*, pp. 86–87.

38. Ibid., p. 88.

39. The use of the word "converse" in this context might be misleading. That which struggles toward articulation in Blanchot's *entretien* is not simply the *opposite* of the Hegelian dialectic and hermeneutical conversation, but is that which both breaks with and makes possible the structure of opposition itself.

40. This is the title of the first section of *L'entretien infini*.

41. Blanchot, *L'entretien infini*, pp. 107–8.

42. Recall Derrida's claim in "Structure, Sign, and Play:" "Play is the disruption of presence. The presence of an element is always a signifying and substitutive reference inscribed in a system of differences and the movement of a chain. Play is always play of absence and presence, but if it is to be thought radically, play must be conceived of before the alternative of presence and absence." See above, note 26.

43. Blanchot, *L'entretien infini*, p. 91.

44. Ibid., p. 99.

45. Blanchot, *Le pas au-delà*, p. 97.

46. Ibid., pp. 105–6.

47. *Le Petit Robert, Dictionnaire de la Langue Française*.

48. Blanchot, *L'entretien infini*, p. 116.

49. Michel Serres, *The Parasite*, p. 12. In view of the importance of negation for the problem of interruption, it is interesting to note that the French word for "meal," *repas*, can be rewritten: *re-pas*.

50. Ibid., p. 13.

51. Ibid., p. 56.

52. Rorty, *Philosophy and the Mirror of Nature*, p. 360.

53. Rorty, *Consequences of Pragmatism*, p. 173, emphasis added.

54. In a para-enthetical aside, Blanchot writes: "Let us recall the terrible monologues of Hitler and of every Chief of State. He enjoyed being alone to speak and, enjoying his haughty solitary speech, imposed it on others, without constraint, as a superior and supreme speech. He participated in the same violence of the *dictare*–the repetition of the imperious monologue" (*L'entretien infini*, pp. 106–7).

55. Ibid., p. 112.

56. Blanchot, *Writing of the Disaster*, pp. 14–15.

57. Quoted in Paul B. Courtright, *Ganesa: Lord of Obstacles, Lord of Beginnings* (New York: Oxford University Press, 1985), p. 80.

58. Ibid., pp. 156–57.

Chapter 10

1. Edmond Jabès, *The Book of Questions: EL, or The Last Book*, trans. R. Waldrop (Middletown, Conn.: Wesleyan University Press, 1984), p. 55.

2. Milan Kundera, *The Unbearable Lightness of Being*, trans. M. H. Heim (New York: Harper and Row, 1984), pp. 121–22.

3. Ibid., p. 5, 6.

4. Ibid., p. 3.

5. Ibid., p. 5.

6. In this context, I use the term "poststructuralism" to refer to a style of interpretation that includes what is commonly labeled deconstruction. Unfortunately, extensive abuse and misunderstanding have rendered the terms "poststructuralism" and "deconstruction" almost useless.

7. This formulation might be misleading. I do not mean to suggest that these three types of interpretation form a dialectical progression in which each grows out of the other. Rather, structuralism, hermeneutics, and poststructuralism repeatedly intersect around common themes, questions, and problems. In many cases, these relationships are indirect and thus must be established rather than discovered. For example, Derrida discusses Gadamer's work only briefly and has not yet considered Ricoeur's work. The relationship between poststructuralism and hermeneutics is especially important in the American context. Richard Rorty's interest in deconstruction and appropriation of hermeneutics have lead many to assume a closer connection between these two ways of reading than actually exists. See above, chapter 9.

8. Quoted in Paul Ricoeur, *The Conflict of Interpretations*, ed. D. Ihde (Evanston: Northwestern University Press, 1974), p. 34.

9. Ibid., p. 40.

10. A supplementary observation might be helpful at this point. I have stressed that in historical-critical analysis, texts are representational and meaning is referential. At first it seems that structuralists reject the notions of representation and reference informing such criticism. More careful reflection, however, suggests that structuralism also remains bound to the mimetic economy of reference. For the structuralist, the referent that establishes the meaning of the text is not extratextual but is a subtext that undergirds the play of signifiers. In other words, structuralism does not call into question the *structure* of representation and reference characteristic of historical criticism. I consider these issues more fully in chapter 12.

11. Claude Lévi-Strauss, "The Effectiveness of Symbols," in *Structural Anthropology*, trans. C. Jacobson and B. G. Schoepf (Garden City, N.Y.: Doubleday, 1976), p. 203.

12. Ferdinand de Saussure, *Course in General Linguistics*, in *Deconstruction in Context: Literature and Philosophy*, p. 159.

13. Ricoeur, *Conflict of Interpretations*, p. 32.

14. Ibid., p. 85, emphasis added.

15. Ibid., p. 96.

16. Ibid., pp. 82, 87.

17. Saussure, *Course in General Linguistics*.

18. Ricoeur, *Conflict of Interpretations*, p. 85.

19. Ibid., p. 87.

20. Ibid., pp. 92–93, emphasis added.

21. Paul Ricoeur, *Freud and Philosophy: An Essay on Interpretation*, trans. D. Savage (New Haven: Yale University Press, 1970), p. 18.

22. Ricoeur, *Conflict of Interpretations*, p. 93. Derrida's notion of undecidability is often confused with the idea of polysemy. As the following text makes clear, there is an important difference between polysemy and dissemination:

> This is why it is not in all rigor a question of polythematicism or of polysemy here. Polysemy always puts out its multiplicities and variations within the *horizon*, at least, of some integral reading that contains no absolute rift, no senseless deviation—the horizon of the final parousia of a meaning at last deciphered, revealed, made present in the rich collection of its determination . . . The concept of polysemy thus belongs within the confines of explanations, within the explication or enumeration, in the present, of meaning. It belongs to the attending discourse. Its style is that of the representative of surface. It forgets that its horizon is framed. The difference between discursive polysemy and textual dissemination is

precisely *difference* itself, "an implacable difference." This difference is, of course, indispensable to the production of meaning (and that is why between polysemy and dissemination the difference is very slight). But to the extent that meaning presents itself, gathers itself together, says itself, and is able to stand there, it erases difference and casts it aside. Structure (the differential) is a necessary condition for the semantic, but the semantic is not itself, in itself, structural. The seminal, on the contrary, disseminates itself without ever having *been* itself and without coming back to itself. Its very engagement in division, its involvement in its own multiplication, which is always carried out at a loss and unto death, is what constitutes it as such a living proliferation. [*Dissemination*, pp. 350–51]

23. Ricoeur, *Conflict of Interpretations*, pp. 50, 38. In anticipation of the next section of this chapter, it is important to note that Ricoeur repeatedly asserts that Lévi-Strauss's structural analysis is more suited to totemic society than to societies and cultures that emerge in the Judeo-Christian context. Hermeneutical analysis is better able to illuminate the complexities of Western history. From this point of view, the polarity between structuralism and hermeneutics can be understood in terms of the opposition between Western and non-Western cultures. Because structuralism is ahistorical and hermeneutics is historical, Ricoeur reinscribes traditional understandings of the West as historical and the non-West as ahistorical. Neither biblical critics nor historians of religion have recognized this aspect of Ricoeur's argument.

24. Ibid., p. 49.

25. Ibid., pp. 42, 32.

26. Søren Kierkegaard, *Concluding Unscientific Postscript*, trans. D. F. Swenson and W. Lowrie (Princeton: Princeton University Press, 1941), p. 272.

27. Kundera, *Unbearable Lightness*, p. 248.

28. Through the association of ideas released by the conjunction of texts here under consideration, an unexpected insight emerges. In one of his most disturbing remarks, Hegel associates Jews with shit. In an early essay entitled "The Spirit of Christianity and its Fate," Hegel writes: "The Jewish multitude was bound to wreck his [Jesus's] attempt to give the consciousness of something divine, for faith in something divine, something great, cannot make its home in feces (*im Kote; Kot:* filth, mire, dung, excrement)" (*Early Theological Writings*, trans. T. M. Knox [Philadelphia: University of Pennsylvania Press, 1971], p. 265). As I have pointed out, Ricoeur maintains that structuralism provides insights into the workings of "nonhistorical" societies but is of limited use when considering "historical" cultures. In developing his account of hermeneutics, Ricoeur consistently draws on the experience of the Jewish people recorded in the Hebrew Bible. If Judaism embodies the historicity of human experience, then Hegel's association of Jews with shit is a function of his effort to subject temporality to the machinations of the eternal Idea.

29. Hegel, *Phenomenology*, p. 14.

30. Ricoeur, *Conflict of Interpretations*, p. 51.

31. Contrary to Ricoeur's reading of structuralism as subverting the philosophy of reflection, it is possible to understand Hegelianism as something like protostructuralism and structuralism as latter day Hegelianism. See, inter alia, Mark C. Taylor, "System . . . Structure . . . Difference . . . Other," in *Deconstruction in Context*, pp. 1–34.

32. Ricoeur, *Conflict of Interpretations*, p. 51.

33. Ibid., p. 52, emphasis added.

34. Ibid., p. 85.

35. Kundera, *Unbearable Lightness*, p. 298.

36. Søren Kierkegaard, *Philosophical Fragments*, trans. H. V. Hong and E. H. Hong (Princeton: Princeton University Press, 1985), p. 51. The Danish word *øieblikket* can also be translated "the blink (*blikket*) of an eye *(øie)*." This momentary blink blinds the philosopher and thus interrupts philosophical vision.

37. Kundera, *Unbearable Lightness*, p. 222.

38. An earlier version of this paper was written in response to a request by an editor of *Semeia*, an experimental journal published by the Society of Biblical Literature (otherwise known as the SBL).

39. Jacques Derrida, "Shibboleth," in *Midrash and Literature*, ed. G. H. Hartman and S. Burdick (New Haven: Yale University Press, 1986), p. 307.

40. Ibid., pp. 325–26.

41. Ricoeur, *Conflict of Interpretations*, p. 28.

42. Derrida, "Shibboleth," p. 320.

43. Ibid., p. 323.

44. Ibid., p. 322.

45. Ibid., p. 315. The use of the phrase *es gibt* is, of course, a reference to Heidegger.

46. Søren Kierkegaard, *The Concept of Anxiety*, trans. R. Thomte (Princeton: Princeton University Press, 1980), p. 83n.

47. Derrida, "Shibboleth," p. 317.

48. Ibid., p. 329.

49. Heidegger, "What Calls for Thinking?" in *Basic Writings*, pp. 350–51. Immediately following this passage, Heidegger refers to Hölderlin's "Mnemosyne" but does not cite the poem's concluding stanza, which suggests a relationship between memory/forgetting/withdrawal/point/sign and mourning:

Beside the fig-tree
My Achilles has died and is lost to me,
And Ajax lies
Beside the grottoes of the sea,
Beside brooks that neighbour Scamandros.
Of a rushing noise in his temples once,
According to the changeless custom of
Unmoved Salamis, in foreign parts
Great Ajax died,
Not so Patroclus, dead in the King's own armour.
And many others died. But by Cithaeron there stood
Eleutherae, Mnemosyne's town. From her also
When God laid down his festive cloak, soon after did
The powers of Evening sever a lock of hair. For the Heavenly, when
Someone has failed to collect his soul, to spare it,
Are angry, for still he must; like him
Here mourning is at fault.

[Friedrich Hölderlin, *Poems and Fragments*, trans. M. Hamburger (Ann Arbor: University of Michigan Press, 1968), p. 501.]

50. Kundera, *Unbearable Lightness*, p. 8.

51. Derrida, "Shibboleth," p. 340.

52. Ibid., pp. 337, 338.

53. Ibid., p. 340.

54. Ibid.

55. Heidegger, *Early Greek Thinking*, p. 76.

56. Levinas, *Otherwise than Being*, p. 69.

57. Ibid., p. 23.

58. Heidegger, *Poetry, Language, Thought*, p. 74.

59. Levinas, *Otherwise than Being*, p. 5.

60. Ibid., pp. 51–52.

61. Levinas, *De dieu qui vient à l'idée*, p. 116.

62. Jacques Derrida, "Edmond Jabès and the Question of the Book," *Writing and Difference*, p. 68.

63. Derrida, "Shibboleth," p. 345.

64. The graphic in Figure 15 is from Edmond Jabès's *EL, or The Last Book*, pp. 52–53.

Chapter 11

1. Unless otherwise indicated, definitions are from the *Oxford English Dictionary*.

2. Shipley, *The Origin of English Words*.

3. Sigmund Freud, "The Uncanny," *The Standard Edition of the Complete Psychological Works of Sigmund Freud*, ed. J. Strachey (London: Hogarth Press, 1964), vol. 17, pp. 224–25.

4. Kierkegaard, *Journals and Papers*, no. 5109. At some points it has been necessary to alter or supplement the translations of Kierkegaard's works. The Danish editions I have used are: *Søren Kierkegaards Papirer*, ed. P. A. Heiberg and V. Kuhr (Copenhagen: Gyldendalske Boghandel, 1912) and *Søren Kierkegaards Samlede Værker*, ed. A. B. Drachmann, J. L. Heiberg, and H. O. Lange (Copenhagen: Gyldendalske Boghandel, 1901).

5. Derrida, *Of Grammatology*, p. 226.

6. Reinhold Heller, *Edvard Munch: The Scream* (London: Penguin Press, 1973), p. 67. Munch's insistence that he did not discover Kierkegaard until 1928 is rendered doubtful by personal correspondence from this period. In his letters Munch indicates that he is *renewing* his acquaintance with Kierkegaard's writings.

7. Ingmar Bergman, *Persona and Shame*, trans. K. Bradfield (New York: Grossman, 1972), pp. 97–98. The frontal shot that accompanies these words is as unsettling as Munch's screaming skeleton.

8. Kierkegaard, *The Concept of Anxiety*, p. 41.

9. See C. G. Jung, *The Theory of Psycho-Analysis*, and Sigmund Freud, *The Standard Edition*, vol. 21, p. 229.

10. Kierkegaard, *Journals and Papers*, no. 5645.

11. Ibid., no. 6107.

12. Maurice Blanchot, *When the Time Comes*, trans. L. Davis (Barrytown, N.Y.: Station Hill Press, 1985), p. 66.

13. Kierkegaard, *Philosophical Fragments*, pp. 44–45.

14. Kierkegaard, *Journals and Papers*, no. 3646.

15. Blanchot, *Le pas au-delà*, pp. 69–70.

16. Kierkegaard, *Philosophical Fragments*, p. 46.

17. Kierkegaard, *Journals and Papers*, no. 3081.

18. Kierkegaard, *Philosophical Fragments*, p. 61.

19. Derrida, "Shibboleth," p. 323.

20. Kierkegaard, *Philosophical Fragments*, p. 37.

21. Derrida, "Shibboleth," pp. 323–24.

22. Ibid., p. 315.

23. Jacques Derrida, "Des Tours de Babel," in *Difference in Translation*, p. 204.

24. Søren Kierkegaard, *Fear and Trembling*, trans. Howard and Edna Hong (Princeton: Princeton University Press, 1983), p. 118.

25. Jacques Derrida, "Foreword: *Fors*: The Anglish Words of Nicolas Abraham and Maria Torok," trans. B. Johnson, in *The Wolfman's Magic Word: A Cryptonymy*, trans. N. Rand (Minneapolis: University of Minnesota Press, 1986), p. xiv.

26. Kierkegaard, *Fear and Trembling*, p. 56.

27. Ibid., p. 76.

28. Ibid., p. 82.

29. Ibid., p. 46.

30. Ibid., p. 113.

31. Ibid., p. 114.

32. Ibid., p. 69.

33. Blanchot, *Faux pas*, p. 34.

34. Julia Kristeva, *Powers of Horror: An Essay on Abjection*, trans. L. S. Roudiez (New York: Columbia University Press, 1982), pp. 2–3. I have altered the translation substantially.

35. Søren Kierkegaard, *The Point of View for My Work as an Author: A Report to History*, trans. W. Lowrie (New York: Harper and Row, 1962), p. 69.

36. Maurice Blanchot, "Interruptions," *Edmond Jabès and the Sin of the Book*, ed. E. Gould (Lincoln: University of Nebraska Press, 1985), pp. 44–45.

37. An uncanny secret held within *cemetery*: the root of both *cemetery* and *home* is *kei*. Joseph Shipley explains that *kei* means "lie down, sleep; settle; hence home, friendly, dear . . . *Kheimai*: lie asleep, whence another euphemism, *cemetery*, a sleeping-place."

38. Derrida, *Fors*, p. xxxv.

39. Kierkegaard, *Philosophical Fragments*, pp. 38–39.

40. Derrida, *Fors*, p. xxi.

41. Ibid., p. xxi.

42. Freud, "The Uncanny," p. 245.

43. Søren Kierkegaard, *Either-Or*, trans. David F. Swenson and Lillian Marvin Swenson (Princeton: Princeton University Press, 1959), vol. 1, p. 450.

44. Ibid., p. 152.

45. Ibid., p. 155.

46. Kierkegaard, *Journals and Papers*, no. 5569.

47. Josiah Thompson, *Kierkegaard* (New York: Knopf, 1973), p. 22.

48. Quoted in Thompson, *Kierkegaard*, p. 27. Ane, who never learned to read or write, might not have known what Michael intended.

49. Quoted in Thompson, *Kierkegaard*, p. 37.

50. Kierkegaard, *Journals and Papers*, no. 5430.

51. As I have noted, Kierkegaard's birthday is May 5th.

52. Søren Kierkegaard, *Stages on Life's Way*, trans. W. Lowrie (New York: Schocken Books, 1967), pp. 236–37.

53. Thompson, *Kierkegaard*, p. 15.

54. Stallybrass and White, *The Politics and Poetics of Transgression*, p. 156. In a chapter entitled "Below Stairs: The Maid and the Family Romance," Stallybrass and White present a brilliant reading of the role of the maid/nurse in Freud's writings by elaborating insights initially advanced by Walter Benjamin. Given the importance of Freud's and Abraham/Torok's analyses of "The Wolf Man" for Derrida's notion of the crypt, Stallybrass and White's account of the relation of the Wolf Man to his maid is of special interest. See especially pp. 149–70.

55. Ibid., p. 155.

56. Freud, "The Uncanny," pp. 227–28.

57. Kierkegaard, *Journals and Papers*, no. 5149.

58. Blanchot, *Death Sentence*, p. 80.

59. "*El*, a word for 'God' in the ancient Semitic languages. The word could be used as either a proper noun or a common noun" (*Harper's Bible Dictionary*, ed. P. J. Achtemeier [New York: Harper and Row, 1985], p. 252).

Chapter 12

1. Martin Heidegger, "The End of Philosophy and the Task of Thinking," p. 70.

2. G. W. F. Hegel, *Science of Logic*, p. 82.

3. Paul Tillich, *The Courage to Be* (New Haven: Yale University Press, 1952), p. 179.

4. Derrida, *Of Grammatology*, p. 14.

5. As will become clear, the intrasubjective nature of the expressive sign does not rule out the possibility of the intersubjectivity of the linguistic referent.

6. In this context, I am emphasizing the intrasubjective nature of the idea. This should in no way obscure the no less important interpretation of ideas as ontological essences that exist prior to and independent of human knowing. I would argue, however, that such ideas actually represent the ontologizing of epistemological structures. One of the primary goals of Hegel's System is to mediate the "subjective" and "objective" interpretation of ideas.

7. A. J. Ayer, *Language, Truth, and Logic* (New York: Dover, 1952), p. 107.

8. R. B. Braithwaite, "An Empiricist's View of Religious Belief," in *Classical and Contemporary Readings in the Philosophy of Religion*, ed. J. Hick (Englewood Cliffs, N.J.: Prentice-Hall, 1965), p. 431.

9. J. L. Austin, *How to Do Things with Words* (Cambridge: Harvard University Press, 1975), p. 1.

10. Ibid., p. 6.

11. Jacques Derrida, "Signature, Event, Context," in *Margins of Philosophy*, p. 321. Derrida also considers the problem of the performative in *Memories for Paul de Man*, trans. C. Lindsay, J. Culler, and E. Cadava (New York: Columbia University Press, 1986). In this context, Derrida develops his argument by carefully analyzing de Man's consideration of the performative in *Allegories of Reading: Figural Language in Rousseau, Nietzsche, Rilke, and Proust*. J. Hillis Miller presents a Derridean reading of performative utterance in *The Ethics of Reading: Kant, de Man, Eliot, Trollope, James, and Benjamin* (New York: Columbia University Press, 1987).

12. Derrida, "Signature," p. 322.

13. Austin, *How to Do Things with Words*, p. 67.

14. The productivity of the imagination is suggested by the etymology of "poetic," which derives from the Greek *poiein*, to make or create.

15. I consider the imagination in more detail below, "Imagine Nothing," p. 215.

16. Gordon Kaufman, *The Theological Imagination: Constructing the Concept of God* (Philadelphia: Westminister, 1981), p. 22.

17. Ibid., p. 29.

18. Ibid., p. 28. It should be clear that this account of language bears important similarities to characteristic features of intentional expressive signification described above.

19. Ibid., p. 264.

20. Wallace Stevens, *Opus Posthumous*, p. 163.

21. For a helpful consideration of the romantic interpretation of the symbol, see Tzvetan Todorov, *Theories of the Symbol*, trans. C. Porter (Ithaca: Cornell University Press, 1982). One of the most informative aspects of Todorov's study is his demonstration that many ideas traditionally traced to Kant's *Critique of Judgment* (1793) or Schiller's *On the Aesthetic Education of Man* (1795) can be found in a little-known work by Karl Philipp Moritz, *Versuch einer Vereinigung und Wissenschaften unter dem Begriff des in sich selbst Vollendeten* (1785).

22. Philippe Lacoue-Labarthe and Jean-Luc Nancy, *The Literary Absolute: The Theory of Literature in German Romanticism*, trans. P. Barnard and C. Lester (Albany: State University of New York Press, 1988), pp. 77–78.

23. Todorov, *Theories of the Symbol*, p. 169.

24. Jacques Derrida, "Economimesis," *Diacritics*, vol. 11, no. 2 (1981), p. 9.

25. Derrida, *Memories for Paul de Man*, p. 135. Derrida makes this point in the course of his analysis of de Man's account of Nietzsche's interpretation of the relation between constative and performative utterance. Derrida observes:

> The rigorous demonstration of "Rhetoric of Persuasion (Nietzsche)" no doubt ends in an aporia, precisely in terms of the couple constative/performative, but this aporia evokes (*fait appel*), in some way situates, the place of evocation through an act of memory. This act calls us back to a time and place "before" oppositions (before the performative/constative opposition but also before that of literature and philosophy, and consequently many others); it therefore procures and promises a "somewhat more reliable point of reference from which to ask the question." This "reliability" will no doubt be precarious and menaced by what renders all "promises" necessary and mad, but it will not promise itself any the less because of this. And what this *act* of memory promises is a thinking of the *act* which theorists of *speech acts* have never thought, not even suspected, even when they defined the performative as an *acting* word. [pp. 133–34]

26. Immanuel Kant, *Critique of Pure Reason*, trans. Norman Kemp Smith (New York: St. Martin's Press, 1965), pp. 130–31.

28. Heidegger, *Kant and the Problem of Metaphysics*, trans. J. S. Churchill (Bloomington: Indiana University Press, 1962), p. 169.

29. Ibid., p. 173.

30. Kant, *Critique of Judgment*, trans. J.C. Meredith (New York: Oxford University Press, 1973), p. 91.

31. John Sallis, *Spacings—of Reason and Imagination in the Texts of Kant, Fichte, and Hegel* (Chicago: University of Chicago Press, 1987), p. 93.

32. Kant, *Critique of Judgment*, p. 58.

33. Ibid., p. 64.

34. Jean-Luc Nancy, "L'offrande sublime," in *Du Sublime* (Paris: Editions Belin, 1988), p. 50.

35. Kant, *Critique of Judgment*, p. 91.

36. Ibid., p. 90.

37. Ibid., p. 101.

38. Ibid., p. 100.

39. Ibid., p. 111.

40. Ibid., p. 92.

41. Sallis, *Spacings*, p. 111.

42. Kant emphasizes the motion of the sublime by associating it with e-motion—*Rührung*. Throughout the *Critique of Judgment*, Kant plays on the difference between *ruhig* and *Rührung*.

43. Kant, *Critique of Judgment*, p. 106. I have, for the most part, followed Salis's translation of this important passage. (Sallis, *Spacings*, p. 126). I have not, however, used the neologism he creates—"tremoring"—to translate *Erschütterung*. Nonetheless, Sallis's explanation of his translation is instructive:

> It is usually to this movement that Kant refers when he contrasts the movement of the mind in the judgment of the sublime with the restful contemplation characteristic of the judgment of taste. In particular, it is to this movement that he refers in a passage in which he again tells how the mind is alternately attracted and repulsed and in which now he in effect names that movement by introducing the word *Erschütterung*, which I propose to translate by recourse to a fabrication that hovers between the isolation, the subject orientation, of *trembling* and the object orientation of *tremor*. [pp. 125–26]

44. To restate Kant's point in a contemporary idiom, while beauty yields

45. Jean-Luc Nancy, "L'offrande sublime," p. 52.

46. Ibid., p. 61.

47. Blanchot, *Le pas au-delà*, p. 8.

48. Blanchot, *Gaze of Orpheus*, p. 129.

49. Sigmund Freud, *The Standard Edition of the Complete Psychological Works of Sigmund Freud*, vol. 6, p. 239.

50. Ibid., pp. 239–40.

51. J. Hillis Miller, "The Critic as Host," p. 219.

52. Blanchot, *Writing of the Disaster*, p. 21.

53. Maurice Blanchot, *L'entretien infini* (Paris: Gallimard, 1969), p. 32.

54. Michel de Certeau, *Heterologies: Discourse on the Other*, trans. B. Massumi (Minneapolis: University of Minnesota Press, 1986), p. 47. De Certeau introduces this term in the course of an analysis of Lacan's discourse of the other. There are important similarities between what I am describing as parapraxical writing and Lacan's discourse of the other.

55. Ibid., p. 100.

56. For a consideration of "anasemic" discourse, see Derrida, *Fors*, p. xi.

57. Michel de Certeau, *La fable mystique: XVIe XVIIe siècle* (Paris: Gallimard, 1982), p. 195. For the most part, the mystics de Certeau considers envision God as beyond, though not discontinuous with being. God, in other words, is the surreal essence of all that is. This surreality remains within the bounds of ontotheology. Nonetheless, many of the rhetorical strategies de Certeau identifies can be reinterpreted in relation to the nonontotheological discourse that I am attempting to describe.

58. J. Hillis Miller, *Ethics of Reading*, p. 21. Charles Winquist also underscores the importance of catachresis. See *Epiphanies of Darkness: Deconstruction in Theology* (Philadelphia: Fortress, 1986), p. 106.

59. De Certeau, *La fable mystique*, p. 199.

60. Ibid., p. 200.

61. Edmond Jabès, *The Book of Questions: El, or The Last Book*, p. 73.

62. Martin Heidegger, *Poetry, Language, Thought*, p. 204.

63. Blanchot, *L'entretien infini*, p. 592.

64. Ibid., p. 632.

65. Ibid., p. 45.

66. Ibid., p. 311.

67. Blanchot, *Writing of the Disaster*, p. 38.